HUMAN ERROR
ELECTION FRAUD

MEL LADNER

HUMAN ERROR
Copyright © 2025 by MEL LADNER

ISBN: 979-8998814426 (hc)
ISBN: 979-8998814402 (sc)
ISBN: 979-8998814419 (e)

All rights reserved. No part of this publication may be reproduced, distributed, or transmitted in any form or by any means, including photocopying, recording, or other electronic or mechanical methods, without the prior written permission of the publisher and/or the author, except in the case of brief quotations embodied in critical reviews and other noncommercial uses permitted by copyright law.

The views expressed in this book are solely those of the author and do not necessarily reflect the views of the publisher, and the publisher hereby disclaims any responsibility for them.

Mel Ladner
917 882 7200
mhl27@aol.com

To all the veterans and patriots from George Washington to the present- day soldiers who served and died defending our rights for free and fair elections, the very bedrock of our democracy. God bless you!

To my great children, my son Dan, my daughter Noel and her husband Dan. I gave them a very tough homework assignment when they were very young. They wrote legal briefs to the United States Court of Appeals for the Second Circuit and to the United States Supreme Court. Thanks you for putting up with my zest and zeal to shine a bright light on our rigged elections! Hopefully "Human Error" can have a positive impact to established free and fair elections in our great country?

To my wife of forty-four years Julia Ladner who passed away. I will always miss you. Thank you for a wonderful life together.

And to my new love, Cindy Schuler, thank you for pointing me in the right direction and remember that in life, always look for better seats.

Please enjoy the book "Human Error" God Bless the United States of America.

IT'S LESS OF ASPIN
DEFENSE SEC'Y QUITS — PAGE 2

IRISH AND BRITS PLEDGE PEACE
CHEERS & JEERS — PAGE 3

DAILY◉NEWS
BROOKLYN EDITION

NEW YORK'S HOMETOWN NEWSPAPER — Thursday, December 16, 1993 — 40¢

THE FRAUD OF ED
EXPOSED

Edward Stancik, top investigator of the city's schools, announces results of scathing school board report.

Corruption and chaos at school board elections

CORTINES ACTS SWIFTLY: PAGES 6 & 7

Bruce Hogenauer's Criminal Record,
the Count Director for the 1993 New York City School Board Election

NYS DOCS Inmate Information - Results

New York State Department of Correctional Services
Inmate Information - Location/Status/Legal Dates/etc.
Back to NYS DOCS Home Page

Information/Error Message:	
(Help) Date of Information:	02/26/99
(Help) DIN (Dept. Identif. Number):	87A4801
Inmate Name:	HOGENAUER, BRUCE
Sex:	MALE
Date of Birth:	07/24/1944
(Help) Race:	WHITE
(Help) Ethnic Origin:	NOT HISPANIC
(Help) Custody Status:	DISCHARGED
(Help) Housing/Releasing Facility:	SING SING
(Help) Date Received (Original):	06/09/1987
(Help) Date Received (Current):	12/16/1988
(Help) Admission Type:	
(Help) County of Commitment:	QUEENS
(Help) Latest Release Date/Type: (Released Inmates Only)	04/17/89 MAXIMUM EXPIRATION
(Help) Crime 1, Description:	UNLAW IMPRISONMENT 1ST
Crime 1, Crime Class:	E
Crime 2, Description:	BAIL JUMPING 1ST
Crime 2, Crime Class:	D
Crime 3, Description:	
Crime 3, Crime Class:	
Crime 4, Description:	
Crime 4, Crime Class:	

If all 4 crime fields contain data, there may be additional crimes not shown here. In this case, the crimes shown here are those with the longest sentences.

(Help) Aggregate Minimum Sentence: 001 Years, 00 Months, 00 Days
(Help) Aggregate Maximum Sentence: 003 Years, 00 Months, 00 Days
(Help) Earliest Release Date:

Under certain circumstances, an inmate may be released prior to serving his or her minimum term and before the earliest release date shown for the inmate.
See "Help" for further information.

(Help) Earliest Release Type:

.../kinqw30?M13-SEL-DINO=87A4801&K01=KINQW30&K02=76B0620&K03=&K04=1&K0 2/26/99

DIRTY SCHOOL DISTRICTS

Shaded districts were cited in a report investigating 1993 community school board elections.

Huge school

Report by city hits an 'archaic,' corrupt system

By PATRICIA MANGAN
Daily News Staff Writer

Widespread fraud, corruption and mismanagement made a mockery of May's "circuslike" school board elections, according to a scathing report that educators hope will renew cries for election reform.

The 123-page report released yesterday capped a 10-month investigation by the office of schools investigator Edward Stancik, who charged that the elections are an "archaic" process "where rules are ignored with impunity and the fear of penalty for one's transgression is virtually nonexistent."

Immediately after the report was unveiled at a packed press conference, Schools Chancellor Ramon Cortines ordered the removal of a Brooklyn elementary school principal and a Bronx school district administrator and launched disciplinary probes of several other school officials named in the report.

"The behavior detailed in the report is extremely disturbing and cannot be tolerated," Cortines said.

The depth of Stancik's probe is unprecedented in the 25-year history of the city's 32 decentralized school

School probes eying 2 bros.

By JOANNE WASSERMAN and VIRGINIA BREEN
Daily News Staff Writers

Call them Brooklyn's Brothers Grim.

The Brighton Beach principal mentioned in yesterday's Board of Education investigation has brushed with trouble before — and so has his brother.

Public School 100 Principal Stuart Posner and PS 154 Principal Harvey Posner are brothers, though they spell their last names differently.

Stuart Posner was accused in yesterday's investigation of sexually harassing staff members and pressuring teachers into making political contributions to help his superior, local school board member Sheldon Plotnick.

Meanwhile, a Brooklyn grand jury is hearing testimony that Harvey Posner hit students at his Windsor Terrace school, the Daily News has learned. Both students and teachers — who were subpoenaed at the school last week — have been called to testify, sources said.

In June, the Daily News reported the complaints of several mothers that Posner, principal for 15 years, had hit their children, all special education students. In one case, a youngster told The News that Posner beat him with a belt. In another, the mother of an 11-year-old said Posner picked her son up by the throat. Another woman said Posner once choked her son, leaving scratch marks on his neck.

Shortly after The News report, the Brooklyn district attorney's office and Board of Education investigators began interviewing students and current and former teachers. The grand jury began hearing the Posner case last week.

New official

District 15 Superintendent William Casey left Posner in PS 154 in September but placed a district administrator in the school to work with students, "dealing with any and all pupil ... discipline."

Posner has denied the charges. Yesterday, his attorney, Phil Kaplan, who also has represented his brother, said Posner was exonerated of similar charges earlier this year.

Yesterday's report, by special investigator Ed Stancik, stated that Stuart Posner "used certain staff members to pressure his teachers to join a local Democratic club." He stacked the club's membership so that it would vote to endorse ... Sheldon Plotnick.

"Posner had his henchmen collect club dues from teachers while they were in the classroom. Other allies made sure that the staff would be in the important club meetings to vote for Plotnick.

"PS 100 teachers reported being the victims of Posner's graphic and aggressive sexual harassment. One teacher likened the staff to 'battered women.'"

Posner did not return calls yesterday. Kaplan said he had not seen the report or heard from Posner.

'A political situation'

"But I don't put much credence in the allegations," he said. "There's no doubt that there's a political situation out there, and who knows who wants retribution?"

Regarding the harassment charges, he said, "The UFT (United Federation of Teachers) is one of the strongest unions in the city," adding, "I doubt if their members can be coerced."

A half-dozen PS 100 teachers reached at home yesterday said they could not comment on the recent allegations against Stuart Posner.

"Look, I'm pretty new, and I don't want to say anything," said one.

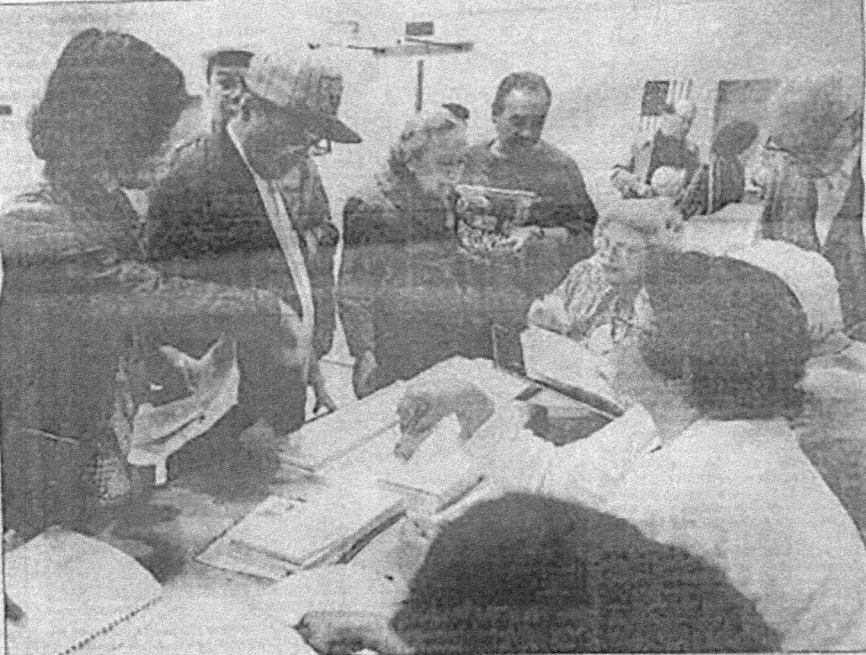

VOTERS line up at sign-in desk at Public School 2 in lower Manhattan to cast ballots in schools election.

election fraud seen

boards, which each control multi-million-dollar budgets and hundreds of school jobs — which critics have charged often are patronage plums.

And its findings fueled long-standing outrage among school officials and parents who have complained that needed reforms continue to languish in the Legislature. "These are systemic problems which exist because the political powers that be want them to exist," said Jon Moscow of the Parents Coalition of Education. "They've got the power and if they want elections to meet kids' needs, they can. Clearly the political establishment has no interest in that whatsoever."

Past complaints

Stancik launched his undercover probe of the May 4 election because of long-standing complaints from districts around the city of gross irregularities in prior elections. Dozens of investigators fanned out throughout the city the day of the election, video-taping the polls. Shortly after the election, complaints started to roll in from parents and school officials in nearly every district.

"May 4 was a day of rampant chaos when ballot boxes were unsealed and sometimes open, ballots, roll books and even inspectors showed up at the polls hours late, others were forced to cast their votes without a modicum of privacy, candidates openly campaigned at the polls, and voters were shuttled to and from different poll sites as time and time again, their voter registration cards did not appear in the proper poll books ..." the report said. "On May 4, voters were forced with a daunting obstacle course, and only those with the most persistence, endurance or luck succeeded in casting a ballot that was counted."

Stancik's investigators found examples of misconduct in about a dozen of the 32 school board elections, and several cases have been

See CHAOS Page 42

HOME SWEET HOME Benjamin Ramos' claimed address, Grant Highway, Bronx (left), and Ramos on Geary Drive in South Plainfield, N.J.

'Chaos to Corruption': excerpts

The following is taken in its entirety from schools Special Commissioner of Investigation Edward Stancik's report "From Chaos to Corruption."

This report describes the problems that beset the 1993 community school board elections, from administrative mismanagement to outright voter fraud. Among the report's most notable findings: Using phony names, undercover investigators "voted" multiple times, while legitimately registered parent voters were turned

Kenneth Drummond

away at the polls. The chaos was so pervasive that one undercover investigator voted 13 times, even twice at the same poll in front of the same inspector.

■ Two Fordham University students who had part-time jobs in School District 10 filled out and cast more than 100 absentee ballots in the names of their unsuspecting fellow students.

■ The principal of a Brooklyn elementary school turned his school into a political power base, coercing his staff to join the local Democratic club and to endorse his ally for reelection to the school board. Teachers who did not attend political club meetings were punished in school. Various teachers reported sexual harassment, and one teacher likened herself and her colleagues to "battered women."

■ Elections commissioners decided which candidates to allow on the ballot in private sessions without having to provide explanations for their actions. At least two commissioners may have been influenced by self-interest and political connections to keep certain candi-

Carmelo Saez

dates' names on the ballot.

■ A Community School Board 1 candidate submitted a nominating petition containing fraudulent signatures. Various candidates backdated petitions and swore falsely to having witnessed signatures.

■ A candidate's son was hired to count ballots in District 11, where his father was a candidate. Meanwhile, an entire box of District 13 ballots was never found, but the ballot count proceeded anyway.

■ Parents of students at 190 schools were disenfranchised due to an administra-

NAMING NAMES
Report details worst cases of fraud in school elections.
See PAGE 42

tive error in the parent voter-registration process.

■ Benjamin Ramos, who was elected to School Board 9, and Kenneth Drummond, who was elected to School Board 12, do not live in their South Bronx districts. Ramos lives in suburban New Jersey and Drummond in a luxury high-rise in Riverdale.

■ A District 9 political group held a fund-raiser, coordinated by Carmelo Saez, for campaign money, but did not account for the thousands of dollars it raised. The money remains unaccounted for today.

■ William Sampol, who was implicated in a 1989 report on corruption in District 27, distributed hundreds of phony flyers endorsing Geraldine Chapey. The flyers were printed on what appeared to be official letterheads of community organizations, but the groups' leaders did not know about or authorize the literature.

Board of Elections didn't care, probe says

By FRANK LOMBARDI
Daily News Staff Writer

Schools investigator Ed Stancik's scathing report on May's chaotic school board elections blasted the city Board of Elections for not preventing "widespread fraud and corruption ... and other horror stories at the polls."

Stancik's probe of the vote in the city's 32 school districts said the "manner by which the decentralized boards elect their representatives is a recipe for disaster," and he blamed the paper ballot system for rampant voter fraud.

Stancik's report also charged that "political influences were exerted and unsavory back-room deals were cut" to allow some candidates on the ballot while others were not.

At a packed press conference yesterday at which he laid out his months-long probe, Stancik said, "The chaotic conditions that reigned in New York City this year ... reflect the Board of Elections' disinterested attitude toward an election it plainly sees as unimportant."

Board of Elections officials denied the charges, blaming the conditions cited by Stancik on the state Legislature's refusal to change "archaic" rules governing school elections.

The election board consists of 10 commissioners — a Democrat and Republican named from each borough by their party leaders.

Among them is Douglas Kellner, a Manhattan Democrat who has been critical of the board. Kellner said the board is being blamed for rules not under its control, though he agreed that some of his fellow board members had handled the petition challenge process in a "cynical way."

Stancik's report also charged that a Bronx Republican district leader, Fred Brown, "used his influence" with Bronx Republican state Sen. Guy Velella and Velella's father, Bronx Election Commissioner Vincent Velella, to restore two ineligible candidates to the ballot.

State Sen. Velella, who is also the Bronx Republican chairman, denied the charge. Stancik's report said Brown was secretly recorded boasting that "it cost a helluva big chip" with the Velellas to get the candidates restored to the ballot.

The matter has been referred to the Bronx and Manhattan district attorneys.

Daniel DeFrancesco, executive director of the Board of Elections, denied Stancik's accusation that the board didn't take the school election seriously. "We take all elections seriously," DeFrancesco said.

He said the board also has been prodding the state Legislature for at least 10 years to change the rules governing school board elections.

— With Zachary Margulis

Probe Eyes Fraud In May Elections For School Board

By Liz Willen
STAFF WRITER

Law enforcement officials are eyeing possible criminal charges resulting from last May's school board elections, including the possibility that some voters cast more than one ballot, sources said.

The allegations are contained in a scathing report to be released tomorrow by Ed Stancik, special commissioner of investigation for New York City schools, according to sources.

The irregularities documented in the report will be referred to criminal prosecutors in the Bronx and Manhattan, sources said, adding that federal prosecutors also may get involved.

The report caps a nearly eight-month investigation of the community school board elections. Sources said Stancik's report describes widespread voter fraud, electioneering, and mismanagement in the archaic paper balloting process.

The report also documents improper behavior by local school board candidates and other officials involved in the elections. Stancik declined to comment yesterday, saying he will wait until his report is released.

New York Newsday last spring described numerous problems in the school board elections, which are conducted every four years with paper ballots despite persistent cries for election reform. The problems ranged from a shortage of interpreters to mix ups in ballot box deliveries to a lack of privacy for voters.

The hotly contested school board elections attracted intense interest — from voters and the media — because it was widely viewed as a battle between the religious right and more progressive forces.

MORE GENERAL NEWS, PAGES 104-109

Contents

Chapter One
Let's Start The Journey 1

Chapter Two
Let's Go To The New York State Court 21

Chapter Three
The Six Year History Of My Federal Court Appearances Fighting Tooth And Nail For A Trial............30

Chapter Four
The Federal Court For The Eastern District Of New York:
The Final Decision Dismissing My Election Fraud Case And Refusing To Give Me A Trial................42

Chapter Five
Traffic Court, Staten Island, New York..54

Chapter Six
Edward F. Srancik Official New York Report:
"From Chaos To Corruption The 1993 School Board Election"
It Totally Disputes The Federal District Court Decision
And Proves That The 1993 School Board Election Was Rigged.
Corrupt And Voter Fraud Did Effect The Outcome Of MY Election. 56

Chapter Seven
Beginning Of The End 66

Chapter Eight
Let's Notify The Parents 71

Chapter Nine
All Aboard On The Way To The U.S. Court Of Appeals..74

Chapter Ten
Decisions Sealing My Case v City Of New York Forever
By The United States Court Of Appeals For The Second Circuit. 92

Chapter Eleven
The U.S. Supreme Court. The Court Of Last Resort! 97

Chapter Twelve
My Conclusions 106

Chapter Thirteen
"The Smoking Gun" The Official Stancik Report:
From Chaos to Corruption, proofs Election Fraud 112

CHAPTER ONE
Let's Start The Journey

My name is Mel Ladner. I ran as a candidate in the 1993 school-board election and gave it my best shot to shine light on the corruption in New York City in the education and election system. I found out that the system works for only a chosen few, so why would anyone want to change it? I won half the case against Proportional Counts Associates, Inc. and Bruce Hogenauer, who ran the school-board election and was awarded $76,741,095.49 (CV96-2190 ILG) by Federal District Judge I. Leo Glasser.

UNITED STATES DISTRICT COURT
EASTERN DISTRICT OF NEW YORK
--X
MELVIN LADNER, Plaintiff,

CV-96-2190 (ILG)

-against-

PROPORTIONAL COUNT ASSOCIATES, INC.;
BRUCE HONGENAUER

Defendants
--X

The summons and complaint in this action having been duly served on the above-named defendants on   1999 and said defendants having failed to plead or otherwise defend in this action, and said default having been duly noted, and upon the annexed declaration of default judgment.

NOW, on motion of Melvin Ladner Pro se plaintiff, it is hereby

OREDERED and ADJUGED that Melvin Ladner, the plaintiff, does recover of Proportional Count Associates, Inc., Bruce Hogenauer, the defendants residing at Proportional Count Associates, Inc. 45 Kraft Avenue, Bronxville, New York, 10708, Bruce Hogenauer 321 West 88th Street, New York, New York 10024, the sum of $50,000,000.00 (Fifty Million dollars) the amount claimed, plus interest in the sum of $ 26,741,095, with $ 0.00 costs and disbursements, and attorney fees in the sum of $ 0.00 $, Amount in all to the sum of $ 76,741,095.49 plus interest at the legal rate in effect on the date of this judgment; and that the plaintiff have execution therefor.

Dated: Brooklyn, New York
Feb. 16 1999

By: _____
Melvin Ladner
60 Kenmore Street
Staten Island, New York 10312
Telephone Number 718-966-5398

The federal court, in its wisdom, separated the case into two parts-one against Proportional Counts Associates, and the other against the people who were responsible for the rigged 1993 school-board election and for hiring convicted felons to run the citywide school-board elections in the city of New York. The Federal District Court, the U.S. Court of Appeals, and even the U.S. Supreme Court all ruled that all corrupt and fraudulent acts in the school-board election was just human error, and I wasn't entitled to a trial. I went all the way to the U.S. Supreme Court, case number 99-5301, asking and fighting for a trial for over six years-Melvin Ladner v. City of New York, 99-5301. The U.S. Supreme Court denied me that trial. Everyone should remember that a trial is a search for the truth. No court ever cited U.S. Marshal Bob Meltzer's sworn testimony in any decision regarding Bruce Hogenauer, the count director for the Staten Island election. He was a convicted felon. I asked why the courts never mentioned Meltzer's testimony about Bruce Hogenauer, prisoner number 03263018, FBI number 486105F in all their rulings, because that would have opened a can of worms. The parents of children who attended the New York City public schools, the taxpayers, and the voters would have seen that the system wasn't working. The case would have brought thousands of lawsuits and perhaps protests in the streets. The amazing part of the story is that the parents of George L. Ebert, of Intermediate Junior High School, 333 Midland Avenue, Staten Island, New York still don't know that their children came into contact with a kidnapper and child molester for five days when the school was in session. The federal courts and the city of New York kept it a secret by not informing the parents that their children were at risk. Bruce Hogenauer fled to Great Britain for three years, where he lived a life of crime. He was apprehended and extradited by Detective Theodore Theologes of the New York City Detective Squad and U.S. Marshal Bob Meltzer on an arrest warrant for kidnapping a minor across state lines to face those criminal charges in a United States court. While being extradited for kidnapping, Hogenauer assaulted Meltzer on the six-and-a-half-hour flight from Great Britain back to the U.S. While he punched and kicked Meltzer on the plane, he screamed that he wanted the marshal to feel what the kidnapped boy felt. Hogenauer may have tried to escape being extradited to the U.S.

HUMAN ERROR: ELECTION FRAUD

(Ed. 3-15-72)

The President of the United States of America

To the Marshal of the United States for the Eastern District of New York and to his Deputies or any or either of them—GREETING:

WHEREAS, complaint on oath hath been made to me, charging that

BRUCE HOGENAUER

did on or about the _____9th_____ day of ____January____, in the year one thousand nine hundred and ___eighty-seven___, at the Eastern District of New York, in violation of Section ___111___, Title 18, United States Code

in that he did assault a federal officer while said officer was engaged in the performance of his official duties

as Set forth in the complaint this day filed in my office, a certified copy of which is hereto attached, against the peace of the United States and their dignity, and against the form of the statute of the United States in such case made and provided.

NOW, THEREFORE, YOU ARE HEREBY COMMANDED, in the name of the President of the United States of America, to apprehend the said __BRUCE HOGENAUER__

and bring __HIS__ bod y ____ forthwith before me or some judge of the United States wherever ___he___ may be found that __he__ may then and there be dealt with according to law for the said offense.

Given under my hand and seal, this __13th__ day of __January__ in the year of our Lord one thousand nine hundred and __eighty seven__

APPROVED:

_____   _____
Asst United States Attorney   United States Magistrate
of the Eastern District of New York   of the Eastern District of New York

☆ U.S. GPO: 1983-619-745

CITY OF NEW YORK
THE SPECIAL COMMISSIONER OF INVESTIGATION
FOR THE NEW YORK CITY SCHOOL DISTRICT
25 BROADWAY, 8TH FLOOR
NEW YORK, NEW YORK 10004

ED STANCIK
SPECIAL COMMISSIONER

**FROM CHAOS TO CORRUPTION:
AN INVESTIGATION INTO THE 1993
COMMUNITY SCHOOL BOARD ELECTION**

TELEPHONE (212) 510-1400
FAX (212) 510-1550

Report Highlights

This report describes the problems that beset the 1993 Community School Board Election, from administrative mismanagement to outright voter fraud. Among the report's most notable findings:

- Using phony names, undercover investigators "voted" multiple times, while legitimately registered parent voters were turned away at the polls. The chaos was so pervasive that one undercover investigator voted fifteen times, even twice at the same poll site in front of the same inspector.

- Two Fordham University students who had part time jobs in School District 10 filled out and cast more than one hundred absentee ballots in the names of their unsuspecting fellow students.

- The principal of a Brooklyn elementary school turned his school into a political power base, coercing his staff to join the local Democratic club and to endorse his ally for reelection to the School Board. Teachers who did not attend political club meetings were punished in school. Various teachers reported sexual harassment, and one teacher likened herself and her colleagues to "battered women."

- Elections commissioners decide which candidates go on the ballot in private sessions without having to provide explanations for their actions. At least two commissioners may have been influenced by self-interest and political connections to keep certain candidates' names on the ballot.

- A Community School Board 1 candidate submitted a nominating petition containing fraudulent signatures. Various candidates "backdated" petitions and swore falsely to having witnessed signatures.

- A candidate's son was hired to count ballots in District 11, where his father was a candidate. Meanwhile, an entire box of District 13 ballots was never found, but the ballot count proceeded anyway.

- Parents of students at 190 schools were disenfranchised due to an administrative error in the parent voter registration process.

- Benjamin Ramos, who was elected to School Board 9, and Kenneth Drummond, who was elected to School Board 12, do not live in the South Bronx. Ramos lives in suburban New Jersey and Drummond lives in a luxury highrise in Riverdale.

- A District 9 political group held a fundraiser to raise campaign money, but did not account for the thousands of dollars they raised. The money remains unaccounted for today.

- William Sampol, who was implicated in a 1989 report on corruption in District 27, distributed hundreds of phony flyers endorsing Geraldine Chapey. The flyers were printed on what appeared to be official letterheads of community organizations, but the groups' leaders did not know about or authorize the literature.

- The Community School Board Election cost New York City millions of extra dollars. More than 10,000 police hours were spent watching cardboard ballot boxes for a nine-day period.

He spent time in prison for kidnapping when he was hired as the count director to run the 1993 Staten Island school-board election. Who would hire such a man to be in charge of the city's paper ballots? It was the City of New York. Hogenauer's criminal record included: 1966 for destruction of private property. 1966 twice for disorderly conduct in New York. 1972 for altering a driver's license in Jersey City, NJ. 1975 for breaking and entering in Mountainside, NJ. 1980 for aggravated harassment in the town of Woodbury, NY. 1983 for kidnapping a minor and crossing state lines in Tampa, FL. For assaulting a federal U.S. marshal. If that wasn't enough, he also used aliases: Bruce William Hogenauer Bruce Hoenover Bruce Anderson Bruce Jack Hogenauer He was held in Her Majesty's Prison at Pentonville,

HUMAN ERROR: ELECTION FRAUD

Great Britain, before being the count director for the 1993 school-board election. Robert A. Meltzer, Supervisor Deputy of the United States Marshal's Service, gave his sworn deposition on August 6, 1997, to my lawyer, Jeff Motelson.

UNITED STATES MARSHALS SERVICE
FIREARM DISCHARGE/ASSAULT REPORT

INSTRUCTIONS:

1. A member of the USMS shall prepare this report within 72 hours whenever he:
   (a) discharges a firearm other than at an authorized firearms range; or
   (b) is the victim of a physical assault while performing a lawful duty.
2. Supervisory personnel shall review and sign the report prior to forwarding to the Chief of Internal Investigations.
3. Legibly complete all applicable items.

USMS PERSONNEL INVOLVED: Name: Robert A. Meltzer | Title: Supervisor DUSM | Credentials No.: 0659 | Assigned District: EDNY

Date of Incident: January 9, 1987 | **Time:** 2:15 pm | **Location of Incident (City, State):** aboard Panam Heath Row Airport London England ☒ Outdoors | **District Where Incident Occurred:** London England

TYPE OF REPORT: ☐ Firearm Discharged ☒ Physical Assault | **Duty Status:** ☒ On Duty ☐ Off Duty | ☐ Working Alone ☒ Working With Partner

TYPE OF ASSIGNMENT IF ON DUTY: Transporting Prisoner Extridition | **TYPE OF INCIDENT:** Assault on Deputy by Prisoner

REASON FOR DISCHARGING FIREARM: ☐ Protect Self ☐ Protect Citizen ☐ Other (Specify) | **WERE THE FOLLOWING NOTIFIED:** FBI ☒ Yes ☐ No | Local Police ☐ Yes ☒ No

LIGHTING CONDITIONS: Indoors: ☒ Good Artificial ☐ Poor Artificial ☐ Other (Specify) | Outdoors: ☐ Daylight ☐ Dusk ☐ Dark

WEATHER CONDITIONS: ☒ Clear ☐ Cloudy ☐ Rain ☐ Snow ☐ Fog ☐ Other (Specify)

DID YOU HAVE PRIOR KNOWLEDGE THAT THE SITUATION INVOLVED A PERSON WITH A DANGEROUS WEAPON? ☐ Yes ☒ No | **TYPE OF PREMISES:** Aircraft-Pan am 747

DID YOU INITIALLY DRAW YOUR FIREARM: ☐ As A Precautionary Measure ☐ When Needed To Fire

OFFICER'S WEAPON(S): ☐ Service Revolver ☐ Other (Specify) No Weapon (firearm) Carried | **OPPONENT'S WEAPON(S):** Fist | **NO. of OPPONENTS** Male: 1 Female: | **NO. ARRESTED** Male: 1 Female: | **NO. OF SHOTS OPPONEN FIRED AT YOU:** 0

NO. OF SHOTS YOU FIRED: n/a | Single Action | Double Action | **DID YOU HAVE TIME TO AIM?** ☐ Yes ☐ No n/a | **DID YOU HAVE TO RELOAD?** ☐ Yes ☐ No n/a

INJURIES: | Not Wounded | Superficially Wounded | Critical | Killed | Unknown
Opponent(s) | ☒ | ☐ | ☐ | ☐ | ☐
Officer | ☒ | ☐ | ☐ | ☐ | ☐

DISTANCE BETWEEN YOU AND OPPONENT WHEN FIRST SHOT WAS FIRED: n/a | **POSITIONS:** Opponent(s) / Officer | Standing ☐ | Sitting ☐ | Crouching ☐ | Lying Down — | Other (Specify) ☐

DESCRIBE PROTECTIVE COVER WHICH YOU USED: n/a | **WERE IMPACT POINT(S) OF FIRED ROUND(S) DETERMINED?** ☐ Yes ☐ No n/a

DESCRIBE THE INCIDENT IN DETAIL: See Attached Memo

(continue on reverse side)

REMARKS: (Include any information that may be used in training programs)

(continue on reverse side)

PREPARED BY (Signature): | **Title:** Supervisor DUSM | **District:** EDNY | **Date:** January ,1
REVIEWED BY (Signature of Supervisor): | **Title:** | **District:** | **Date Forwarded:**

COPY 3 — USMS EMPLOYEE'S COPY | FORM USM-133 (Ex. 3-23-7)

The transcript begins on page seven, line two:

Jeff: In the course of your duties for the Unites States Marshal's Service, have you been assigned any tasks involving one Bruce Hogenauer?

Bob: Yes, I have.

Jeff: When were you first assigned any duties concerning Mr. Hogenauer? Bob: In 1987. Jeff: What duties were you assigned at that time?

Bob: I was assigned to be involved in the extradition of Mr. Hogenauer from England, Great Britain, to the United States.

Jeff: Who gave you that assignment? Bob: That was from headquarters.

Jeff: At the time that you were assigned to such duties, was Mr. Hogenauer under apprehension?

Bob: Yes, he was.

Jeff: Where had he been apprehended, Sir?

Bob: He was apprehended in Great Britain, and they were holding him in the jail there for extradition.

Page eight, line five, to page eight, line twenty-one: Jeff: From which authorization or jurisdiction?

Bob: New York City had a kidnapping warrant on him.

Jeff: For approximately what period of time had there been an outstanding warrant for the arrest of Mr. Hogenauer for kidnapping at the time of apprehension?id Bob: Since approximately 1984, I believe. Jeff: Were the kidnapping charges Baldomestic or United States charges concerning the kidnapping?"

Bob: Yes, they were.

bali Jeff: At the time that Mr. Hogenauer was known to have left the country, was he arca fugitive from justice?

Bob: I believe he was.

From page eleven, line twenty-three, to page twelve, line fifteen:

Jeff: At the time you took Mr. Hogenauer into custody, did he initially make any attempt of flight from your custody?

Bob: When we first got on the plane, the English police officers turned Mr. Hogenauer over to myself and Mr. Theologes, and they left, of course, and the plane started to back from the gate. At that point, I was sitting in the middle seat of three seats. There were seats in the plane on the left side of the plane, and Mr. Hogenauer was in the window seat, and my partner was in the aisle seat. At that point, Mr. Hogenauer proceeded to strike me in the head with his fists, and I don't know if that was an escape attempt or not, but it could be construed as one.

From page thirteen, lines fourteen to twenty five:

Jeff: Following that attack on you, what did you do?

Bob: I restrained him, subdued him, and he was handcuffed.

Jeff: Immediately prior to, during, or immediately after the attack upon you, did Hogenauer say, shout, or otherwise communicate with you verbally?

Bob: Yes. He said after the attack that he did it because he wanted me to know what the boy was going through. I took that to mean the boy that he kidnapped. From page fifteen, lines two through ten:

Jeff: As of the time of your extradition of Mr. Hogenauer back to the United States, did Mr. Hogenauer have a prior criminal record?

Bob: Yes, he did.

Jeff: What did that consist of?

Bob: Numerous charges from forgery to, I believe, assault.

The 1993 school-board election count was held in George L. Ebert Intermediate School, Midland Avenue, Staten Island, New York 10306 on Staten Island while the school was in session. The count lasted five days, and Hogenauer and his staff set up for three more days in the school gym while school was in session. Children from the ages of five to eleven came into contact with a child molester, kidnapper, and forger, not only in school but in the bathrooms. I went to the nearest bathroom in the school during the count. As I walked down the hall to the bathroom, I heard two boys screaming, as they ran out of the bathroom. I barely glanced at them running down the hall.

When I opened the door, I saw Hogenauer washing his arms, which had bleeding scratches on them. I asked if he was OK. He said he cut himself opening boxes. I didn't make anything of it until I found out years later he was a kidnapper and child molester. If someone advertised in the Sunday *New York Times* looking for someone to commit election fraud, he wouldn't find a better candidate than Hogenauer to be the count director for the Staten Island school-board election. With a résumé like his, it would be hard to find someone else with an arrest record for fraud, destruction of private property, arson, altering a driver's license, breaking and entering, assault, the use of aliases, and harassment. There was a bonus in the hiring of Hogenauer, because he was also a child molester, kidnapper, and fugitive from justice who assaulted a federal officer. Who in his right mind would hire such a person as count director? The New York City Board of Elections did.

Archibald Robertson of Proportional Counts Associates was Hogenauer's supervisor, who referred to Hogenauer as being between situations. That meant jail. Robertson's sworn testimony with Jeff Motelson, my lawyer, on April 2, 1997 included these lines from pages 102-3, lines eighteen to ten: (Ms. Le Goff, the attorney for New York City, objected to the form of a question.)

Mr. Rotenson was Hogenauer's Boss

```
1                    Robertson
2      District 31 did you notice that Mr. Hogenauer
3      was talking about invading aliens?
4              MS. LE GOFF:  Objection to the
5          form of the question.
6      A.    I just used that example.  I don't
7      think he talked about invading aliens.
8      Q.    Did he talk about any other bizarre
9      subject, that you recall?
10             MS. LE GOFF:  Objection to the
11         form.
12     A.    Mr. Hogenauer seemed to be mentally
13     troubled.  I don't recall the specific
14     instance.  I do know that police officers
15     called me about him as a reference they told
16     me of some trouble deep trouble that Mr.
17     Hogenauer.
18     Q.    What did the police officer tell you?
19             MS. LE GOFF:  Objection to the
20         form of the question.
21     A.    Do we have to go into that question?
22     Q.    Please, we need an answer for the
23     record.
24     A.    He molested some young people,
25     according to the police officers.
```

                                                              103
                        Robertson
Q.   Did the officer report that Mr. Hogenauer had been arrested in suspicion of committing such an offense?

A.   He was calling me as a former "employer," and I explained that I knew his family and I was shocked.

Q.   Was that in 1993 that you received that call?

A.   I think it was '94.

Q.   When you spoke to the officer, was it your understanding that Mr. Hogenauer was incarcerated?

A.   Couldn't guess. I mean he was the subject of serious allegations, I can tell you that.

Q.   Had the bizarre call that you received from Mr. Hogenauer preceded the call from the officer?

A.   Oh, yes.

Q.   Did you relate to the officer the bizarre call from Mr. Hogenauer that you received?

A.   Not specifically. I just detected some mental instability.

The 1993 school-board election was city wide. Millions of New York City residents were eligible to vote. The City of New York was responsible for a free and fair election. After reading the evidence presented in this book, the reader can decide if the city should be held criminally responsible for failing to hold a free and fair election. An open trial would have established that. By having an open trial, it would have brought to light that the election was far from being fair and honest. The ballot boxes sat in the Staten Island election headquarters for nine days before the count began. It was against state and federal law to open a sealed ballot box without a court order. No court order was received. Barbara Kett, the chief clerk, and her deputies of the board of elections, admitted they opened the sealed ballot boxes before the ballots were counted and altered the ballots by putting her initials on hundreds, perhaps thousands, of ballots before the count. Another fact the court never cited was that the sealed ballot boxes were stored for nine days before the count in the Staten Island Board of Elections headquarters on Bay Street, where Barbara Kett and her deputies had their offices. A lot could happen in nine days.

I received information from a friend's wife who worked at the Staten Island Board of Elections that Kett was caught going into sealed ballot boxes during the nine-day storage period. We also had a witness named Charles Zappla who worked at the Board of Elections. He gave his sworn deposition to Jeff Motelson, my lawyer, on June 11, 1996. Zappla took pictures that were evidence showing the 1993 school-board ballots on the floor and in laundry bins.

From page eighty-one, line two of the deposition:

Jeff: The ballots?

Zappla: Being on the floor? Jeff: Yes. Zappla: They knew.

Jeff: Did you tell anyone? Zappla: Yes. Jeff: Who?

Zappla: Barbara Kett or Arnold Thompson. Jeff: When did you tell them?

Zappla: We brought the ballots downstairs for garbage, and we asked Barbara Kett or Arnold Thompson, I don't recall who. They said to put them to the side, and when we took ballots out of the containers, we put them on the floor on the side, and then they just got destroyed.

Page eighty-three, line three:

Jeff: How are you sure?

Zappla: I know. I'm positive about that.

Jeff: at the time you took the pictures, were you working for the Board of Elections?

Zappla: Yes, I was.

Jeff: Did anyone else tell you to take the pictures?

Zappla: People seen me taking pictures around the office.

Barbara Kett, chief clerk for the Staten Island Board of Elections, gave her sworn deposition on December 22, 1995, stating, from page twenty:

Jeff: Were the pencil marks on the ballots cast in the election erasable? Kett: I guess so, if somebody had an eraser.

Jeff: Were pencils provided at voting stations for voters to use? Kett: Yes. On page twenty-four, lines thirteen to fifteen:

Jeff: Who engaged the services of Proportional Counts Associates for that job? Kett: The City of New York.

On page twenty-four, line nineteen, Jeff asked:

Jeff: Who is Bruce Hogenauer?

Kett: He was the director of the count for Staten Island, Richmond Count. From page twenty-five, line two:

Jeff: Where did you meet him (Hogenauer)? Kett: IS2, Midland Avenue. Jeff: Is that also known as Egbert School? Kett: Yes.

From page twenty-five, lines thirteen through fifteen:

Jeff: Where at the school did you meet him?

Kett: I met Hogenauer at the count site in the school gymnasium.

Jeff: Did you have any conversations with him when you met him?

Kett: Yes.

Jeff: What was the sum and substance of that conversations?

Kett: Off the record, I told him he was an idiot. That's not allowed, I guess.

From page fifty-one, line eighteen:

Jeff: In the May 4, 1993 school -election in Staten Island, were voters allowed to use those sample ballots for ballot voting?

Kett: Some areas.

From page fifty-eight, line three:

Jeff: Did Bruce Hogenauer inform you that there were sample ballots that were in the May 4, 1993 election that came to his attention at the Egbert site?

Kett: No.

From page 160 line four:

Kett: We do not have possession of the stubs. (They destroyed 24,000 ballot stubs and the protest sheets I filled out at the count site.)

From page 165, lines three-nine:

Jeff: Have you ever initialed ballots before the school-board election on May 4, 1993?

Kett: No.

Jeff: Have you ever initialed ballots again after the school-board election of May 4, 1993?

Kett: No.

From page seventy-five, lines eight to twelve:

Jeff: How many ballots did you initial before the count?

Kett: A lot of them.

From page eighty-five, line eighteen:

Jeff: Did you open ballot boxes which contained votes in them to make changes on election district written on those ballots?

Kett: Yes.

Jeff: Did you open boxes at the site to make those changes?

Kett: Yes.

Jeff: Did you take the tape off the cardboard boxes to allow the top of the boxes to be removed?

Kett: Sometimes.

Barbara Kett, chief clerk of the Staten Island Board of Election, just confessed to committing crimes with intent to alter ballots not yet counted. Kett had no court order to open sealed ballot boxes.

I called the New York City Police to the count site and the New York City Board of Elections to file a formal complaint about the count director counting sample ballots. I filed a protest about counting sample ballots.

The court used the defense of human error for opening sealed ballot boxes without a court order. The court never cited the fact that when I requested Hogenauer to stop the count, he refused. I called the New York City Police Department to stop the count when BMK initials appeared on thousands of ballots. Two ballot boxes were also missing. I protested over as many of the altered ballots that Hogenauer would let me.

When the police arrived at the count site, I showed them the ballots I protested. Half of the handwritten numbers were in both ink and pencil on the same ballot! Hundreds of ballots with had the number 11, with the first digit in ink and the second in pencil. It was amazing to me that the ballots were the 11 were all my votes, which coincidentally put me out of the race.

There were sample ballots counted with my being put out of the race. It's easy to change paper ballots. If I received a number one on the ballot, and someone had access to the sealed boxes, all he had to do was add another number one to create the number eleven. It was that easy to fix an election and put me out of the race.

I called 911 for the police to come to the count site and stop the count. They arrived from the 122 Precinct. The police captain made a phone call to someone, but no one stopped counting the ballots. I made a police report about voter fraud. The story of the protested ballots and protest sheets ran in the Staten Island Advance newspaper the following day.

The reporter for the Advance and eyewitness to the voter fraud was Laura D'anglea, who quickly wrote up the story.

The election system has been getting away with rigged elections for years.

When there is a repeated pattern of election fraud, it's called historical corruption. That was what the FBI agents told me when they came to my house after I made a formal complaint to the FBI about election fraud.

The people in the system didn't think they'd be caught. If someone was caught, nothing happened, and nothing changed. The sad part was they were right. The Board of Elections admitted to destroying sheets, eliminating evidence of voter fraud. The court ruled that this, too, was human error.

The destroyed ballot stubs were the check and balance for a fair election. Each ballot had the same number on the ballot and on the stub attached at the bottom. When someone voted, there were two boxes, one for the ballot and another for the stubs. If there was fraud, the stub wouldn't match the ballot. If there were more stubs than ballots, that should send up a red flag that something was wrong. That, too, was ruled human error.

Sample ballots were a different color-yellow. The real ballots were white. Hogenauer counted the samples as real ballots. After I protested to stop the count, I filled out protest sheets explaining that the samples were being counted, and there were no stubs or ed/ ad numbers, so there was no way to tell where the sample ballots came from. As far as anyone knew, thousands of sample ballots were stuffed into the ballot boxes.

The more I protested, the more Hogenauer cheated me. My chances of winning the election were nil to none.

Dead people also voted in the 1993 school-board election. I hired a private investigator who used a sample list of ten voters in the election to check. Four of them were already dead, but they somehow voted in the election. Their names were Thomas Reilly, Pasquale Delio, Theresa Bellia, and Ronald Ross. The more we investigated the 1993 school-board election, the more it became clear that the same fraud was happening in other elections. It's easy to copy the names of dead people from the newspaper obituaries and use them to vote in local and nationwide elections.

Robert Brull, the private investigator, checked the obituaries with the board of elections voter record. He went to the recorded addresses and interviewed neighbors and made round-robin investigations. He included date of birth, date of death, the board of elections data banks, driver's licenses, and arrest records. He concluded that four of the ten people he checked were dead before the 1993 school-board election in Staten Island.

If anyone wishes to check this story, go to Google and search the U.S. Supreme Court website. Look for case 99-5301, Melvin Ladner v. City of New York. The name of the case is all anyone will see. The content has been deleted. If someone is lucky, he might be able to read the lower court's ruling. That ruling was a whitewash to prevent a trial. New York City lawyers feared that the parents would find out about Hogenauer's criminal record regarding child molestation and kidnapping would be revealed at the trial. The parents would be in an uproar if they knew the truth.

Free and fair elections are the foundation of a free society. Without free and fair elections, we have a country that doesn't truly represent the people. I campaigned for six months. I participated in over twenty forums, debates, and one live two-hour debate on TV. I demanded we have an audit and a criminal investigation where the missing $5 billion was going, because it wasn't reaching the classrooms to buy books and supplies. The final straw was discovering the corruption regarding rented space to relieve overcrowding. Public officials were making a nice living from the kickback from awarding contracts to landlords for renting space. There was no way I would win a school-board election.

Using the New York City school system as an example, I gave speeches in my campaign in 1993 that the system was headed toward bankruptcy, and it wouldn't stop there. The way the school system went, there would go our country and our future.

What made me a loser was that in all my speeches, I said it and meant it that my top agenda was to audit the $7.5 billion school-board budget. If someone we're stealing from the school budget, his number-one plan would be to prevent me from winning that election, and a lot of careers depended on that. After one of my speeches, I was invited out for coffee. The person, a retired principal, had his eyes on Staten Island politics and hinted that if I played ball, I might have a future in politics. I had many enemies by insisting on an audit, and he asked if I were serious about that. He seemed concerned about whether I'd keep the same administrators in place if I were elected.

I said I was very serious about changing the system and replacing the administrators. I added that whoever sent him could go screw themselves. He left the shop abruptly, and I had to pay the bill.

Melvin H. Ladner

My name is Melvin H. Ladner and I am a conservative and proud of it. My wife and I reside in Annadale and have been Staten Island residents for more than 20 years. My most impressive credential is being a parent to two wonderful children — my daughter, who is currently attending public school, and my son, who graduated Tottenville High School and is in college.

I am an advocate of parents' rights, optional prayer and saluting the flag in school. Being a retired police officer and United States Special Deputy Marshal, I have vast experience in criminal investigations which I feel will be a tremendous asset due to the fact that $5 billion of the budget is disappearing every year.

I belong to the following organizations: Patrolmen's Benevolent Association; 10-13 Association; Shorim Society of the New York City Police Department; the Fraternal Order of Police; and the Blue Knights intentional law enforcement organization. I also am certified as a fire safety director.

    I did receive a lot of support from law enforcement, parent groups, and newspapers. I gained more support from parents who volunteered to make phone calls and put up signs. I had over 100 volunteers working on my campaign. The New York Post endorsed me. My name was mentioned on Reverend Fallwell's TV Station twenty-four hours a day to support my candidacy. During Sunday prayer services in church, they couldn't support me, but they helped as best they could. My plan was to receive a little more than one ninth of the votes to win. There were twenty- four candidates in the election. I always displayed a study during my speeches. The U.S. Chamber of Commerce in 1990 stated that the New York City school system had a budget of $7.5 billion, but only $2 billion reached the classrooms for teachers, supplies, and services. $5 billion was missing, and very little of that could be accounted for. In fact, in 1992-1993, New York City schools sent letters to parents begging for money and asking them to donate books, pencils, paper, toilet paper, and other supplies to the schools.

Student textbooks were so outdated that the pictures of airplanes in them had propellers. The world maps in the books had countries that no longer existed. There was a shortage of textbooks, and students had to share the outdated books in the classroom. That was pretty bad for a $7.5 billion school budget.

What made me decide to run was when my daughter came home with a letter from her school to donate toilet paper to the school, because they didn't have any. The teachers were buying toilet paper for the students, but their salaries were low to begin with. It turned out that the teachers were paying for most of the necessary supplies so they could teach their students.

I found out that Bill Clinton's daughter was attending a private school and was paying less than the New York City school system spent on each student. The deeper I looked into the situation, the more corruption I found. Someone had to fix the education in the New York City School system, because that represented our country's future. I made endless phone calls to open the eyes of our politicians and city leaders to no avail. I wrote a letter to the editor of the Staten Island Advance. They published some of my articles that stated, *The New York City school system has a $7.5 billion budget, and $5 billion of the budget is missing.* The only thing I got in return was to be attacked for trying to expose the corruption.

STATEN ISLAND ADVANCE ■ THURSDAY, FEBRUARY 23, 1995   A 9

wsuit charges election fraud

board candidates claim '93 elections were fixed

D'ANGELO
WRITER

May 1993 Staten Islunity School Board re "fixed" and "fraudr of unsuccessful cane filed a $2 million ederal court.

,adner, of Annadale, y Carl, of Stapleton, lost the election bes of imaginary and were counted against

harges that legitimate s were replaced with stuffed with votes for rival candidates.

"There were multiple votes cast by the same people in the same handwriting, and the boxes were opened before tabulations and were debased," said Jeffrey M. Motelson, the attorney representing the candidates.

Motelson said the proportional voting system used in community school board elections is "most susceptible to problems of tampering."

Under this system voters rank the candidates according to their preferences. The process is vastly different from the at-large system used in most other elections, where the preferred candidate is chosen by pulling a lever.

The suit names as defendants the City of New York, the Board of Elections, the Board of Education and chief clerk of the Staten Island Board of Elections, Barbara M. Kett. Corporation Counsel attorney Patricia LeGoff is representing the defendants.

U.S. District Court Judge I. Leo Glasser denied the city's motion to dismiss the lawsuit on procedural grounds earlier this month.

Ms. LeGoff said that the defense has not yet responded to the complaint. "We're still in the process of investigating the allegation," she said.

A response will be submitted by the end of March, she said.

The suit alleges that the chief clerk, Ms. Kett, allowed fraud to occur in the "casting, securing, transfer, tabulation and entering of elections results." The suit charges that she herself tampered with votes and failed to properly seal ballot boxes.

Ladner and Carl say the fraudulent election subjected them to scorn, contempt and ridicule, deprived them of their civil rights, caused embarrassment, anguish and pain, and subjected them to stigma and irreparable harm as far as becoming viable political candidates in the future.

nant heads for Fort Wadsworth

y office to move from Manhattan

F REPORT

ommand that oversees ontracts and employs 0 and 150 workers will ort Wadsworth March nnounced yesterday. y operating in downattan, the unit, known Contract Management new building that had been built as headquarters for the Navy.

Rep. Susan Molinari reported earlier this month that a unit of the Defense Logistics Agency (DLA) would be moving into office space in the Fort. The contract-management command reports to the DLA, which is based in Al- is made up of military personnel and civilians who are experts in such areas as product assessment, price-cost analysis, technical analysis and acquisition, according to Lt. Col. Larry Epstein.

While the move may not offer a direct economic benefit to Staten Island, it helps in the effort, spearheaded by Ms. Molinari, to keep the Fort in the hands of the federal government. Two thirds of ment to become part of the Gateway National Recreation Area network.

Last week Coast Guard Commandant Robert Kramek testified before a House subcommittee that Staten Island is "very attractive" as the place to relocate from Governors Island. If the Coast Guard were to transfer its harbor operations to Rosebank, it would take over 160 units of housing

What made the U.S. great is its public education system. It is the feeding system for the country's colleges and universities, where most innovation comes from. If the link becomes broken at the public school level, the U.S. will eventually fail. That explains why we have more foreign students attending our colleges and universities. Why are Third-World countries beginning to overtake us? It was time to wake up to the situation. The future is in public education. That means discipline for students, prayer in schools, and parents taking responsibilities for their children's education. Certain school subjects should allow parents to opt their children out. The basics of reading, writing, history and arithmetic should be required.

I asked why we didn't have courses in business for students starting sixth grade. We had to change the subjects so children could learn how to start and run their own businesses. That would be a great foundation for any child. We could have summer programs to run businesses for students, with half the profits going to the school that funded the program. It seemed like a no-brainer except in the world of New York City education. I was booed off the stage. The New York City education system is so overcrowded, students have to share seats. There aren't enough classrooms for students, so the school system used temporary buildings that were dangerous for kids. It takes at least seven years to build a school, and time had already run out for the students in the class of 2000, who had seven years before graduation.

I offered a plan to rent commercial space to relieve overcrowding using an open, fair process by landlords to rent their properties. The plan could have relieved overcrowding in one year. To my amazement, the system liked the idea, only I learned after the election that the chosen few landlords who rented commercial space to the system had inflated the rent and gave kickbacks to school officials. They were indicted for this, but it still happened. The school system was very good at corruption.

My education policy was to make the system simple, because the simpler the system, the easier it would be to manage and teach. We could do away with most of the administrators in the system, with the money saved being used in the classrooms.

The problem with my policy was I would be doing away with thousands of administration and office jobs. My policy proposal opened a can of worms. There was no way anyone would let me win the election. Think how much could be saved on administrative costs. What could the students and teachers do with an extra $5 billion a year?

People heckled me, and there were demonstrations at my appearances. The situation got crazier and crazier as the election neared. Most elected officials ran to add jobs and didn't care about the education system. The more jobs they created, the more endorsements they would have for their next election.

Meanwhile, the parents and taxpayers who depended on the success of the education system came out to support me. My policy was being noticed. I gathered more and more support from parents.

The more I told the truth, the more the members of the education system attacked me. Parents backed me in large numbers, and I received more invitations to speak at events.

I refused to take or ask for money during my campaign. I wanted to run a grass-roots campaign. If someone wanted to change the New York City school system, he could sign up to volunteer. Over 100 people did, and they did everything they could. Not surprisingly, teachers and school personnel volunteered to work for my campaign. I felt I was on a roll.

NEW YORK STATE
FRATERNAL ORDER OF POLICE
EMPIRE STATE LODGE
166 W. OLD COUNTRY ROAD ■ HICKSVILLE, NEW YORK 11801
(516) 433-4455 FAX (516) 433-4473

April 13, 1993

ROBERT N. LUCENTE
PRESIDENT

WILLIAM LOMBARD
PAST PRESIDENT

LEROY J. MOLINI
EXECUTIVE VICE PRESIDENT

VINCENT CANNATELLA
VICE PRESIDENT

ROY DINKLE
VICE PRESIDENT

PAUL KELLER
VICE PRESIDENT

MIKE TAYLOR
VICE PRESIDENT

AL TRAVERS
VICE PRESIDENT

VINCENT FLYNN
SECRETARY

PETE GALLO
RECORDING SECRETARY

ROSS PATERNOSTRO
TREASURER

CHARLES CAPUTO
CONDUCTOR

RODNEY CHIN
GUARD

JOSEPH BOSCO
GUARD

JOHN SORICELLI
TRUSTEE CHAIRMAN

ROBERT N. LUCENTE
NATIONAL TRUSTEE

MSGR. ROBERT N. O'CONNELL
NEW YORK STATE CHAPLAIN

KATHLEEN MAHON, ESQ.
CHIEF COUNSEL

DENNIS J. PAPPAS, ESQ.
CHIEF FINANCIAL COUNSEL

ANN POWERS, ESQ.
ASSOCIATE COUNSEL

Mel Ladner
60 Kenmore St.
Staten Island, NY 10312

Dear Mel,

On behalf of the New York State Fraternal Order of Police and its 14,000 members, this is to advise that we fully support you in your candidacy for the Staten Island School Board.

We wish you much success in your efforts to obtain this goal in the upcoming elections.

Fraternally,

Robert N. Lucente
President

RNL:sw

"BACK THE BADGE"...SUPPORT LAW ENFORCEMENT

There was an off-Broadway play called *Perfect Election*. It toured in the New York City schools, and it was about me and my education policy. The actor playing me was draped in an American flag.

I saw the play, and it was terrible. It was highly political and slanted the truth against me and my policy. I walked out, shaking my head, but at least my campaign was being noticed.

I was grading a federal prison in Beekman Hospital in Lower Manhattan when I met a Roman Catholic priest who was there to aid and comfort the patients.

I showed him articles about corruption in New York City's school system from the *Staten Island Advance*. I told him about the corruption and missing money from the school budget and my proposed policies. I said I planned to run for the school board. If successful, I would get rid of all thirty-two school boards and turn 110 Livingston Street into a condo.

That was the headquarters of New York City's Board of Education. There were more administrators than there was space to hold them. They used bathrooms as offices. I went there to serve federal court papers and had to visit six different offices to get the job done. Every office was overcrowded with administrators.

One of the offices I went to was in a converted men's bathroom, where I saw six desks being used by principals, assistant principals, and teachers. On one wall stood three porcelain urinals behind two of the principals' desks. Most of the principals and teachers were currently under suspension and couldn't work in the schools. They stayed at the office for two to five years, fully paid until their hearing came up. By the time they received a hearing, most of the witnesses were gone.

I told the priest how I was being attacked by the same people who could have solved the school problem, the administrators of the school system. He told me a story about Jesus, Who was attacked for the same reason- telling the truth. That opened my eyes to the fight I was in. It was a war for the education of our children and future of our country. The priest gave me his blessing and said he would pray for me. I thanked him and left feeling God was on my side.

I made a promise to myself. *Let the war begin. We will take no prisoners, and I'll take the battle as far as I can, even to the U.S. Supreme Court. With the help of friends and family, I'll fight a fair fight and let the chips fall where they may. I swear to God.*

Education is the future of our children and our country. I felt people would understand that the education system was failing. All I had to do was open the parents' eyes. I decided to run for public office and change the cesspool that was the New York City school system.

CHAPTER TWO
Let's Go To The New York State Court

I saw a friend of mine, Jeff Motelson, a great lawyer who worked at the law offices of Moskowitz, Passman, and Edelman, and told him the facts regarding election fraud. I went into all the details, aided by someone working in the board of elections who kept me informed concerning all the cheating and fraud. I'll call her Betty. Her husband and son-in-law were in the Blue Knights Motorcycle Club with me. The stuff the New York Board of Elections was getting away with made me want to cry.

Jeff listened to my case and said, "I'll look into the case and speak to Shelly, my partner. I'll get back to you."

I really liked Jeff, but he didn't know what he was getting into. When he accepted the case of Ladner v. City of New York, he said, "I'll do the best I can." The City of New York fought extremely hard to keep the corrupt election in place, bringing in their top lawyers against us.

Jeff was surprised when we had a hearing held in the corporation council's ex-offices. He said he'd been trying cases against the City of New York for over twenty years, and he never went to a corporation council's ex- offices before a hearing.

The plush offices looked like they were in the top 100 businesses in the

U.S. I was impressed. "We just hit the big time," I told Jeff. Jeff filed the lawsuit for election fraud with the New York State Court. The City of New York went to the State Court and filed a motion to bring Ladner v. The City of New York to federal court. Jeff argued it should stay with the New York State Court, but that court ruled there were federal issues in election fraud. The City of New York won, and we were dragged into federal district court to appear before the Honorable Judge I. Leo Glasser. Judge Glasser was an old-time, no-nonsense federal judge. Nothing got past him. He got mad when he read the complaint. Judges, like many people, often read the New York newspapers and watch local TV. He knew from those sources what was going on with the school- board election.

The City of New York argued that the case should be dismissed, because it was in the wrong court and should be held in New York State Court. The City of New York used every trick and were successful in getting the case moved to federal court due to the federal civil rights issues in the case. We objected, hoping to stay in New York State Court.

I stood with Jeff before the judge, shaking my head, wondering how the City of New York could get away with it. Judge Glasser took a couple days to rule. He said there had been only one other federal election fraud case in the history of the U.S., involving Susan B. Anthony. I felt I was in good company to be with the woman whose face appeared on the silver dollar because of her efforts to gain women the right to vote. That also showed how hard it was to fight a corrupt election system.

Susan B. Anthony was arrested and charged with voter fraud for checking the Male box when she voted during the time when women weren't allowed to vote. Bush v. Gore was about technical issues regarding the Florida vote, not about fraud.

Judge Glasser ruled that it was a federal case. It wasn't just common election irregularities. We were in the correct federal court. We began all the motions, depositions, and entering of evidence for the trial. All witnesses gave depositions before the trial. It took days just for one witness. During the testimony, both sides put in their evidence. I was very proud of Jeff. He was prepared and very professional in his cross-examinations. Things were going well for our side. During the pretrial hearing, Judge Glasser awarded me $50,000,000 plus $26,000,000 interest for a total of $76,000,000 against Proposal Counts Associates for not defending the case. That's right. Bruce Hogenauer refused to testify. He was served with a subpoena and still didn't testify.

After that hearing, I felt wealthy and told Jeff that Judge Glasser had to be the real deal. The city lawyers were furious. One of them, Pat Le Goff, was hyperventilating at hearing the amount. It was a priceless moment.

"The award of $76 million will smoke out the witnesses," Jeff told me.

"They'll show up to testify now."

I still felt rich. Hogenauer never did show up.

"The City of New York is fighting the law of Ladner v. City of New York and the facts of the fraud case?" I asked. "If you don't have a case, you fight the law."

I kept asking myself why the city fought so hard to change a corrupt educational and election system. I didn't figure out until later that it wasn't about the education system. It was a case about fraud in the entire New York State election system.

I told the city lawyers we'd work together to fix the educational system, and I would drop all criminal and civil cases against the city. They never got back to me.

I hired a collection agency to try to collect the $76 million. I gave them the information, and Judge Glasser signed the order with the seal of the court. It was official. I was suddenly worth $76 million.

The hard part was collecting the money. The collection agency got back to me in three days. I was told that Proportional Counts Associates was a shell corporation and had no assets. I was rich for only three days.

That raised another important question. How could the City of New York hire a shell corporation PAC to run a citywide election? The contract given as evidence stated, among other things, that PCA had an insurance bond for the 1993 school-board election. PCA never bought any insurance. Who was responsible for PCA having that insurance? It was New York City.

What was really interesting was that the collection agency found out that the account director, Bruce Hogenauer, checked into the Kirby Forensic Psychiatric Hospital part of the city's prison system on Wards Island for the criminally insane. That immediately raised a red flag in my mind. What was going on?

I didn't know his criminal record when he checked into the hospital for the criminally insane and refused to testify.

Kirby Forensic Psychiatric Center
Verna Greenall, M.D.
Executive Director

WARD'S ISLAND, NY 10035 • (212) 427-9003
NEW YORK STATE OFFICE OF MENTAL HEALTH
James L. Stone, MSW, Commissioner

212-427-9003

AFFIDAVIT

STATE OF NEW YORK}
COUNTY OF NEW YORK} ss:

I, Gayla Laiken, being duly sworn, depose and say:

As director of medical records for Kirby, I am in charge of documenting the movements of the patients.

Bruce Hogenauer, dob 7/24/44, has been an inpatient at Kirby Forensic Psychiatric Center from 11/21/95 to the present. Mr. Hogenauer has never been placed on leave since his admission to Kirby.

Gayla G. Laiken, RHIA

Sworn to before me
this 8th Day of June, 2000.

Patricia Albin
Notary Public

PATRICIA ALBIN
Notary Public, State of New York
No. 03-4622335
Qualified in Bronx County
Commission Expires April 30, 2001

Affiliated with New York University Medical Center
Accredited by Joint Commission on the Accreditation of Health Care Organization
AN EQUAL OPPORTUNITY/AFFIRMATIVE ACTION EMPLOYER

God works in mysterious ways. What were the odds that I would know a person who once arrested Bruce Hogenauer? I used to work as a U.S. special deputy marshal. U.S. Marshal Bob Meltzer was my supervisor when I was in the service. I was a member of the Blue Knights Motorcycle Club, and so was Bob. All the members were law- enforcement people, active or retired. We had a great time during our Sunday rides.

We had a motorcycle ride to Old Greenwich, Connecticut, for a barbecue. The party was sponsored by the local chapter of the Blue Knights. We toured Old Greenwich with a police escort and were invited into George C. Scott's mansion. Then we took a motorcycle ride to their private beach for a pig roast, fun, and games.

Whenever cops got together, there were plenty of laughs. It was my turn to tell a story, and Bob Meltzer was in the group listening to my account of what happened in federal court the other day. I had them spellbound.

"I was awarded $76 million, and while you were touring George's mansion, I was looking for a place to buy and live in. Maybe I should get the Helmsley Mansion."

The Helmsley Mansion looked like a castle. Ralph Vigalante, president of our chapter of the Blue Knights, joked, "Remember, Mel, you meet the same people on the way up as you do on the way down."

We joked about it for an hour. When I told them that Hogenauer was being put into the Kirby Institute for the Criminally Insane and refused to testify, and he looked very strange, and the mood became serious.

When Bob Meltzer heard the man's name, he asked, "What did he look like, and how old was he?"

I described the man with his flaming red wig.

"That might be the child molester and kidnapper who assaulted me on a plane when I was extraditing him from England. Call me at the marshal service tomorrow afternoon. If this is who I think it is, there's no way he should be allowed in any school."

As I continued talking to Bob about Hogenauer, the more we were sure it had to be the same man.

"Can I come down to see his mug shot?" I asked. We made a date to meet.

I met Bob at the marshal's office. We had coffee and talked about our motorcycle rides, then opened a folder of his old criminal cases and flipped through it. They seemed to be filed according to years and names. He went through half the files for the year 1987 until he pulled up a sheet with Hogenauer's picture and rap sheet attached. As soon as I saw the picture, I knew it was the same man.

The more I read from Hogenauer's rap sheet, the more I knew that was the Rosetta stone that would change the school-board election system for the better. I had New York City by the balls, and I would use the info. The city wouldn't be able to stop me now. The newspaper article of Bruce Hogenauer being arrest for Kidnapping.

Syracuse Herald Journal, Wednesday, October 26, 1983, Page 3

Hill lawmakers may attempt sizable spending cuts and tax increases this year ;lo the federal budget deficit. -Jlut the chances for success are question- ;i ible. 'A group of House Democrats Tuesday a plan to raise S73 billion in in th e next three years the mandated by the congression- "ally approved budget, v A merican people face a game of deficit one of the groups's leaders, Hep. Donald Pease, D- said at a press conference. stakes are tragically noting that inter est rates could soar 'and unemployment climb again unless -the federal budget deficit is brought control. -The coalition of freshman lawmakers "and veteran liberals, backed by House 'Speaker Thomas O'Neill, plan to offer amendments to an S8 billion tax re- form bill that the House will consider Thursday. If acc epted, the two amendments, along with one already proposed by Ways and Means C ommittee Chairman Dan Rostenkowski, D-Ill., would bring the package's total re venue up to billion. Each amendment would be sub- ject to a separate vote on t he House floor. The administration opposes any tax in- creases, except the loo phole closing and extension of tax rules contained in the Ways and Means Commi ttee basic billion bill. Although that legislation has bipartisan support, it is unlikely that Re- publicans will support any of the Demo- cratic amendments offered to raise the bill's total revenue. In the Senate, Finance Committee C hairman Robert Dole, R-Kan., said his committee would begin work this week on a package of at least billion in budget savings, including both spending cuts and tax increases. "If we're only going to do billion to billion (in tax why d o any- Dole said during a committee meeting Tuesday. "We'll try to come up wit h a major plan to reduce the deficit." He told reporters later that he would a im for at least billion in budget savings over three years. But, so far there is little indication that his col- leagues share his enthusiasm. Pease said li beral members of the House Democratic Study Group will offer a 31.7 billion am endment to close loopholes and raise taxes for certain busi- ness and wealthy inviduals. In a related effort. Democratic freshmen will offer a billion amend ment to limit the ben- efits of the final stage of President Rea- gan's three-year 25 percent tax cut to per person, similar to one the House approved earli er this year. The liberals' plan includes a new 10 percent luxury tax on jewel s, furs, ex- pensive cars, and non-commerical boats and airplanes. OPI Telpcho to [KIDNAP SUSPECT ARRESTED. FBI agents force a protesting Bruce William Ho- ge nauer, center, into a car after arresting him at a Clearwater. Fla.. marina on a kidnap- ping warrant. Hogenauer is accused of kidnapping 12-year-old Michae l Sammartino of Queens, N.Y. Agents made the arrest as the two were stepping o ff a fishing party boat.] John Anderson stumps in California for new party By U nited Press International John Anderson, who ran as an independent for preside nt in 1980, took his efforts to organize a new political party to California today. Anderson, 61, stopped short Tuesday of saying he would run for presiden t again in 1984, but said he hoped to be the standard bearer of a new group ca lled the "National Unity Party." The former GOP congressman from Illinois cite d recent polls by his group indicating that up to 15 percent, or more than 10 million people, currently would favor him over other candi- dates. In 1980, An derson pulled 7 percent of the vote. a figure that would entitle him to millio n in federal funds should he run again. He said the new party's goal would be the "basic reform of the political process" in a coun- try undergoing "system ic failure." Much of that failure can be blamed on the monopoly held by the Re publican and Democratic parties. Ander- son said. Another straw poll in Indian

Caption for photo on previous pg.

http://newspaperarchive.com/us/new-york/syracuse/syracuse-herald-journal/1983/10-26/page-3

June 11, 2014

Bruce Hogenauer's bail set at $500,000 dollars.

		ASSUMED 10/24/83	INST ABBR M/FL	18	03263-018
HOGENAUER, Bruce William					OTHER (EXPLAIN)
PRISONER'S ALIAS					
DOB 7/24/44	DOB 39	RACE ☒W-1 ☐N-2 ☐I-3 ☐C-4 ☐S-5 ☐O-6			
EMERGENCY ADDRESS 119 Fredica Ave. N. Clearwater, FL	BIRTHPLACE NY, NY	SEX ☒M ☐F	COLOR HAIR Blo	COLOR EYES Blu	HEIGHT 509	WEIGHT 165
VIOLATOR ☐PAROLE ☐MANDATORY RELEASE ☐PROBATION	PROPERTY IN CUSTODY ☐U.S. MARSHAL ☐JAIL	OFFENSE Kidnapping S/NY		SOCIAL SECURITY NO. 111-34-9921	
SENTENCE				SENTENCE TYPE ☐CONCURRENT ☐MINORITY	

20. Date Sentence Begins	21. Date Appeal Filed	22. Date Elected Not To Serve	23. Date Sentence Rewritten	24. Reason Sentence Rewritten ☐ELECTED ☐COURT	25. Detainer on File ☐YES ☐NO

26. INSTITUTIONS TO WHICH COMMITTED (INCLUDE ALL TIME FROM DETENTION UNTIL FINAL DISPOSITION)	29. DATE COMMITTED (MO. DAY, YR.)	30. DATE RELEASED (MO. DAY, YR.)	31. DAYS BOARDED	32. ACTION OR DISPOSITION
Arrested by FBI 10/24/83 Hillsborough Cnty Jail	10/24/83			$500,000 C/S

COPY 1 - TO ACCOMPANY PRISONER

Plaintiffs Exhibit 4
Date 8/6/17
Reporter: MB

STATE OF NEW YORK
EXECUTIVE CHAMBER
ALBANY 12224

GEORGE E. PATAKI
GOVERNOR

May 16, 1995

Mr. Mel Ladner
60 Kenmore Street
Staten Island, NY 10312

Dear Mr. Ladner:

Thank you for writing to me regarding alleged cheating in your 1993 school board election.

This is an extremely serious issue. Election fraud is incomprehensible and un-American. It undermines the entire base of our democratic process of selecting candidates.

I have forwarded your letter to the Office of the Counsel to the Governor to have the matter looked into.

Very truly yours,

Timothy S. Carey
Director
Intergovernmental Relations

I called the newspapers, 60 *Minutes*, NBC, CBS, ABC, and Governor Pataki's office of the State of New York, to leave messages about the information I had. A couple of reporters called back. The problem I encountered was that the election was years in the past. It was old news, so no one cared. I felt like the boy who cried "Wolf!" and no one listened. That was the first time I felt I was in over my head and had no control over the outcome of the case.

A political friend who heard about the award given to me called. "You really caught them that time cheating in the election. I've known for years that the Staten Island elections were rigged."

I was still waiting for a response from my calls to the media. I told him about meeting the priest, who said, "Changing the educational and election system is something martyrs are made for."

My friend understood what I meant.

It was great going to court. The city was hit hard by the dispositions and court appearances. More and more corruption was being exposed concerning the school-board election. With every deposition we heard, more fraud came out. The more the city lawyers stalled the trial, the more the federal courts heard about the depositions and evidence showing it was a lot more than a rigged schoolboard election system. It had ramifications for the entire state. Since I had two people working inside the Staten Island Board of Education, I was given information concerning the lies and plans they were ready to try. The officials on the board were very good at cover-ups.

I never learned what the City of New York did, but somehow, they moved the case away from Judge Glasser. I was told he made a trial date, then suddenly, the case was handed to Judge Gershon. No matter how many times I asked, I never was told why the judge was changed.

I kept asking for a trial date. It was always going to be after the next deposition or motion. We were in federal court for over five years. Over one hundred court appearances, depositions, and evidence was given without a trial date. There were so many legal papers that I wondered if Jeff's office could hold them all. There were endless boxes of legal papers, pictures, and videos. The City of New York made a motion at one point that we didn't have enough evidence and no laws were broken for a trial. The idea was laughable.

CHAPTER THREE
The Six Year History Of My Federal Court Appearances Fighting Tooth And Nail For A Trial

This is a history of all the court appearances and motion just in Federal District court:
HISTORY OF THE CASE IN FEDERAL COURT DISTRICT COURT
https:// ecf.nyed.uscourts.gov/cig- bin/DktPrt.pl? 6694412672844- L_923_0-1 2/16/2006
ATTORNEY TO BE NOTICED

Defendant
Board of Elections of the City of New York represented by **Daniel S. Feder**
(See above for address)
LEAD ATTORNEY
ATTORNEY TO BE NOTICED

Patricia A. Le Goff
(See above for address)
LEAD ATTORNEY
ATTORNEY TO BE NOTICED

Defendant
New York City Police Department represented by **Daniel S. Feder**
(See above for address)
LEAD ATTORNEY
ATTORNEY TO BE NOTICED

Patricia A. Le Goff
(See above for address)
LEAD ATTORNEY
ATTORNEY TO BE NOTICED

Defendant
New York City Board of Education represented by **Daniel S. Feder**
(See above for address)
LEAD ATTORNEY
ATTORNEY TO BE NOTICED
OTTE

Patricia A. Le Goff
(See above for address)
LEAD ATTORNEY
ATTORNEY TO BE NOTICED

Defendant Barbara M. Kett
As Chief Clerk of the Staten Island Board of Elections represented by **Daniel S. Feder**
(See above for address)
LEAD ATTORNEY
ATTORNEY TO BE NOTICED

Patricia A. Le Goff
(See above for address)
LEAD ATTORNEY LATE
ATTORNEY TO BE NOTICED

Defendant
Staten Island Board of Elections represented by **Daniel S. Feder**
(See above for address)
LEAD ATTORNEY
ATTORNEY TO BE NOTICED

Eastern District of New York-Live Database Version 2.5 Release-Docket Report Page 2 of 13 https://ecf.nyed.uscourts.gov/cig-bin/DktPrt.pl? 6694412672844-L_923_0-1 2/16/2006

Patricia A. Le Goff
(See above for address)
LEAD ATTORNEY
ATTORNEY TO BE NOTICED

Defendant
Richmond County Board of Elections represented by **Patricia A. Le Goff**
(See above for address)
LEAD ATTORNEY
ATTORNEY TO BE NOTICED

Third Party Plaintiff New York City represented by **Daniel S. Feder**
(See above for address)
LEAD ATTORNEY
ATTORNEY TO BE NOTICED

Third Party Plaintiff New York City Police Department represented by **Daniel S. Feder**
(See above for address)
LEAD ATTORNEY
ATTORNEY TO BE NOTICED

ThirdParty Plaintiff New York City Board of Education represented by **Daniel S. Feder**
(See above for address)
LEAD ATTORNEY
ATTORNEY TO BE NOTICED

Third Party Plaintiff Barbara M. Kett represented by **Daniel S. Feder**
(See above for address)
LEAD ATTORNEY
ATTORNEY TO BE NOTICED

Third Party Plaintiff Staten Island Board of Elections represented by **Daniel S. Feder**
(See above for address)
LEAD ATTORNEY
ATTORNEY TO BE NOTICED

Eastern District of New York-Live Database Version 2.5 Release-Docket Report Page 3 of 13 https://ecf.nyed.uscourts.gov/cig-bin/Dkt Prt.pl? 6694412672844-L_923_0-1 2/16/2006

Richmond County Board of Elections v. ThirdParty Defendant Proportional Counts Associates, Inc. represented by **Archibald E. Robertson, Jr.**
45 Kraft Avenue Bronxville, NY 10708 (914) 3378900
LEAD ATTORNEY
ATTORNEY TO BE NOTICED

The federal court record of all the appearances Date Filed # Docket Text

6/17/1994 1 NOTICE OF REMOVAL FROM SUPREME COURT, COUNTY OF RICHMOND, FILING FEE $120.00 RECEIPT # 163109 (Greene, Donna) (Entered: 06/20/1994)

6/17/1994 CASE REFERRED to Magistrate Joan M. Azrack (Greene, Donna) (Entered: 06/20/1994)

7/05/1994 2 ORDER dated 6/30/94 that defts' time to answer extended to 7/22/94. (signed by Judge I.L. Glasser on letter dated 6/27/94 from Daniel S. Feder). (Greves, Liz) (Entered: 07/05/1994)

7/19/1994 3 Letter dated 7/15/94 from Christine Victor to Mr. Feder advising that Mag Azrack has scheduled an initial conference on 8/10/94 at 2PM. (signed by Judge I. L. Glasser on letter dated 6/27/94 from Daniel S. Feder). (Greves, Liz) (Entered: 07/19/1994)

7/26/1994 4 Entire file received from County Clerk of Richmond County this date. (Greves, Liz) (Entered: 07/27/1994)

8/10/1994 5 ORDER dated 8/8/94 that defts' time to answer extended to 8/26/94 conference scheduled for 10/14/94 at 11:30AM before Magistrate Joan M. Azrack (signed by Magistrate Joan M. Azrack on letter dated 8/4/94 from Daniel S. Feder). (Greves, Liz) (Entered: 08/10/1994)

8/24/1994 6 Defts' MOTION to dismiss. Motion hearing set for 9:30AM 10/7/94 [6-1] motion. (Greves, Liz) (Entered: 08/24/1994)

8/24/1994 7 Defts' MEMORANDUM in support of [6-1] motion to dismiss. (Greves, Liz) (Entered: 08/24/1994)

10/13/1994 8 ORDER dated 10/11/94 that return date for defts' motion to dismiss adjourned from 10/7/94 to 10/28/94 at 9:30AM. (signed by Judge I. L. Glasser on letter dated 10/6/94 from Jeffrey M. Motelson). (Greves, Liz) (Entered: 10/13/1994)

10/19/1994 9 ORDER dated 10/13/94 that conference adjourned from 10/14/94 to 2/21/95 at 11AM before Magistrate Joan M.Azrack. (signed by Magistrate Joan M. Azrack on letter dated 10/12/94 from Patricia Le Goff). (Greves, Liz) (Entered: 10/19/1994)

Eastern District of New York-Live Database Version 2.5 Release-Docket Report Page 4 of 13 https://ecf.nyed.uscourts.gov/cig-bin/DktPrt.pl?66944412672844-L_923_0-1 2/16/2006

10/20/1994 10 AMENDED COMPLAINT by Melvin Ladner, Timothy Carl, (Answer due 10/30/94 for Staten Island Board of Elections, for Barbara M. Kett, for NYC Board of Education, for NYC Police Dept., for Board Elections New York City) amending against the Richmond County Board of Elections. (Greves, Liz) (Entered: 10/20/1994)

10/24/1994 11 Pltffs' Memo of Law in opposition to defts' motion to dismiss. (Greves, Liz) (Entered: 10/25/1994)

10/24/1994 12 AFFIDAVIT by Timothy Carl in opposition of defts' motion to dismiss. (Greves, Liz) (Entered: 10/25/1994)

10/24/1994 13 AFFIDAVIT by Melvin Ladner in opposition of defts' motion to dismiss. (Greves, Liz) (Entered: 10/25/1994)

10/24/1994 14 AFFIDAVIT of Raquel F. Samuels re: service of supplemental summons & amended complaint upon the City of NY, Board of Elections of the City of NY, Police Dept, Board of Elections of the City of New York, Staten Island Board of Elections, Richmond County Board of Elections, & Barbara Kett on 10/20/94. (Greves, Liz) (Entered: 10/25/1994)

10/27/1994 15 LETTER dated 10/25/94 from Patricia Le Goff to Judge Glasser re: advising that the return date of defendants' motion to dismiss has been adjourned to 12/2/94 on consent of the parties. (Conte, Daniela) (Entered: 10/27/1994)

11/02/1994 16 ORDER dated 10/26/94 that hearing on defts' motion to dismiss adjourned to 12/2/94. (signed by Judge I. L. Glasser on copy of letter dated 10/25/94 from Patricia Le Goff (Greves, Liz) (Entered: 11/02/1994)

12/01/1994 17 ORDER granting permission to withdraw defts' [6-1] motion to dismiss. Order granting deft permission to move to dismiss the amended complaint and notice the motion for 1/13/95. (signed by Judge I. L. Glasser) (endorsed on letter dated 11/25/94 from Patricia Le Goff to Judge Glasser) (Greves, Liz) (Entered: 12/01/1994)

12/23/1994 18 Defts' MOTION to dismiss. Motion hearing set for 9:30AM 1/13/95 [18-1] motion. (Greves, Liz) (Entered: 12/27/1994)

01/03/1995 20 LETTER dated 12/28/94 from Patricia Le Goff to Mr. Motelson confirming that return date of motion to dismiss has been adjourned from 1/13/95 to 1/18/95 at 4PM. (Greves, Liz) (Entered: 01/03/1995)

01/18/1995 21 Copy of LETTER dated 1/12/95 from Jeffrey M. Motelson to Ms. Le Goff confirming that return date of motion to dismiss has been adjourned from 1/18/95 to 1/27/95 at 9:30AM. (Greves, Liz) (Entered: 01/18/1995)

01/20/1995 22 Special Commissioner Ed Stancik's Investigation into the 1993 Community Schoolboard election. (Greves, Liz) (Entered: 01/23/1995)

Eastern District of New York-Live Database Version 2.5 Release-Docket Report Page 5 of 13 https:// ecf. nyed.uscourts.gov/cig- bin/DktPrt.pl? 6694412672844-L_923_0-1 2/16/2006

01/20/1995 23 AFFIDAVIT by Timothy Carl in opposition to defts' [18-1] motion to dismiss. (Greves, Liz) (Entered: 01/23/1995)

01/20/1995 24 AFFIDAVIT by Melvin Ladner in opposition to defts' [18-1] motion to dismiss. (Greves, Liz) (Entered: 01/23/1995)

01/20/1995 25 MEMORANDUM by Melvin Ladner, Timothy Carl in opposition to defts' [18-1] motion to dismiss. (Greves, Liz) (Entered: 01/23/1995)

01/27/1995 26 Calendar entry: Before Judge Glasser on 1/27/95 case called. Court Reporter D. Pereira. Counsel for all sides present. Motion to dismiss 1985 claim is granted with leave to replead within 30 days. Motion to dismiss under 12(b)(6) is denied. (Greves, Liz) (Entered: 01/30/1995)

02/09/1995 27 MEMO/ORDER dated 2/8/95 that defts' motion is granted as to Section 1985(3) claim with the pltffs' granted leave to replead that aspect of their complaint. In all other respects dfts' motion is denied. CM (signed by Judge I. L. Glasser).. (Greves, Liz) (Entered: 02/09/1995)

02/21/1995 28 Calendar entry: Before Mag Azrack on 2/21/95 initial conference held. Discovery to be completed by 9/12/95. Defts to answer 3/24/95. Pltff to amend by 3/10/95. Next conference scheduled for 9/12/95 at 10:30AM before Magistrate Joan M. Azrack. (Greves, Liz) (Entered: 02/23/1995)

03/17/1995 29 AMENDED COMPLAINT by Melvin Ladner, Timothy Carl, (Answer due 3/27/95 for The Richmond County Board of Elections, for Staten Island Board of Elections, for Barbara M. Kett, for NYC Board of Education, for NYP Police Dept., for Board of Elections for New York City) amending [10-1] amended complaint. (Greves, Liz) (Entered: 03/20/1995)

04/17/1995 30 ANSWER to 2nd AMENDED COMPLAINT & THIRD-PARTY COMPLAINT by NYC Board of Elections, NYC Police Dept., NYC Board of Education, Barbara M. Kett, Staten Island Board of Elections, the Richmond County Board of Elections against Proportional Counts Associates, Inc. (Greves, Liz) (Entered: 04/17/1995)

04/19/1995 31 ANSWER to 2nd Amended Complaint & 3rd party complaint by NYC Board of Elections, NYC Police Dept., NYC Board of Education, Barbara M. Kett, Staten Island Board of Elections, the Richmond County Board of Elections against Proportional Counts Associates, Inc. (Greves, Liz) Modified on 04/20/1995 (Entered: 04/20/1995)

06/06/1995 32 RETURN OF SERVICE executed as to Proportional Counts on 5/1/95. (Asreen, Wendy) (Entered 06/07/1995)

09/18/1995 33 LETTER dated 9/8/95 from Matthew K. Breitman to Ms. Falcone confirming that status conference & discovery deadline adjourned on consent to 11/17/95 at 10AM. (Greves, Liz) (Entered 09/18/1995)

11/22/1995 34 Calendar entry: Before Mag Azrack on 11/22/95 conference held. Discovery to be completed by 3/4/96. Next conference 3/4/96 at 11AM before Magistrate Joan M. Azrack. (Greves, Liz) (Entered 11/27/1995)

02/02/1996 35 LETTER dated 1/31/96 from Magistrate Azrack's chambers to all counsel rescheduling the 3/4/96 conference for 4/1/96 at 11:00. (Asreen, Wendy) (Entered: 02/02/1996)

02/02/1996 Status conference reset for 11:00 on 4/1/96 before Magistrate Joan M. Azrack. Conference for 4/1/96 at 11:00. (Asreen, Wendy) (Entered: 02/02/1996)

04/08/1996 36 Calendar entry: Before Mag Azrack on 4/8/96 discovery conference held. Discovery to be completed by 7/17/96. Next conference scheduled for 7/16/96 at 10:30AM before Magistrate Joan M. Azrack. (Greves, Liz) (Entered: 04/09/1996)

07/16/1996 37 Calendar entry: Before Mag Azrack on 7/16/96 at 10:30AM. Plaintiff to complete counting of ballots within 2 weeks. Plaintiff must subpoena Edward Stancik personally. Deft to provide list of inspectors present for 5/4 election. No order will be issued. Next status conference set for 9/12/96 at 4:00PM. (Dobkin, David) (Entered: 07/18/1996)

08/15/1996 CASE reassigned to Judge Nina Gershon. (Vaughn, Terry) (Entered: 08/15/1996)

09/12/1996 38 Calendar entry: Before Mag Azrack on 9/12/96 for a Conference. Set Status Conference for 10:00 10/2/96 before Magistrate Joan M. Azrack Re: Deposition issue. (Piper, Francine) (Entered: 09/16/1996)

09/12/1996 39 Calendar entry: Before Mag Azrack on 10/3/96 at 10:15AM. Plaintiff application to take deposition of Stancik denied at this time. Plaintiff to take deposition of Cominsky and 2 deputies Brenner and Coughian. (Dobkin, David) (Entered: 10/08/1996)

12/12/1996 40 Calendar entry: Before Mag Azrack on 12/12/96 at 11:00AM, case called. Conference adjourned to 12/19/96. (Lui, Lin) (Entered: 12/17/1996)

12/19/1996 41 Calendar entry: Before Mag Azrack on 12/19/96 at 2:15 p.m., case called. Next conference scheduled for 2:30 3/6/97 before Magistrate Joan M. Azrack. Deposition of Robertson to occur by 2/10/97. No further discovery permitted until deposition of Robertson. (Lui, Lin) (Entered: 12/26/1996)

01/13/1997 42 ANSWER by Proportional Counts to [30-1] third-party complaint. (Greves, Liz) (Entered: 01/14/1997)

03/06/1997 43 Calendar entry: Before Mag Azrack on 3/6/97 at 2:30 p.m., case called. Next conference scheduled for 4/10/97 at6 11:00 a.m. before Magistrate Joan M. Azrack. (1) Pltff to serve nonparty deposition on Robertson for deposition by 2nd week of April. (2) Status 4/10/97. (3) Pltff to provide deft with access to videotapes. (Lui, Lin) (Entered: 03/07/1997)

04/10/1997 44 Calendar entry: Before Magistrate Azrack on 4/10/97 at 11:00 a.m., conference adjourned to 5/8/97. (Lui, Lin) (Entered: 04/14/1997)

05/08/1997 45 Calendar entry: Before Magistrate Azrack on 5/8/97 conference held. Discovery to be completed by 7/1/97. Deft to advise re: dispositive Eastern District of New York motion. Next conference scheduled for 7/1/97 at 11:30AM before Magistrate Joan M. Azrack. (Greves, Liz) (Entered: 05/13/1997)

07/15/1997 46 Calendar entry: Before Magistrate Azrack on 7/15/97 at 11:30AM, case called. Telephone conference set for 10:30 7/25/97. (Lui, Lin) (Entered: 07/16/97)

07/23/1997 47 ORDER dated 7/21/97 that the deposition of Robert Meltzer be taken at the offices of Moskowitz, Passman, & Edelman on 8/5/97 at 10AM; that upon such deposition that Robert Meltzer shall produce copies of the records of the assault upon him by Bruce Hogenauer, & a certified copy of Mr. Hogenauer's criminal record. (signed by Magistrate Joan M. Azrack). (Greves, Liz) (Entered: 07/23/1997)

07/24/1997 49 Calendar entry: Before Magistrate Azrack on 7/24/97 conference held. Discovery is closed except for issue of Hogenauer. Deft to serve pltff with summary judgment motion by 9/19/97. (Greves, Liz) (Entered: 07/30/1997)

07/30/1997 48 COPY OF LETTER dated 7/25/97 from Alessandra F. Zorgniotti to Mr. Motelson, confirming Mag. Azrack's order issued during the telephone conference on 6/24/97. (Lui, Lin) (Entered: 07/30/1997)

07/30/1997 53 Calendar entry: Before Mag. Azrack on 7/30/97, case called. (1) Deft. to provide letter confirming that she has produced all receipts concerning the ballots. (2) Deposition of Marshal Meltzer to be completed by 9/19/97. (Lui, Lin) (Entered: 08/05/1997)

08/05/1997 50 LETTER dated 7/25/97 from Jeffrey M. Motelson to Judge Azrack, requesting that Mr. Meltzer's deposition and record production not be recalled. (Lui, Lin) (Entered: 08/05/1997)

08/05/1997 51 LETTER dated 7/30/97 from Alessandra F. Zorgniotti to Mag. Azrack, requesting that the Court deny pltff.'s request to reopen discovery to produce documents which do not exist and would be irrelevant is they did exist. (Lui, Lin) (Entered: 08/05/1997)

08/05/1997 52 LETTER (not dated) from Steven V. Roque to Mr. Motelson, requesting that authorization be provided pursuant to 5 U.S.C. Section 552a. (Lui, Lin) (Entered: 08/05/1997)

08/12/1997 54 ORDER dated 8/12/97 GRANTING Alessandra F. Zorgniotti's request until 10/17/97 to serve pltffs with defts' motion for summary judgment. (signed by Magistrate Joan M. Azrack on letter dated 8/12/97 from Allessandra F. Zorgniotti). (Greves, Liz) (Entered: 08/12/1997)

10/15/1997 55 Calendar entry: Before Judge Gershon on 10/15/97 at 5:00 p.m., case called for pre-motion conference. Counsel for all sides present. Briefing schedule for motion for summary judgment is as follows: Deft.'s motion is due 11/21/97. Pltff.'s response is due 12/11/97. Deft.'s reply is due 12/19/97. (Lui, Lin) (Entered: 10/16/1997)

12/01/1997 56 ORDER dtd. 11/13/97 Schedule regarding summary judgment motion. Deft's to serve pltff. 12/19/97; Pltff's opposition 1/23/98; Reply papers on ltr. dtd. 11/5/97 from Alessandra F Zorgniotti (signed by Judge Nina Gershon). (Jackson, Ramona) (Entered: 12/01/1997)

02/19/1998 57 ORDER dtd. 1/23/98 Opposition to motion for summary judgment to 2/13/98. Deft's time to reply 3/6/98 on ltr. dtd. 1/21/98 from Jeffrey M. Motelson. (signed by Judge Nina Gershon) (Jackson, Ramona) (Entered: 02/19/1998)

02/25/1998 58 ORDER dtd. 2/17/98 Application Granted on ltr. dtd. 2/11/98 from Jeffrey M. Motelson Pltff's opposition by 2/27/98; Reply to March 20,1998. (signed by judge Nina Gershon) (Jackson, Ramona) (Entered: 02/25/1998)

03/16/1998 59 ORDER dtd. 3/13/98 Application GRANTED on ltr. dtd. 3/11/98 from Alessandra F. Zorgniotti enlargement of time to reply to pltff's opposition to deft's summary judgment motion to April 10,1998. (signed by judge Nina Gershon) (Jackson, Ramona) (Entered: 03/16/1998)

03/30/1998 60 LETTER dated 3/20/98 from Jeffrey M .Motelson to Ms. Zorgniotti opposition papers to motion for summary judgment. (Jackson, Ramona) (Entered: 03/30/1998)

04/16/1998 61 ORDER dtd. 4/7/98 Application GRANTED on ltr. dtd. 4/6/98 from A. Zorgniotti request enlargement of time for deft's to reply to pltff's opposition to April 30,1998. (signed by Judge Nina Gershon) (Jackson, Ramona) (Entered: 04/16/1998)

05/05/1998 62 LETTER dated 4/30/98 from Alessandra F. Zorgniotti to Judge Gershon notify the court of deft's motion for summary judgment. (Jackson, Ramona) (Entered: 05/05/1998)

05/05/1998 63 MOTION by The Richmond County, Staten Island Board, Barbara M. Kett, NYC Board of Education, NYC Police Dept., Board of Elections, New York City for summary judgment, Motion hearing set for 10:00 2/6/98 [63-1] motion. (Jackson, Ramona) (Entered: 05/05/1998)

05/05/1998.64 MEMORANDUM by The Richmond County, Staten Island Board, Barbara M. Kett, NYC Board of Education, NYC Police Dept., Board of Elections, New York City in support of [63-1] motion for summary judgment. (Jackson, Ramona) (Entered: 05/05/1998)

05/05/1998 65 Declaration of BARBARA M. KETT by The Richmond County, Staten Island Board, Barbara M. Kett, NYC Board of Education, NYC Police Dept., Board of Elections, New York City re: [63-1] motion for summary judgment with attached exhibits. (Jackson, Ramona) (Entered: 05/05/1998)

05/05/1998 66. Supplemental Declaration of BARBARA M. KETT, The Richmond County, Staten Island Board, Barbara M. Kett, NYC Board of Education, NYC Police Dept., Board of Elections, New York City re: in support [63-1] motion for summary judgment. (Jackson, Ramona) (Entered: 05/05/1998)

05/05/1998 67 REPLY MEMORANDUM OF LAW by The Richmond County, Staten Island Board, Barbara M. Kett, NYC Board of Education, NYC Police Dept., Board of Elections, New York City in further support [63-1] motion for summary judgment. (Jackson, Ramona) (Entered: 05/05/1998)

05/05/1998 68 Declaration of ALESSANDRA F. ZORGNIOTTI with attached exhibits Volume 2 OF 2 The Richmond County, Staten Island Board, Barbara M. Kett, NYC Board of Education, NYC Police Dept., Board of Elections, New York City Re: [63-1] motion for summary judgment. (Jackson, Ramona) (Entered: 05/05/1998)

05/05/1998 69 Declaration of THOMAS F. COMISKEY The Richmond County, Staten Island Board, Barbara M. Kett, NYC Board of Education, NYC Police Dept., Board of Elections, New York City re: [63-1] motion for summary judgment with attached exhibits. (Jackson, Ramona) (Entered: 05/05/1998)

05/05/1998 70 Declaration of ALESSANDRA F. ZORGNIOTTI The Richmond County, Staten Island Board, Barbara M. Kett, NYC Board of Education, NYC Police Dept., Board of Elections, New York City re: [63-1] motion for summary judgment with attached exhibits volume 1 of 2. (Jackson, Ramona) (Entered: 05/05/1998)

05/05/1998 71 Rule 56.1 Statement (formerly Rule 3(g) by Timothy Carl, Melvin Ladner re: in opposition to [63-1] motion for summary judgment. (Jackson, Ramona) (Entered: 05/05/1998)

05/05/1998 72 MEMORANDUM by Timothy Carl, Melvin Ladner in opposition to [63-1] motion for summary judgment with affidavit of service of all documents attached. (Jackson, Ramona) (Entered: 05/05/1998)

05/05/1998 73 Declaration of TIMOTHY CARL Timothy Carl, Melvin Ladner Re: support [63-1] motion for summary judgment. (Jackson, Ramona) (Entered: 05/05/1998)

05/05/1998 74 Declaration of MELVIN LADNER Timothy Carl, Melvin Ladner Re: [63-1] motion for summary judgment with attached exhibitsvolume one of two. (Jackson, Ramona) (Entered: 05/05/1998)

05/05/1998 75 Declaration of Melvin Ladner Timothy Carl, Melvin Ladner Re: [631] motion for summary judgment with attached exhibits volume two of two. (Jackson, Ramona) (Entered: 05/05/1998)

05/12/1998 76 LETTER dated 5/8/98 from Alessandra F. Zorgniotti to Judge Gershon, enclosing a copy of the Notice of Claim discussed in Plaintiff's Response to Defendants' Motion for Summary Judgment and in Defendant's Reply, footnote 3. (Reddy, Lisa) (Entered: 05/12/1998)

05/28/1998 77 LETTER dated 5/6/98 from Alessandra F. Zorgniotti to Judge Gershon trying to reach Mr. Robertson to serve reply papers. (Jackson, Ramona) (Entered: 05/28/1998)

06/19/1998 78 Calendar entry: Before Judge Gershon Civil Cause for conf. Ct Rep. Shelly Silverman Case called. Oral argument on deft's motion for summary judgment. (Jackson, Ramona) (Entered: 06/24/1998)

06/24/1998 79 Declaration of Melvin Ladner Re: in further opposition to [63-1] motion for summary judgment. (Jackson, Ramona) (Entered: 06/24/1998)

06/24/1998 80 Supplemental MEMORANDUM by Melvin Ladner in opposition to [63-1] motion for summary judgment. (Jackson, Ramona) (Entered: 06/24/1998)

07/01/1998 83 Calendar entry: before Judge Gershon-Civil Cause for Telephone Conference held. Case called. Telephone Conference. See Transcript. (Galeano, Sonia) (Entered: 07/07/1998)

07/06/1998 81 TRANSCRIPT filed of telephone conference before Judge Gershon for dates of 7/1/98 at 10:00a.m. Plaintiff counsel: Jeffrey Motelson. Defense counsel: Paul Marks. CR. Frederick Guerino. (Dobkin, David) (Entered: 07/06/1998)

07/06/1998 82 LETTER dated 06/26/98 from Michael D. Hess, Corp. Counsel to Judge Gershon submitting this letter as plaintiffs' response to the defendants' counsel's letter to the Court dated 06.24.98. (Galeano, Sonia) (Entered: 07/06/1998)

07/07/1998 84 ORDER dtd. 6/24/98 Application to file response by 7/31/98 GRANTED on ltr. dtd. 6/24/98 from Alessandra F. Zorgniotti request the court not accept pltff's supplemental papers as they are defective and not in compliance with court's 6/19/98 order. (signed by Judge Nina Gershon) (Jackson, Ramona) (Entered: 07/07/1998)

07/29/1998 86 Second Supplemental Declaration of BARBARA M. KETT Board of Elections Re: in reply to pltff's supplemental response to deft's motion for summary judgment. (Jackson, Ramona) Modified on 07/29/1998 (Entered: 07/29/1998)

07/29/1998 85 REPLY MEMORANDUM OF LAW by Richmond County, Staten Island Board, Barbara M. Kett, NYC Board of Education, NYC Police Dept., Board of Elections, New York City in further support [63- 1] motion for summary judgment (Jackson, Ramona) (Entered: 07/29/1998)

07/31/1998 86 LETTER dated 7/27/98 from Jeffrey M. Motelson to Judge Gershon, re: copies of ballots submitted by the plaintiffs and defendants in this matter. (Reddy, Lisa) (Entered: 07/31/1998)

09/15/1998 87 OPINION & ORDER dtd. 9/14/98 Deft's motion for summary judgment is GRANTED. Pltff's motion for summary judgment is DENIED. (signed by Judge Nina Gershon). Copies mailed. (Jackson, Ramona) (Entered: 09/15/1998)

09/15/1998 Case closed. (Jackson, Ramona) (Entered: 09/15/1998)

09/17/1998 88 JUDGMENT dtd. 9/16/98 (pltff's take nothing of the deft's; that the pltff's motion for summary judgment is DENIED; AND, that the deft's motion for summary judgment is GRANTED). Copies mailed. (Jackson, Ramona) (Entered: 09/17/1998)

09/17/1998 Received defts' exhibits Y-original community school district 31 ballots in support of defts' supplemental reply memo. (see documents filed 7/27). Placed in vault for safekeeping and to be returned to defts upon application. (Glenn, Marilyn) (Entered: 09/17/1998)

09/18/1998 89 NOTICE OF APPEAL by Pro-Se Melvin Ladner Fee Paid $105.00. Receipt #211102. Notice of Appeal and certified copy of docket sent appealing [88-1] judgment order, [871] order. (Vasquez, Liz) (Entered: 09/21/1998)

09/18/1998 Notice of Appeal and certified copy of docket to USCA: [89-1] appeal. (Vasquez, Liz) (Entered: 09/21/1998)

09/22/1998 90 LETTER dated 7/27/98 from Alessandra F. Zorgniotti to Judge Gershon enclosed copies deft's memo. of law dtd. 7/27/98 etc. (Jackson, Ramona) (Entered: 09/22/1998)

09/22/1998 Certified and transmitted record on appeal to U.S. Court of Appeals: [89-1] appeal. This record consists of doc# 26,27,29,31,42,48,54,62- 76,78-80,82-85-89. Missingdoc# 1-25,28,30,32-41,43-49,5053,55-61,77,81,90. Acknowledgment requested. (Vasquez, Liz) Modified on 09/22/1998 (Entered: 09/22/1998)

09/22/1998 Memo. dtd. 9/22/98 has been sent to Admin. Manager requesting a search on the missing docs. in this case, when located will be transmitted to the USCA. (Vasquez, Liz) (Entered: 09/22/1998)

10/05/1998 Transmitted 1st supplemental record on appeal: [89-1] appeal. This record consists of docs# 1-21,23-46, 48-60,76,77,81-84 sent only to the USCA. (Vasquez, Liz) (Entered: 10/05/1998)

10/13/199891 Acknowledgment from USCA received re: [89-1] appeal.Acknowledgment signed by N.J. on 10/7/98. USCA# 98-9285. (Vasquez, Liz) (Entered: 10/15/1998)

10/13/199892 Acknowledgment from USCA received re: [89-1] appeal.Acknowledgment signed by N.G. on 10/7/98.USCA# 98-9285. (Vasquez, Liz) (Entered: 10/15/1998)

06/11/1999 93 MANDATE OF USCA (certified copy) Re: [89-1] appeal. It is Ordered, Adjudged and Decreed that the judgment of the District Court is AFFIRMED. Issued as Mandate 6/8/99. Acknowledgment returned to USCA. Judge notified. USCA#98- 9285. (McGee, Maryann) (Entered: 06/15/1999)

08/03/1999 94 Record on appeal returned from U.S. Court of Appeals: [89-1] including documents 22,24,25,27-46,48-60,62-89. Document 26 was not returned. [Copy if this receipt sent to Fred Nunnery do Court of Appeals]. (Johnson, Tanya) Modified on 08/03/1999 (Entered: 08/03/1999)

08/03/1999 95 First Supplemental Record on appeal returned from U.S. Court of Appeals including documents 1-16. (Copy sent to Fred Nunnery do Court of Appeals.) (Per-maul, Jenny) (Entered: 08/03/1999)

CHAPTER FOUR

The Federal Court For The Eastern District Of New York: The Final Decision Dismissing My Election Fraud Case And Refusing To Give Me A Trial

DICISION FOR THE U.S. DISTRICT COURT FOR THE EASTERN DISTRICT OF NEW YORK

The Order of the U. S. District Court for the Eastern District of New York dismissing the case of Ladner v. City of New York. After reading the order do you agree with the court that I don't have enough evidence for a trial? Remember a trial is the search for the truth, Isn't it amazing that the Federal District Court in their opinion dismissing my case never divulges the Count Director, Bruce Hogenauer's, criminal past, which a jury would be shocked to learn.

OPINION AND ORDER UNITED STATES DISTRICT COURT FOR THE EASTERN DISTRICT OF NEW YORK Ladner v. City of New York UNITED STATES DISTRICT COURT FOR THE EASTERN DISTRICT OF NEW YORK

September 14, 1998

MELVIN LADNER and TIMOTHY CARL, Plaintiffs, against THE CITY OF NEW YORK, THE BOARD OF ELECTIONS OF THE CITY OF NEW YORK, THE POLICE DEPARTMENT OF THE CITY OF NEW YORK, THE BOARD OF EDUCATION OF THE CITY OF NEW YORK, BARBAR a.m. KETT, as Chief

Clerk of Staten Island Board of Elections, THE STATEN ISLAND BOARD OF ELECTIONS, and THE RICHMOND COUNTY BOARD OF ELECTIONS,

Defendants! Third-Party Plaintiffs,-against- PROPORTIONAL COUNTS ASSOCIATES, INC., Third-Party Defendant. The opinion of the court was delivered by: GERSHON OPINION AND ORDER GERSHON, United States District Judge:

Plaintiffs Melvin Ladner and Timothy Carl, two unsuccessful candidates in the May 4, 1993 election for Community School Board, District 31 ("Community School Board 31") in Staten Island, New York, bring this action pursuant to 42 USC.?? 1983 and 1985(3) alleging violations of the Due Process and Equal Protection Clauses of the Fourteenth Amendment. Defendants City of New York, Board of Elections of the City of New York ("Board of Elections"), the New York City Police Department "fn1*, the Board of Education of the City of New York, Barbara Kett, Chief Clerk of the Staten Island Borough Office of the Board of Elections, the Staten Island Board of Elections and the Richmond County Board of Elections *fn2* move for summary judgment pursuant to Rule 56 of the Federal Rules of Civil Procedure dismissing the amended complaint.

Plaintiffs also move for summary judgment, on the ground that defendants destroyed ballot stubs and stub boxes, which, they claim, were vital to their proof. The third-party defendant, Proportional Counts Associates, Inc., an independent company hired to do the actual counting of ballots for the election, has answered.

FACTS:

Unless otherwise indicated, the following facts are undisputed.

On May 4, 1993, the Board of Elections of the City of New York conducted a city- wide election in which nine members were elected to each Community School Board. Plaintiffs were two of the 25 candidates for the nine seats on the Community School Board 31, which comprised all of Staten Island. Plaintiffs, who describe themselves as adhering to a conservative political philosophy, campaigned for election on a platform opposing the

"Children of the Rainbow" curriculum as promoted by then-New York City Chancellor of Schools Joseph Fernandez and then-New York City Mayor David Dinkins.

Staten Island was divided by the Board of Elections into three Assembly Districts ("ADs"), the 59th, 60th, and 61st. Within each AD, there were numerous Election Districts ("EDs") and the resulting entities were called "ED/ADs." For example, the 41st ED within the 60th AD was called the "41/60 ED/AD." Some ED/ADs were divided into sub-EDs or assigned an "H" designation; these were areas consisting of individual apartment buildings, developments or nursing homes which had enough registered voters to make up an independent sub-ED within the main ED territory. As a result, some ED/ADs had more than one ballot box. Although all of Staten Island was divided into separate ED/ADs, a single site, such as a school, frequently served as the polling site for several different ED/ADs. By statute, the Board of Elections is authorized to combine certain ED/ADs with one another if there are not enough registered voters to maintain an independent ED/AD. N.Y. Elec. L.? 4104(5) (a). For the 1993 school- board election, the Board of Elections combined the 37th ED/60th AD ("37/60") into the 95th ED/60th AD ("95/60") and the 101st ED/60th AD ("101/60") into the 90th ED/60th AD ("90/60"). As a result, the 95/60 ballot box was used to collect ballots from 37/60 and 95/60, and the 90/60 ballot box was used to collect ballots from 101/60 and 90/60.

In accordance with New York Education Law? 2590-c(7), the 1993 school-board election was conducted using a proportional representation voting procedure. See generally Campbell v. Board of Education, 310 F. Supp. 94, 98-102 (E.D.N.Y. 1970). At the polls, each registered voter was given a paper ballot which included the names of the 25 candidates for election to Community School Board 31. Each ballot designated the particular ED/AD where it was to be voted; the ballots themselves, however, were not individually numbered. The order of the names of the candidates on the ballots was rotated by ED/AD so that each candidate's name had an equal opportunity to appear on top, middle or bottom of the ballots. Voters were instructed to vote by preference. That is, they were directed to mark, using a pen or pencil, a "1" by their first choice candidate, a "2" by their second choice candidate, and so forth. Voters could mark as many choices as they pleased. Voters were directed to fold the completed ballot and give it to the election inspectors, who would place it in the ballot box. Attached to all ballots were ballot stubs,

which were numbered from 1 to 500. The ballot stubs were used primarily to enable election officials to know how many ballots had been distributed. After marking their preferences on the ballot, voters were instructed to place the ballot stub in the stub box. Sample ballots were provided upon request to voters while they waited to vote. Sample ballots were identical to the official ballots except that they were printed in a different color and the stubs were printed without numbers. The sample ballots were buff colored and the official ballots were white.

During the election, Barbara Kett, who was responsible for the administration of the 1993 election for Community School Board 31, was informed that many voters had mistakenly cast sample ballots, instead of official ballots, in the ballot boxes. The Board of Elections later determined that the sample ballots should be counted because they were cast by registered voters. During the election, Kett was also notified by election inspectors at four polling sites, which housed the ballot boxes for more than one ED/AD, that they had ballots which did not reflect the proper ED/AD. Kett went with two clerks, Jill Jackson and Marion Kaminski, to each of these sites and confirmed that the police had mistakenly delivered ballots to the wrong ED/AD voting tables within that polling site.

Kett and the two clerks temporarily suspended voting and moved the unused ballots to their correct ED/AD tables. After opening the ballot boxes to verify that ballots had been cast in the wrong ED/AD ballot boxes, they corrected, in ink, the ED/AD designation on each ballot to reflect the proper ED/AD. They then marked each correction with their initials, "BMK," "JJ," and "MK," respectively. Kett explains that she did not see how the votes were cast and made no changes to the voting sections of the ballots. The ballots were returned to their ballot boxes, and voting recommenced.

When the polls closed at 9:00 p.m. on May 4, 1993, the ballot boxes and stub boxes at each polling site were sealed. Election inspectors filled out ballot box certificates, which accounted for the total number of ballots cast at each ED/AD. There was a total of approximately 24,000 votes cast in this election for Community School Board 31. The ballot boxes were moved from the polling places to police precinct houses and eventually to the central counting site. Each time the ballot boxes were moved, election officials used "tick-off" sheets, listing all the ballot boxes, for accounting purposes.

The count was conducted at the Egbert Intermediary School in Staten Island from May 13, 1993 to May 18, 1993.

Under the system of proportional representation set forth in Section 2590-c of New York Education Law, ballots are counted by ED/AD in an order determined by lot. As an initial matter, all of the first choices marked on the ballots are counted.

This system was described in Campbell, as follows:

After all of the first preferences are counted, and the total number of valid ballots cast in the school district becomes known, a formula is applied to determine whether any candidates have been elected. To win, a candidate's votes must surpass a quota determined by dividing the total number of valid ballots cast in the school district by one more than the number of offices to be filled (in this case, the number is 10, since 9 board members are to be elected in each school district), and then adding one to this total.

If any candidate reaches this quota figure, all ballots cast for him in excess of that number are to be awarded to the second choice marked on them....

A similar procedure is utilized to remove candidates. First, after the transfer of surplus votes described above, all first-preference votes credited to candidates receiving the fewest votes are to be transferred to the second choices indicated on the ballots.

Upon completion of this transfer, the candidate remaining who has the lower number of votes is declared defeated, and his second preference votes are transferred to the remaining undefeated candidates. Once transfers are sufficient to enable a candidate to pass the quota, he is declared elected, and all subsequent preferences attributed to him are transferred to the candidate with the next highest preference. This process is continued until all but the desired number of elected officials have been eliminated. Campbell, 310 F. Supp. at 99.

Neither Kett nor any personnel from the Board of Elections participated in the counting of the ballots. The task was contracted out to an independent company, Proportional Counts Associates, Inc., the third-party defendant in this case.

The Staten Island Count Director was Bruce Hogenauer, an employee of Proportional Counts Associates, Inc.

Plaintiffs attended the count and observed several election irregularities, which form the bases for their complaint in this action. Objecting to these election irregularities, Ladner filed a protest sheet.

Defendants deny that any such protest sheet was ever submitted. For purposes of this motion, Ladner's allegation regarding the filing of the protest sheet is accepted as true. Plaintiffs observed that, during the random draw which determines the box order for counting purposes, the boxes for 37/60 and 101/60 were not located when those boxes were announced.

Plaintiffs notified Count Director Hogenauer and demanded that the count be stopped until the boxes were located. Hogenauer refused, and the election count proceeded. It is unrefuted that, since the Board of Elections had previously combined several ED/ADs, including 37/60 and 101/60, with other ED/ADs, the allegedly missing ballot boxes never in fact existed. Plaintiffs observed "hundreds or thousands" of ballots being counted, with writing in ink on them, bearing the initials "BMK," "JJ," or "MK." Carl Dec. P 15; Ladner Dec. P20. Plaintiffs showed Hogenauer these altered ballots, marked some of these ballots with a red "P" for protest, and demanded the count be stopped. Hogenauer counted them over their protest. Defendants' explanation for the initials on certain ballots is set forth above. Plaintiffs observed numerous sample ballots, instead of official ballots, being counted. As noted above, defendants acknowledge that, in this election, some sample ballots were cast and counted, and that the Board of Elections advised Hogenauer to count the sample ballots because they had been cast by registered voters.

Plaintiffs observed "hundreds, if not thousands" of ballots which appeared to be voted in identical handwriting, with scores of identical patterns." Carl Dec. P 15; Ladner Dec. P 20. Plaintiffs believe that these "identical" ballots were "stuffed" into the ballot boxes. Defendants deny that any ballots were altered. Hogenauer investigated this allegation during the count and determined that the handwriting was not similar and therefore included the challenged ballots in the count.

Plaintiffs observed "hundreds (if not thousands) of ballots" where the "1" and "2" votes for them had been altered to "11" and "12," with new candidates chosen as "1"and "2." Carl Dec. P 15; Ladner Dec. P 52. Defendants again deny that any ballots were altered.

Plaintiffs noticed that there were more than one ballot box from a single AD/ED at the count site. Defendants acknowledge that, since some ED/ADs were divided into sub EDs or given an "H" designation, there were multiple ballot boxes for certain ED/ADs.

Plaintiffs observed ballot boxes which, plaintiffs believed, had been opened and later resealed with tape. They noticed that the re-taping had peeled away portions of the paper boxes. Defendants acknowledge that, since the ballot boxes were moved several times, they required some re-taping.

Plaintiffs saw ballot boxes being counted without including the absentee ballots from that ED/AD. Hogenauer explained that the absentee ballots were treated separately and, therefore, the absentee ballots from all the ED/ADS would be counted together at the end of the count.

Plaintiffs also saw that ballots which were in the wrong ED/AD boxes had been counted. Defendants acknowledge that, if ballots from the wrong ED/AD were counted, it was done pursuant to New York Election Law? 9- 108(4) which requires the counting of misplaced ballots.

After the count, the election materials were removed from the Egbert Intermediate School. There were nine sealed boxes, one for each winning candidate, containing the ballots which elected each candidate. A tenth box contained the spoiled or void ballots and an eleventh box contained the exhausted ballots. (Exhausted ballots were those ballots which could not be transferred to other candidates during the count because all the candidates identified by the voter had already received the requisite number of votes to be elected.)

These eleven boxes, which contained all the ballots, were locked in a secure room at the Staten Island Borough Office, where they have been continuously maintained. The remaining over 300 empty ballot boxes, the stub boxes, and the approximately 24,000 ballot stubs were discarded. When the count was completed on May 18, 1993, plaintiffs were not among the nine winning candidates. The final results of the 1993 city-wide school-board election were certified by the Board of Elections on June 1, 1993.

Plaintiffs filed a notice of claim with the New York City Comptroller on September 27, 1993, alleging election fraud. Thereafter, plaintiffs commenced this action in New York State supreme court and, since plaintiffs alleged only violations of federal law, defendants removed the action to this court on the basis of federal question jurisdiction. On February 9, 1995, the Honorable I. Leo Glasser, District Judge, denied defendants' motion to dismiss plaintiffs' Section 1983 claims, but granted the motion to dismiss the conspiracy claim under Section 1985(3) with leave to replead Ladner v. City of New York, 1995 WL 62687 (E.D.N.Y.).

On March 14, 1995, plaintiffs filed an amended complaint. Pursuant to a July 1996 Order of the Honorable Joan Azrack, Magistrate Judge, plaintiffs inspected the original ballots at the Staten Island Borough Office of the Board of Elections. Based on their observations at the inspection, plaintiffs now allege additional election irregularities, specifically, that the approximately 24,000 ballot stubs and Ladner's protest sheet had been destroyed, and that there had been a significant "diminution" in the number of

sample ballots and fraudulent ballots. Finally, based on an anonymous tip after the election, plaintiff Ladner hired a private investigator, who claimed to find that 4 people "arose from the dead, to register and to cast their ballots for the school board candidates of their choice" during the 1993 election. Ladner Dec. P 37.

DEFENDANTS' MOTION FOR SUMMARY JUDGMENT Pursuant to Federal Rule of Civil Procedure 56(c), summary judgment should be granted if "the pleadings, depositions, answers to interrogatories, and admissions on file, together with the affidavits, if any, show that there is no genuine issue as to any material fact and that the moving party is entitled to a judgment as a matter of law." *Celotex Corp. v. Catrett*, 477 US 317, 322, 91 L. Ed. 2d 265, 106 S. Ct. 2548 (1986). It is the movant's burden to demonstrate the absence of any genuine issue of material fact. See *Adickes* v. S.D. Kress &Co., 398 US 144, 175, 26 L. Ed. 2d 142, 90 S. Ct. 1598 (1970). A material fact is one whose resolution would "affect the outcome of the suit under governing law," and a dispute is genuine "if the evidence is such that a reasonable jury could return a verdict for the non-moving party." *Anderson v. Liberty Lobby, Inc.*, 477 US 242, 248, 91 L. Ed. 2d 202, 106 S. Ct. 2505 (1986). The nonmoving party, however, "must do more than simply show that there is some metaphysical doubt as to the material facts." *Matsushita Elec. Indus. Co., Ltd. v. Zenith Radio Corp.*, 475 US 574, 586, 89

L. Ed. 2d 538, 106 S. Ct. 1348 (1986). Summary judgment is proper "against a party who fails to make a showing sufficient to establish the existence of an element essential to that party's case, and on which that party will bear the burden of proof at trial." Celotex, 477 US at 322.

Section 1983 Claims In order to maintain an action under 42 USC.? 1983, plaintiffs must demonstrate conduct committed by a person acting under color of law that deprived them of rights, privileges, or immunities secured by the Constitution or the laws of the United States. Here, plaintiffs allege that their rights to due process and equal protection of the laws as guaranteed by the Fourteenth Amendment were violated by defendants' "fraudulent election acts, in causing, permitting and/or allowing widespread fraud in the casting, tabulation and entering of ballots and results in the Staten Island School-Board elections." Amended Complaint P 16.

"It has been said often and with great force that there is no right more fundamental in our country than the right to vote." Gelb v. Board of Elections in the City of New York, 950 F. Supp. 82, 84 (S.D.N.Y. 1996) (citing Wesberry v. Sanders, 376 US 1, 11 L. Ed. 2d 481, 84 S. Ct. 526 (1964)). Where there is an adequate state law remedy, however, mere election irregularities rarely rise to the level of a federal constitutional violation. In Powell v. Power, 436 F.2d 84 (2d Cir. 1970), voters sought relief pursuant to Section 1983, alleging that state officials had abridged their rights to due process and equal protection by allowing unqualified voters to cast ballots in a primary election. In declining to find a federal violation, the Court of Appeals for the Second Circuit explained:

Were we to embrace the plaintiffs' theory, this court would henceforth be thrust into the details of virtually every election, tinkering with the state's election machinery, reviewing petitions, registration cards, vote tallies, and certificates of election for all manner of error and insufficiency under state and federal law. Absent a clear and unambiguous mandate from Congress, we are not inclined to undertake such a wholesale expansion of our jurisdiction into an area which, with certain narrow and well-defined exceptions, has been in the exclusive cognizance of the state courts. Id. at 86.

The Court recognized that a Section 1983 action to remedy errors in the election process allegedly violating the Equal Protection Clause does not lie unless the state action constituted "intentional or purposeful discrimination." Id. at 88.

The Court also held that the Due Process Clause "offer[s] no guarantee against errors in the administration of an election," noting instead that "New York Election Law?? 145, 330(2) provide a method for correcting such errors as are made. " Id. The Court concluded by stating that it could not "believe that the framers of our Constitution were so hypersensitive to ordinary human frailties as to lay down an unrealistic requirement that elections be free of any error." Id.

The Second Circuit recently "reaffirmed. [its] holding in Powell." Gold v. Feinberg, 101 F.3d 796, 802 (2d Cir. 1996). In Gold, a judicial decree, issued the day before the primary election, which removed one candidate from the ballot, resulted in delays in the arrival of voting machines at approximately one-third of the election districts; votes being miscounted because of the improper placement of templates over ballots; and ineligible candidates remaining on the ballot. The district court concluded that these election irregularities constituted a due process violation under Section 1983 and issued a preliminary injunction prohibiting election officials from certifying the election. The Second Circuit, however, reversed the district court, finding that there was no evidence of "intentional deprivation of the right to vote." Id. at 798. Specifically, it held that "there are no substantiated allegations of any wrongful intent on the part of state officials All of the irregularities alleged to have occurred were the direct result of a late-issued judicial order." Id. at 801. It therefore rejected the district court's conclusion that certain longstanding practices of the Elections Board regarding the delegation of undue amounts of oversight responsibility to subordinates, which the district court had characterized as "foolish decisions," "constituted willfulness within the meaning" of Section 1983. Id. The Court also rejected the district court's suggestion that the "requirement of willfulness established by Powell should no longer be required because of the passage of 25 years in the Second Circuit and a change of attitude." Id.

The Court then reaffirmed that where there exists a state law remedy to the election irregularities that is fair and adequate, human error in the conduct of elections does not rise to the level of a Fourteenth Amendment Constitutional violation actionable under?

1983 in the absence of willful action by state officials intended to deprive individuals of their constitutional right to vote. Short of that, human error is something we all have to live with. Id. at 802.

Due Process Violations The election irregularities alleged by the plaintiffs in the present case do not rise to the level of a federal constitutional violation. Several of plaintiffs' allegations of election irregularities are unsubstantiated by any evidence in the record. As to those claims where there exists an issue as to whether an election irregularity occurred, there is no factual issue as to any wrongful intent by election officials to deprive individuals of their constitutional right to vote. Nor can it be said that any of the irregularities rendered the election so pervasively unfair as to require a federal remedy under the Due Process Clause. Therefore, plaintiffs' due process claims must be dismissed.

MISSING BOXES:

Plaintiffs allege that the ballots were counted even though the ballot boxes for 37/60 and 101/60 were missing. Plaintiffs' allegation of missing boxes, however, is unfounded because, since the Board of Elections combined 37/60 into 95/60 and 101/60 into 90/60 before the election, the allegedly missing ballot boxes never existed. The ballot box certificate for 90/60 recorded that there were 68 ballots from 90/60 and 2 ballots from 101/60 in that ballot box, and the ballot box certificate for 95/60 recorded that there were 79 ballots combined from 37/60 and 95/60. Plaintiff Ladner contends that the ED/ADS in question could not have been combined; he claims that he "obtained proof that in fact 419 voters were reported at 101/60 alone on the 5-493 date of election, before 8:00 a.m." Ladner Dec. P24. The local newspaper article, upon which plaintiff relies, indicated that, by 8:00 p.m. (not a.m.), there had been 419 votes cast at P.S. 60. While P.S. 60 was listed as the polling site for 101/60 ED/AD, it was also the polling site for at least three other ED/ADs, 88/60, 89/60 and 90/60. Therefore, that 419 voters had cast ballots does not constitute evidence that there was a separate ballot box for 101/60.

Plaintiffs also contend that 37/60 and 101/60 could not have been combined with other ED/ADs because they were included in the list of ED/ADs for the random draw and on one of the "tick-off" lists used by election officials to account for the ballot boxes during moving. This inclusion alone does not establish any willful intent on behalf of state officials. At most, it can be said that some election officials were negligent in mistakenly including these ballot boxes on certain lists when, in fact, they did not exist.

Altered Ballots with Initials "BMK," "JJ," and "MK"

There is no dispute that defendant Barbara Kett and two clerks opened ballot boxes, corrected the ED/AD designations on numerous ballots, and added their initials to the corrections. However, there is no evidence that any alterations were made to the votes cast on the initialed ballots or that the corrections had any effect on the outcome of the election. It is undisputed that Kett and her clerks opened ballot boxes and changed the ED/AD designations for the purpose of ensuring that ballots would be counted in their correct ED/AD. Whether or not opening ballot boxes and making alterations to a cast ballot violated state election law, as plaintiffs suggest, no federal constitutional violation has been shown.

SAMPLE BALLOTS:

Plaintiffs have established that numerous sample ballots were cast and counted. Again, there is no evidence to suggest that the outcome of the election was affected by the use of sample ballots in lieu of official ballots. In fact, the Board of Elections decided to count the sample ballots so as not to disenfranchise registered voters who mistakenly cast such ballots. This decision was not a violation of plaintiffs' rights under the Constitution.

"Stuffed" Ballots with Identical Handwriting and Identical Sequence of Votes:

Plaintiffs allege that ballot boxes were stuffed with numerous ballots. Plaintiffs have two bases for this claim: an identical sequence of votes on as many as ten ballots as well as other pairs of ballots with an identical sequence of votes; and the alleged identity of the handwriting on ballots with an identical sequence of votes. To support their claim, plaintiffs now submit photocopies of approximately seventy-five ballots.

That votes were cast for an identical sequence of candidates does not in itself create an issue of fact that there was an election irregularity, much less a constitutional violation. Indeed, identical sequencing of votes on various ballots is not surprising, because it is undisputed that, in this election- where nine candidates were to be selected from a pool of 25- some candidates campaigned together as a coalition and handed out "palm cards" listing candidates in sequential order to voters. Even apart from that, from a total of approximately 24,000 ballots cast in this election for Community School Board 31, it cannot be considered suspicious that ten ballots, or even more, would be cast for the same sequence of candidates.

More importantly, plaintiffs have not established an issue of fact as to whether a single hand wrote more than one ballot. Plaintiffs have not proffered a handwriting expert, but merely express their own lay opinions that the ballots are identical. Plaintiffs' photocopied ballots and the original ballots, to which they correspond, have been carefully reviewed by the court. Comparison of the ballots fails to reveal anything whatever in support of plaintiffs' claim. Review of the photocopies of the ballots reveals no similarity, much less identity, in the handwriting alleged to be the same. Review of the original ballots not only confirms this assessment but establishes beyond a doubt that any claim of identity is based in plaintiffs' imagination and not on the evidence. "When no rational jury could find in favor of the nonmoving party because the evidence to support its case is so slight, there is no genuine issue of material fact and a grant of summary judgment is proper." Gallo v. Prudential Residential Services, Inc., 22 F.3d 1219, 1224 (2d Cir. 1994). Since the evidence supporting plaintiffs' claim of identical, stuffed ballots is so slight, no rational jury could find in their favor on this claim.

Ballots Altered From "1" and "2" Votes for Plaintiffs to "11," "12" and Other Votes Plaintiffs also claim that numerous ballots were altered. Specifically, they claim that "1" and "2" votes for plaintiffs were changed to "11,""12" or other votes for them. Again, plaintiffs do not offer any handwriting expert to support their claims, but instead rely on their own unsupported opinions. Plaintiffs submit photocopies of approximately sixtyfive ballots in support of this claim.

Basically, plaintiffs claim that every vote that contains a downstroke, such as a "4,"","14," or "17," which was cast for one of them, was originally a "1," and every vote, such as a "12" or "22," which contains a "2," was once a "2" vote for them. This argument is frivolous. It is not supported by any evidence, either on the ballots themselves or external to the ballots. The claim appears to be based on wishful thinking, not reason.

Even on the occasional ballot where there are marks indicating that a number may have been changed, there is no evidence to suggest that the change was not made by the voter at the time of the vote.

Plaintiffs have offered no evidence, for example, suggesting that the changes were made with a writing instrument different from that used to cast the original ballot, and examination of the original ballots reveals no sign of fraud.

In sum, plaintiffs have adduced no issue of fact as to whether the ballots were marked by anyone other than the voter during the act of choosing the preferential order of the candidates.

Duplicate Ballot Boxes From a Single ED/AD Plaintiffs' claim that they observed more than one ballot box from a single ED/AD is not an election irregularity at all. Several ED! ADs were divided into

sub-ED/ADs or "H" designations, requiring separate ballot boxes; in those instances, there was more than one ballot box from a single ED/ AD at the count site.

Ballot Boxes Which Required Re-taping Defendants acknowledge that, since the boxes were moved several times before the ballots were counted, the boxes needed to be re-taped. Contrary to plaintiffs' suggestion, there is no evidence that the boxes were opened for any unlawful purpose.

Ballot Boxes Counted Without Absentee Ballots Hogenauer informed plaintiffs that the absentee ballots would be counted, not with their assigned ED/AD, but altogether, after all the ballots cast at the polling sites had been counted.

Whether or not counting the absentee ballots separately from the rest of the ballots amounts to a state election law violation, as plaintiffs suggest, it does not amount to a constitutional violation. Ballots Which Were Counted From Incorrect ED/AD Ballot Boxes Contrary to plaintiffs' assertions, that some ballots were counted despite being located in the wrong ED/AD ballot box was not only permissible, it was required by New York Election Law? 9-108(4).

Destruction of 24,000 Ballot Stubs and Stub Boxes Plaintiffs claim that the destruction of all 24,000 ballot stubs and the stub boxes constitutes a willful act of election fraud.

Plaintiffs, however, have failed to explain how the availability of the ballot stubs would be necessary or even helpful to verify the alleged inaccuracy of the election results. Since the official ballots are not numbered at all, there is no correlation between the official ballots and the numbering of the ballot stubs, which run from 1 to 500 in each ED/AD. Therefore, the ballot stubs would be useless to determine if a particular ballot was fraudulently cast.

Kett explained that the ballot stubs are used primarily for knowing how many ballots have been distributed and are of limited value to calculating how many votes were actually cast. She explained that the number of stubs in the stubs box do not always match the number of ballots in the ballot boxes because, for example, voters often fail to place the stub in the stub box or, if a voter spoils a ballot, the stub for that ballot is still placed in the stub box, and the voter is given a new ballot, with another stub attached.

Moreover, unlike ballots and voting records, New York Election Law? 3- 222 does not require the retention of ballot stubs and stub boxes.

Finally, since the ballot stubs and other election materials were removed immediately after the election as a matter of course before this action was filed or noticed, there is no indication that any public officials discarded the ballot stubs with any wrongful intent.

Diminution of "Altered" or Sample Ballots and Destruction of Protest Sheets:

Plaintiffs have provided no evidence beyond their own conclusory statements that there has been a "significant diminution" of these ballots to support their claim that there were fewer sample ballots, altered ballots and protest sheets at the July 1996 ballot inspection than they observed during the original count. Plaintiffs make no effort to quantify how many ballots no longer exist; nor do they offer any basis for their opinions. Given the undisputed evidence regarding the manner in which the ballots have

been secured since the election count, plaintiffs' references to a "diminution" at the ballot inspection are insufficient to create an issue of fact.

DEAD VOTERS:

Plaintiffs' allegation that four dead people, Thomas Reilly, Pasquale Delio, Theresa Bellia and Ronald Ross, voted in the 1993 school-board election lacks support and fails to implicate any wrongful intent on behalf of state officials. Plaintiffs rely upon newspaper obituaries, Voting Activity Lists and Voter Registration Lists to contend that these four individuals fraudulently voted in this election. Examination of these documents, however, does not reveal the voting histories for these individuals. In contrast, Voting History Lists (which are public documents used by the Board of Elections to record personal information for each voter) collect the voting history information, including the date and type of election voted in, which ED/AD voted in, and which type of ballot was used. The Voting History Lists for the four individuals indicate that none of them voted in the 1993 school-board election in question. Therefore, plaintiffs' claim of dead voters in this election lacks any basis.

Finally, it should be noted that the New York courts have jurisdiction to provide a remedy under New York law for the election irregularities as to which there may be a fact issue. See N.Y. Elec. L.?? 16-100 et seq. Judicial proceedings challenging Community School-board elections are subject to the New York election laws. See N.Y. Educ. L.? 2590c(6). Plaintiffs make no showing that New York courts cannot provide a fair and adequate remedy other than to argue that the irregularities are so serious as to require federal court intervention. As shown above, plaintiffs have been unable to establish an issue of fact as to their claims of serious irregularities.

EQUAL PROTECTION VIOLATIONS

Plaintiffs have also failed to demonstrate that defendants engaged in any intentional effort to discriminate against plaintiffs on the basis of their conservative political philosophy. See Power v. Powell, 436 F.2d at 88. In the amended complaint, plaintiffs allege that former Mayor David Dinkins, a Democrat, and defendants worked together to prevent plaintiffs from being elected to Community School Board 31 because plaintiffs campaigned on a politically conservative platform. Plaintiffs do not offer any evidence beyond a newspaper article setting forth Mayor Dinkins' involvement in a City- financed voter drive for the school-board election at issue and the fact that Barbara Kett was a member of the Executive Committee of the Richmond County Democratic Party Organization, to suggest that they were intentionally discriminated against because they are conservative politicians. The newspaper article, even were it not inadmissible hearsay and unusable to defeat summary judgment, see FED. R. CIV. P. 56(e), merely states that Mayor Dinkins committed $635,000 to mail cards to all of the City's registered voters. Although the campaign was non-partisan in nature, an unnamed mayoral aide was reported to state the belief that, if more New Yorkers voted, they would reject "conservative candidates and support [Mayor Dinkins's] educational policies. "These comments do not establish that any constitutional violation occurred during the election. Since plaintiffs have failed to demonstrate intentional discrimination, their Section 1983 claims for violations of the Equal Protection Clause must be dismissed.

Conspiracy under Section 1985(3) Plaintiffs have also failed to demonstrate any evidence of a conspiracy among the defendants to violate their rights to equal protection of the laws. In the amended complaint, plaintiffs alleged that Mayor Dinkins conspired with defendants in violation of 42 USC.? 1985 (3) to prevent their election. To prevail on a Section 1985(3) claim, plaintiffs must prove that defendants (1) engaged in a conspiracy; (2) for the purpose of depriving, either directly or indirectly, any person of the equal protection of the laws; (3) acted in furtherance of the conspiracy; and (4) deprived such person of the exercise of any right or privilege of a citizen of the United States. New York State N.O. W. v. Terry, 886 F.2d 1339,1358 (2d Cir. 1989). Here, there is no evidence of a conspiracy.

Plaintiffs again merely point to the involvement of Mayor Dinkins, a Democrat, in a City-financed voter drive and the fact that Barbara Kett is a member of the Executive Committee of the Richmond County Democratic Party to suggest there was a conspiracy against plaintiffs, who were politically conservative. Summary judgment therefore should be granted dismissing plaintiffs' conspiracy claims.

PLAINTIFFS' MOTION FOR SUMMARY JUDGMENT

Plaintiffs contend that, in failing to preserve the ballot stubs and stub boxes, defendants destroyed "vital, essential evidence," which, they allege, could have been used to verify the ballots cast. They argue that, because defendants participated in the destruction of such evidence, summary judgment must be granted against defendants. In support of this proposition, plaintiffs cite product liability cases in which the plaintiffs or third-party plaintiffs destroyed the product which caused the injury before the defendants had an opportunity to inspect the defective product, making it impossible for defendants to defend the case. See, e.g., Thiele v. Oddy's Auto and Marine, Inc., 906 F. Supp. 158 (W.D.N.Y. 1995). Such cases are clearly inapplicable here.

As previously explained, plaintiffs have failed to demonstrate how the ballot stubs could demonstrate willful election fraud in this case. New York Election Law does not require the retention of ballot stubs. N.Y. Elec. L.? 3-222. Therefore, plaintiffs' motion for summary judgment must be denied.

CONCLUSION

Defendants' motion for summary judgment is granted. Plaintiffs' motion for summary judgment is denied. The Clerk of Court is directed to enter judgment dismissing the complaint. SO ORDERED. NINA GERSHON United States District Judge Dated: Brooklyn, New York September 14, 1998.

CHAPTER FIVE
Traffic Court, Staten Island, New York

I received a parking summons for an expired meter. It was SOP to have a trial in traffic court. In that court, they have over 100 trials a day. The defendants don't know how lucky they are to be afforded a trial. Citizens in our country take trials for granted. Imagine if someone had to make motion after motion just for a trial. After dealing with federal court for five years, I couldn't believe that all I had to do was ask for a trial, and the traffic court had one. It was no big deal to have a trial and be able to search for the truth at a trial in traffic court. Having a trial was a gift from the government.

In traffic court, a citizen has the constitutional right to defend him or herself and bring witnesses and evidence into his defense. I never gave a thought about the right to a trial. I thought they were a constitutional right for all. When a court ruled that someone didn't have the right to a trial, that was going down a very dangerous, slippery slope.

The U.S. constitution states that every citizen is entitled to his or her day in court. What would happen if traffic court denied trials, because someone didn't like a citizen's defense?

I testified to the true events in traffic court and used the defense or human error. I forgot my reading glasses that day and didn't read my watch correctly, missing the time when my meter expired. When I went to the meter to add more money and extend the time, I saw a parking ticket on the windshield. The time had already expired.

The traffic court judge was fair and interpreted the law correctly. I agreed with the judge's decision that I was guilty of the offense of an expired parking meter. I also agreed with the judge's interpretation of the law, that there was no defense using human error. I paid the fine, thinking, *This is the real world, where common sense rules. Could it be that the traffic court judge has the smartest mind in the whole United States court system?*

I later learned that the traffic court judge was much smarter than the United States Court of Appeals and the United States Supreme Court combined. The traffic court judge the is only U.S. court where I had a real trial. He heard the evidence and the defense of human error. He ruled, saying that such a defense was nonsense.

"Human error!" the judge said. "That's a new one on me."

The courtroom erupted with laughter. The judge couldn't stop laughing, even as he found me guilty. I showed him the federal district court decision, and he read it with a puzzled expression.

"Is this a joke?" he asked. "No. It's the real deal," I replied.

"You've been railroaded. I can cite at least ten case laws that state there is no such defense as human error. I just ruled against you on the same grounds."

I was at a hearing office in Staten Island, New York.

"Let some average, law-abiding citizen use the defense of human error with the IRS and see what the IRS does," the judge added. I knew what the answer would be. I rested my case.

Many years' latter I received a summons for not shoveling snow from my sidewalk while I was on vacation and out of the country. I made the motion of the affirmative defense, that it was just human error! That I did not look at the weather report while on vacation.

I introduce the ruling into evidence of affirmative defense of human error that the U.S. court of appeals and U.S. Supreme court ruled in dismissing my case of election fraud. The New York City court ruled correctly that there is no such defense of Human Error even when you commit a minor infraction of not shoveling my walk. The ruling makes sense for the second time.

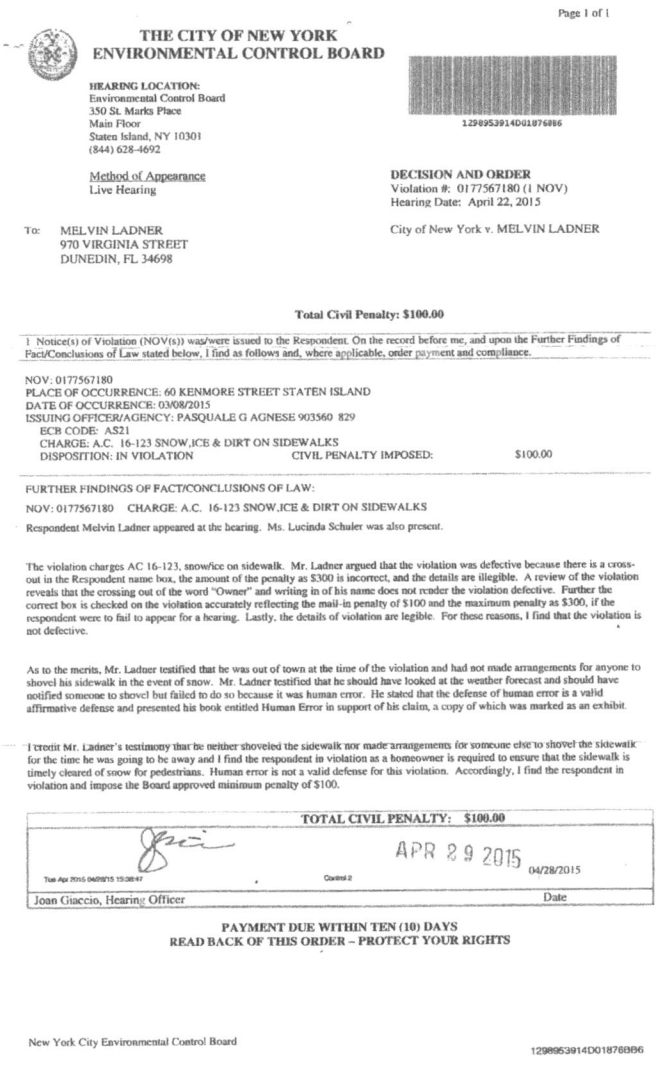

CHAPTER SIX
Edward F. Srancik Official New York Report:
"From Chaos To Corruption The 1993 School Board Election"
It Totally Disputes The Federal District Court Decision
And Proves That The 1993 School Board Election Was Rigged.
Corrupt And Voter Fraud Did Effect The Outcome Of MY Election.

EDWARD F. STANCIK REPORT: FROM CHAOS TO CORRUPTION. CITY OF NEW YORK THE SPECIAL COMMISSIONER OF INVESTIGATION FOR THE NEW YORK CITY SCHOOL DISTRICT EDWARD F. STANCIK, SPECIAL COMMISSIONER FROM CHAOS TO CORRUPTION: AN INVESTIGATION INTO THE 1993 COMMUNITY SCHOOL-BOARD ELECTION

Even when Ladner v. City of New York was still in federal court, fighting for the students of the city of New York for a better education and safety from a kidnapper and child molester, nothing changed. The education system became even more corrupt, yet the city fought hard to keep the system intact. City lawyers prevented me from having a trial to search for the truth to change the education system. They kept tying us up with endless motions and depositions. I figured that eventually, the city would run out of witnesses and motions, but I was wrong.

The city's plan was to win just one motion to dismiss the case. The city made the motion to bring the case to federal court and won over our objections. Then the city moved that we were trying the case in the wrong court, and it should be held in state court! In federal court, the city of New York moved to dismiss the case, even after Judge Glasser ruled that federal court was the right court.

Jeff kept asking for a trial and a date. The city of New York constantly objected. The judge kept granting the city motions for more evidence and depositions. That went on for five years. I thanked God that Jeff didn't quit the case.

I understood what Moses must have felt when he and his followers were lost in the desert for forty years, wandering endlessly. God must've had a reason for the endless delay. I was fighting for the education and safety of our children. How could New York City deny me a trial when the court had the Edward F. Stancik report in evidence that spelled out in detail the election fraud committed in the 1993 school board election.

The Stancik report also introduced as evidence, a video that detailed one hour and seven minutes of voter fraud, the names of those who committed the fraud, and the crimes that they performed in the 1993 school-board election?

The investigation I began was released in December, 1993, by Edward F. Stancik, City of New York, the Special Commissioner of Investigation for the New York City School District. When we received the 125-page report detailing one hour and seven minutes of voter fraud in the 1993 school board election Below is a summary of the full report. You can access it at https://go.gale.com showing who-what-where occurred in the 1993 School Board Election and other elections. However, We submitted the report into evidence. How could the federal district court deny me a trial with all the documented evidence the court had of voter fraud in the 1993 school board election?

Below is a summary of the full report. You can access it at https://go.gale.com showing who-what-where occurred in the 1993 School Board Election and other elections. However, I discovered Ed Stancik's name is misspelled - SRANCIK on the site! Was this done on purpose to prevent people from accessing the information which proves, beyond a reasonable doubt, that my election and other elections are rigged?

The Edward Stanchik report of the 1993 New York City School board election: CITY OF NEW YORK THE SPECIAL COMMISSIONER OF INVESTIGATION FOR THE NEWYORK CITY SCHOOL DISTRICT EDWARD F.STANCIK, SPECIAL COMMISSIONER FROM CHAOS TO CORRUPTION: AN INVESTIGATION INTO THE 1993 COMMUNITY SCHOOL- BOARD ELECTION By: ROBERT M. BRENNER, Deputy Commissioner REGINA A.

LOUGHRAN, Special Counsel THOMAS COMISKEY, Supervising Investigator TRACY KRAMER, Intelligence Analyst EXECUTIVE SUMMARY Our ten-month investigation closely examined the integrity of the May 1993 New York City Community School-board election. School-board elections are at the heart of decentralization, which should enable local communities to exercise control over the education of their children. Local board members have a direct impact on the quality of education in the district. The thirty-two boards elected last May set policy for their districts and control budgets in excess of $100 million, as well as thousands of educational jobs.

We found widespread fraud and corruption as well as administrative mismanagement in many areas of the election process. Both of these present serious dangers, because, when they flourish, parents and community members are denied the voice decentralization was designed to give them. A brief summary of our most-illustrative findings follows.

PARENT VOTER REGISTRATION

Poor planning and coordination by the Board of Elections and the Board of Education once again had a disastrous impact on the registering of parent voters. While in Manhattan anyone could pretend to be a parent and cast as many votes as names he or she could make up, duly registered parents lost their votes through administrative fumbling.

- In Community School District 2, one undercover investigator voted fifteen l times under fifteen different fictitious names. He even voted twice in front of the same poll inspector. Another investigator voted ten times in District 6 using fictitious names.
- Due to administrative errors, each of the 25 fictitious "parents" had valid voter registration cards waiting for them at the polling sites.

- Parent voters from 190 schools, who had legally registered in and before 1989, lost their right to vote in 1993 when principals at those schools failed to return their certification lists. The Board of Education did not ensure that the lists were completed and returned.

ELECTION DAY

School-board elections should be conducted with a seriousness and integrity that reflect their importance to the community. The chaotic conditions that reigned in New York City this year instead reflect the Board of Elections' disinterested attitude toward an election it plainly sees as unimportant.

- Parents and other registered voters lost their votes in a host of ways. Parent voters were turned away because the Board of Elections had sent their cards to the wrong sites, or because the inspectors did not know to look for them in a oll separate roll book 2 made up for parent voters. When two school districts shared one voting site these sites were known as "split district" sites-voters from one district were often given the ballots for the other. On some occasions, the ballots for only one district were available. Sample ballots virtually identical to the real thing were not marked as samples, with the result that many wound up filled out and dropped into the ballot boxes. Once again, disenfranchisement could be avoided only by sacrificing integrity concerns, and the Board of Elections was forced to count the sample ballots as valid.
- Voters were afforded little dignity or privacy. At best the voting "booth" was a small cardboard divider. At worst, it was a bench shared with other voters. Often, voters had to fight off candidates or their supporters telling them how to vote. The most basic security precautions, such as sealed ballot boxes, were ignored.
- One of our investigators actually lifted the top off the box to insert his ballot inside. The attending inspector just laughed.
- Widespread electioneering was tolerated. One candidate approached voters at the Ramirez Senior Citizens Home in District 7 as they were voting and repeated her slogan, "Carmen Arroyo #1." As our investigator was marking his ballot in another district, a woman approached him with a list of candidates and said, "these ten here…it's a good decision." Similar scenes were witnessed throughout the city.
- Essential materials such as roll books, ballots, and ballot boxes were often hours late in arriving at their sites. At one site, voting commenced only after a voter found the ballots in a corner of the gymnasium.

THE VOTE COUNT

Despite widespread irregularities cited by investigators and journalists in the 1989 vote count, the Board of Elections seemed disinterested in improving the integrity of the 1993 count. Two means of getting a more-honest count were obvious: attract new contractors to perform the count, and automate the count to reduce opportunities for fraud. The Board of Elections did neither. With almost no effort to find new contractors, the Board awarded the job to the only bidder, Proportional Count Associates (PCA), who had won the contract for three of the last four elections. Predictably, PCA delivered a far-from satisfactory performance.

- Though automation was recognized as an important tool to improve integrity, the Board of Elections did not explain what automation meant either in its contract or in the pre-bid conference.
- The Board of Elections did not consult with its own computer unit on the software PCA wanted to use. The software was only tested once, with no Board of Elections personnel present.
- In District 11, PCA hired candidate Rodney Saunders' son Keith to count ballots. In District 13, PCA hired Candidate Marilyn Mosely's campaign workers to count ballots.
- In District 13, PCA lost a ballot box containing at least thirteen ballots. The ballots were never recovered.
- Tally sheets and vote stubs, mechanisms designed to guard against ballot stuffing, were routinely ignored.

THE COST:

What the School-board election lacks in integrity and decorum, it makes up for in cost. The price, both in dollars and in police manpower, is staggering. The police cost is particularly troubling, since it is directly attributable to the paper ballots and complex ballot counting system used only in the School- board election.

- The Board of Elections spends approximately $4 million on the Community School-board election, about the same as it does on a general election.
- For each of the eight days between Election Day and the start of the count, a total of thirty police officers and three sergeants spent full eight-hour shifts guarding the cardboard ballot boxes in warehouses.
- For each day of the counting, a total of ninetysix police officers and nine sergeants spent full shifts guarding the count sites.
- Thus, at a time when New Yorkers are increasingly concerned about their safety, the School-board election required that the police spend almost 10,000 crime- fighting hours watching boxes. In addition to the gross mismanagement described above, our investigation also uncovered cases of deliberate fraud and misconduct.

VOTER FRAUD

Impossibly the most egregious fraud perpetrated in an election already riddled with improprieties, unsuspecting Fordham University students were duped into participating in the 4 Community School-board election in the Bronx. Two Fordham seniors who worked part-time in the District 10 office cast more than one hundred votes in the names of their fellow students to help a District 10 candidate get elected.

- Nicole Avallone and Jean Marie Gildea, two Resident Advisors at Fordham, filled out absentee ballot applications for their fellow students, obtained the ballots, and cast them- all without the consent and knowledge of their unsuspecting classmates.
- Students from as far away as Hawaii and California were surprised to find themselves registered to vote in the Bronx.
- James Sullivan, director of Pupil Personnel in District 10, orchestrated Avallone and Gildea's efforts.

UNDUE POLITICAL INFLUENCE

Our investigation revealed that the pressure suffered by educators to get involved in political campaigns is not limited to any one district. To the contrary, we found that teachers and school staff in District 21 in Brooklyn were pressured to participate in political campaigns. In District 9 in the Bronx, school employees were tapped to throw a fundraiser. School employees feel that they have no choice but to pay their political dues.

- Stuart Possner, principal of PS 100 in District 21, used certain staff members to pressure his teachers to join a local Democratic Club. He stacked the Club's membership so that it would vote to endorse one of his supporters on the School Board, Sheldon Plotnick. Many of the teachers do not live in the neighborhood of the Club, let alone in Brooklyn. Possner had his henchmen collect Club dues from teachers while they were in the classroom. Other allies made sure that the staff would be at the important Club meetings to vote for Plotnick.
- Teachers who did not attend Club meetings were punished in school the next day.
- PS 100 teachers reported being the victims of Possner's graphic and aggressive sexual harassment. One teacher likened the staff to "battered women" who see no way out of their destructive environment.
- In District 9, School Board Member Carmelo Saez coordinated efforts for a fundraiser which was attended by almost every principal in the District and many other District employees. Virtually every task needed to pull off the fundraiser was accomplished using District personnel and resources. Although many thousands of dollars were raised, the distribution of the proceeds remains a mystery.

PETITION REVIEW

The petition-review process is replete with arcane rules and secrecy that give political insiders an advantage over parents and community members without political clout. The secretive process makes it easy for politicians and commissioners to cut deals behind the scenes to favor certain candidates.

- The manner in which the Commissioners of the Board of Elections held the hearings to review the challenges to candidates' petitions raised serious questions about the integrity of the process.
- In closed-door meetings, Board of Elections commissioners voted to place District 12 candidates Randy Glenn and Ed Cain and District 8 candidates Ciro Guerra and Steven Eskow on the ballot, despite the fact that all four candidates fell short of the requisite two hundred nominating signatures. No record of the vote or proceedings was made. Bronx Republican District Leader Fred Brown was captured on tape saying that "it cost a helluva chip" to get State Senator Guy Velella to contact his father, Elections Commissioner Vincent Velella, to restore Glenn and Cain to the ballot. The integrity of the petition review process was further compromised by the fact that Elections Commissioner Paul Mejias had business interests in both districts.
- At the same time, District 10 Candidate Herbert Suss was excluded from the ballot for a technical violation. A political outsider, Suss was not given the same consideration afforded to the well connected candidates in Districts 12 and 8.

PETITIONS

Community School Board candidates violated petition rules in a variety of ways for a variety of reasons. Our investigation revealed that for whatever reason, candidates largely disregarded the rules, opening the door to forgeries.

- Sister Elizabeth Kelliher, a long-time Board member in Community School District 1, broke the law to secure the requisite number of nominating signatures. Kelliher used one set of volunteers to collect nominating signatures on her petitions, then asked others who were not present when the signatures were obtained to swear falsely that they had witnessed them.
- Forged signatures appear on several pages of Kelliher's petitions.
- Kenneth Drummond and Veronica James, candidates in District 12, used school 6 employees to collect signatures and then had others sign as the witness. Drummond and James were indicted by a New York County Grand Jury as a FR result of their petition scheme and their cases are pending.
- In District 10, candidate Marvin Kamiel obtained and circulated petition pages before the official start of the petition period. Kamiel's wife, Harriet, signed as the subscribing witness for signatures which she did not collect.

Many signature collectors left the date blank so they could "backdate" petition pages. Others left the candidate's name blank so that the pages could be distributed to fellow candidates in need of nominating signatures.

RESIDENCY FRAUD

Candidates all too often ignored or circumvented the requirement that they live in the district they seek to serve as school board members. People with minimal, if any, ties to the local school district create sham addresses or otherwise misrepresent their true homes to get elected to the school boards. As a result, genuinely concerned parents and community members are denied that opportunity.

- Kenneth Drummond, who was already removed from School Board 12 once before for not living in District 12, still lives in a luxury high-rise in Riverdale. In a secretly recorded conversation, he admitted that he installed a telephone in a South Bronx apartment to convince investigators he lives there.
- School Board 9 member Benjamin Ramos claimed to live in an apartment within the confines of that District for the purpose of running for the school board. We found substantial evidence indicating that Ramos lives in South Plainfield, New Jersey.

CAMPAIGN ADVERTISING

Even campaign advertising was infiltrated by fraud. In one district, when genuine endorsements were not forthcoming, a candidate's supporter brazenly enacted a fraudulent advertising scheme.

- In Community School District 27, it seemed that Candidate Geraldine Chapey was the lucky recipient of endorsements by the Gateway Republican Club and a junior high school parents association. In fact, William Sampol, who was implicated in a 1989 report on corruption in District

27, circulated phony flyers. He signed them as "president emeritus," but he has never been the president of either organization, and both groups said they deliberately decided not to endorse any school-board candidates this year.

FINANCIAL DISCLOSURE

Surprisingly few candidates disclose their finances as required by law. Leaving the public without this information makes it easier for candidates to pressure school employees to contribute to their campaigns.

- The financial disclosure rules were routinely violated, but no one enforced a penalty. More than twenty-five percent of the candidates ignored the financial disclosure requirements altogether.
- The CSA PAC 10, a political action committee supporting candidates in District 10, raised over ten thousand dollars, but inaccurately and falsely reported how they spent the money.

RECOMMENDATIONS

The events chronicled in this report make it clear that the present system of electing representatives to the local school boards must be changed dramatically. In addition to systemic recommendations, we have made disciplinary recommendations to the Chancellor, and we have referred evidence of criminal activity and conflict of interest to the appropriate adjudicating agencies.

- Proportional voting should be eliminated.
- Votes should be cast on the voting machines used in the general elections.
- The impact and advantages of moving the election to coincide with the general election should be evaluated.
- The Board of Education should immediately begin planning a complete overhaul of the parent voter registration process. The current contradictory mandates of the Education and Election Laws with respect to parent voter certification should be reconciled.
- All decisions made by the Board of Elections regarding candidates for Community School Boards must be made in public and on the record.
- The financial disclosure requirements for Community School Board candidates should be tightened, clarified, and enforced. Candidates who fail to Tech comply should not be sworn in as board members.
- The Board of Education should require more detailed disclosure of residency status 8 from Community School Board candidates.
- The Board of Education should extend "whistleblower" protection to the students of the New

FROM THE NEW YORK TIMES ARTICLE BY SAM DILLON

Report Assails Board of Elections on School Vote in May By SAM DILLON Published: December 16, 1993

Announcing the results of a 10-month inquiry yesterday, the New York City school system's top investigator accused the Board of Elections of "gross mismanagement" of the city's community school board elections in May and called for a sweeping overhaul of the process.

Edward F. Stancik, special commissioner of investigation for the New York City school district, detailed several instances of petition fraud, political coercion exercised by school officials, and other campaign and Election Day wrongdoing, as well as one case of outright ballot-stuffing in the Bronx.

"We found widespread fraud and corruption as well as administrative mismanagement in many areas of the election process," Mr. Stancik said. "The problem is that the Board of Elections just does not treat these elections seriously."

In no case, however, did the investigation find that fraud or corruption had affected the outcome of an election, he said. Report Is Disputed

Daniel DeFrancesco, executive director of the Board of Elections, disputed the report's findings. "The idea that we don't take these elections seriously is really unfounded," Mr. DeFrancesco said. "We pride ourselves on the conduct of any election we run. I think this report is based on hearsay and a lot of he-said and she-said kind of stuff."

Mr. Stancik turned over evidence of what he said were at least eight election-related crimes to Federal and state prosecutors, and he recommended that a Brooklyn principal, a Bronx school board member and a Bronx district administrator be removed from their posts. Schools Chancellor Ramon C. Cortines responded by immediately ordering local school boards to discipline the three educators.

"The behavior detailed in the report is extremely disturbing and cannot be tolerated," Mr. Cortines said in a statement. "I have directed the boards to take immediate disciplinary action and indicated to them that, if necessary, I am prepared to exercise my authority under the law."

The three educators were Stuart Possner, principal of Public School 100 in District 21 in Brooklyn, accused of coercing most of the school's teachers into participating in the campaign and of sexually harassing some of them; James Sullivan, director of pupil personnel for District 10 in the Bronx, accused of orchestrating a ballot-stuffing scheme, and Benjamin Ramos, a school board member in District 9 in the Bronx, accused of falsely claiming Bronx residency.

Mayor David N. Dinkins issued a statement yesterday calling Mr. Stancik's report "deeply disturbing." Job Prospects as Motive

At stake in the May 4 elections were the 288 seats on the city's 32 nine- member community school boards, whose members set policy for the city's 850 elementary and junior high schools. The major findings of fraud occurred in six districts, Bronx Districts 8, 9, 10 and 12, Brooklyn District 21 and Manhattan District 1. Mr. Stancik said the common motivation for the fraud appeared to be the prospects of local jobs in the districts, whose budgets range from $80 million to $125 million each, rather than differing philosophies about education.

Mr. Stancik's report also accused the Board of Elections of "gross mismanagement" for failing to plan properly for the elections, train election inspectors, mark sample ballots adequately and suppress polling site politicking on Election Day.

In perhaps the most egregious incident involving the Board of Elections leadership, Mr. Stancik's report quotes from a conversation taped by an undercover investigator that suggests that Vincent J.

Velella, one of the board's 10 commissioners, intervened to restore four Bronx school board candidates to the ballot after they had been disqualified because they lacked the necessary 200 signatures on their nominating petitions. The report suggests that Mr. Velella acted after receiving a call on behalf of the candidates from his son, state Senator Guy J. Velella.

The report acknowledges that Mr. Stancik's investigators were unable to prove any wrongdoing in the incident, but concludes "that the integrity of the entire process is suspect." Both Vincent J. Velella and his son, speaking yesterday in separate phone interviews, denied involvement in any wrongdoing.

"This guy Stancik is looking for publicity," Vincent J. Velella said. "He's a biased individual who's trying to crucify me because my son is a state senator." Most Egregious Fraud'

Mr. Stancik said he has turned over evidence regarding the incident to the New York County District Attorney, where he said a parallel investigation is under way, as well as to the Bronx County District Attorney.

Although the report concludes that the elections were marred by "widespread fraud," it points to just one case of attempted ballot-stuffing, which occurred in District 10 in the Bronx. The outcome was not affected, Mr. Stancik said.

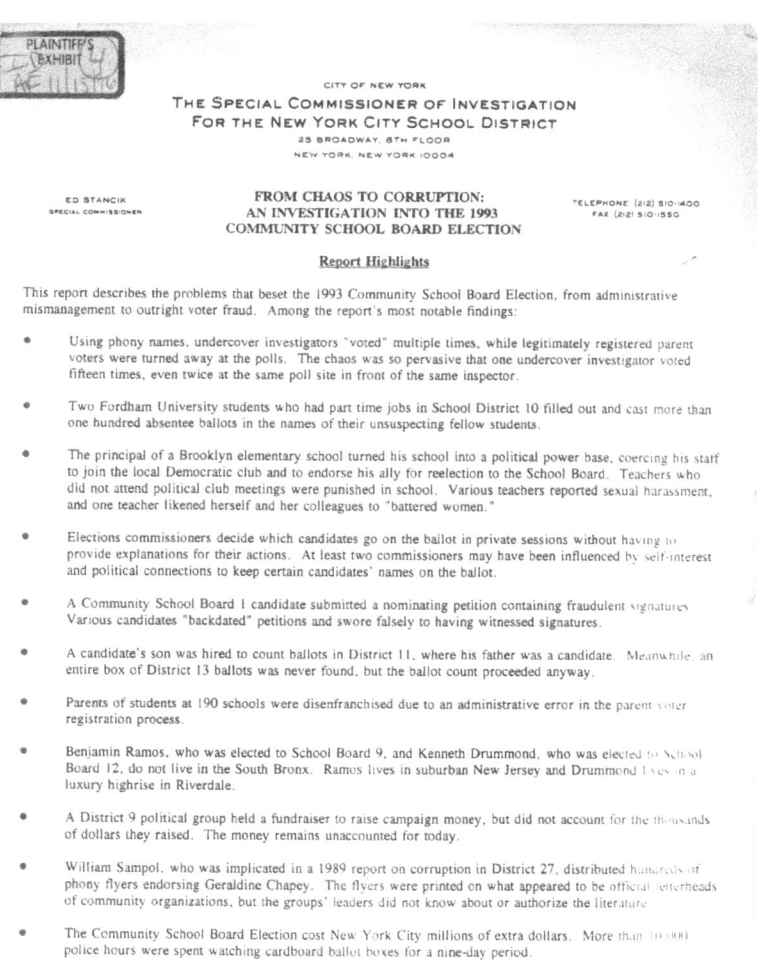

In what the report called the election's "most egregious fraud," two Fordham University students working as temporary employees of District 10 in the Bronx, which includes Bedford Park, Kingsbridge and Riverdale, filled out 117 absentee-ballot applications using the names of unsuspecting fellow university students and cast them on behalf of Edward McCarthy, a lawyer who subsequently won election. The two students worked under the direction of Mr. Sullivan, the report said.

In Brooklyn's district 21, which includes the Midwood, Coney Island, Brighton Beach sections, the report detailed how Mr. Possner pressured P.S. 100 teachers to join a Democratic club, to pay dues that amounted to campaign contributions, and punished teachers who did not cooperate.

Mr. Stancik recommended changes in the laws and procedures governing the elections to eliminate proportional representation, to allow for the use of voting machines instead of paper ballots, to open the Board of Elections' meetings to public scrutiny, and to tighten disclosure requirements for campaign financing and residency requirements.

The leaders of several parent organizations and education advocacy groups who monitored the voting yesterday hailed many of Mr. Stancik's findings and recommendations. At the same time, some expressed reservations about some of the report's sweeping claims, like the characterization of balloting this year as marred by "rampant chaos" when thousands of polling sites functioned smoothly on May 4.

"This report is an indictment of the Board of Elections and the sloppy administration of school voting that we've been criticizing for years," Judith Baum, who monitored the elections for the Public Education Association, a nonprofit organization.

CHAPTER SEVEN
Beginning Of The End

This was the beginning of the end for New York City corrupt school boards. With the end of the corrupt school boards, there would have to be accountability in the educated system. I accomplished what I set out to do when I made a promise to God and myself-I would give the children of New York City a better life.

To finish the job, I will focus on the New York City Board of Education until my job is done. Something happened. I couldn't explain when or where the case *Ladner v. the City of New York* changed. but the case became more focused on going after the New York City Board of Elections.

The investigations and testimony was mostly about going after the corrupt New York City Board of Elections. By going after the New York City Board of Elections, we were trying to change the whole United States election system. That's a lot to do, based on a citywide school-board election.

After the Stancik report came out, we called more and more officials of the New York City Board of Elections.

I worked on the Ronald Reagan presidential campaign in 1984 and was on Reagan's A Team. When they needed a task force to travel to solve a campaign problem, we did what we could legally to fix the problem. It was really interesting working in the Reagan campaign. I remember just filling out 1 or 2 signatures on petitions, so if the democrats challenged Reagan's petitions, we would lose only one or two signatures instead of forty on an entire sheet. Back in 1984, if the Democrats won a challenge on the petition sheet, the candidate lost all the signatures on the whole sheet. I worked the northeast conference on Forty-Second Street in New York City for Reagan's campaign. I was on the stage next to the speakers, running their tape recorder and taping the speeches for the White House. A pollster-I believed it was Lyn Nofziger-went back in history explaining presidential elections for the past 30 years. When he got to the Kennedy v. Nixon election, the whole audience erupted in laughter, especially when he mentioned Mayor Daley from Chicago. They all knew that Nixon lost the election because of the fraud perpetrated by Mayor Daley. Daley had so many dead people vote for Kennedy in the 1960 election they ran out of names to use from graves.

Working on President Ronald Reagan's campaign in 1984, I learned that running for office is a rough sport. Almost anything goes as far as running for elected office. Still, you still have to obey the law when you run for office, which President Reagan's campaign did they obeyed all the laws. Reagan won the election fair and square.

What I learned is you can win an election only to lose through voter fraud. In a national election, like the presidential election, if you want to cheat, you don't have to commit voter fraud in all fifty states. Your opponent just has to commit voter fraud in the states that have the most electoral votes, like Florida, New York, Ohio, and California. It's not who gets the most votes in a national election. It's who wins large states.

How do we accomplish this? By registering voters who are known not to exist, like dead people, or people who are ineligible to vote. Campaign workers or friends can impersonate nonvoting voters using aliases at the election polls or using absentee voting ballots. Voters can be prevented from voting by destroying voter registrations or simply stopping qualified voters from voting. One can also commit voter fraud the old-fashioned way by stuffing the ballot boxes. If enough ineligible voters in certain swing districts are illegally registered in the state, you can win that state.

Another way it's done is by changing the tabulation of the count on election day. The people at the poll site call in the tabulation of the count after the election. All they have to do is call in the wrong total votes by reporting the total vote to the board of elections. The workers at the board of elections have weeks to change the voting machine or ballot boxes to match the fraudulent vote numbers. Is this done? Damn right it is.

The federal courts must prosecute voter fraud cases to keep American democracy intact. The integrity of the election system is the bedrock of society, the very heart of our government. If people allow corrupted elections to exist in the country, it's just a matter of time before a corrupt government takes over. It's inevitable. Nothing changed in New York City elections. In 2013 the elections are still being rigged and dead people are still voting as the following article states:

The New York Post Article. By Carl Campanile December 30, 2013 13:29 PM. *The New York Post* The Dead Can Vote in NYC 12/30/13: New York: Police Prove How Easy Voter Impersonation is next door to the Brennan Center. Death doesn't necessarily disqualify you from voting in New York City. Investigators posing as dead voters were allowed to cast ballots for this year's primary and general elections, thanks to antiquated Board of Election registration records and lax oversight by poll workers, authorities said. The election board's susceptibility to voter fraud by people impersonating the departed was uncovered during a massive probe of the agency by the Department of Investigation. The probe uncovered 63 instances when voters' names should have been stricken from the rolls, but weren't even though some of them had died years before. "The majority of those 63 individuals remained on the rolls nearly two years-and some as long as four years since a death, felony conviction, or move outside of New York City," said DOI Commissioner Rose Gill Hearn. Undercover DOT agents were able to access voting booths in 61 instances- including 39 dead people, 14 jailbirds and eight nonresidents. Only twice were the agents blocked.

It was easy to scam the system because poll workers did not closely check birth dates or signatures of the ineligible voters. In all cases, probers voted for a fictitious "John Test" instead of a real candidate

During the Bush v. Gore election in Florida, voter fraud wasn't mentioned. Instead, people tried to change the election on technicalities. That was the easy way out. There must have been an agreement not to mention voter fraud. A blind person could find voter fraud in Dade County, Florida.

I didn't realize I was attempting to change the election system until I was already in the United States Court of Appeals. I was right about the election fraud in the 1993 school-board election, but I was in over my head in attempting to change the whole election system. Still, fraud is fraud, and, in a free society, we deserve free and fair elections.

I called Edward F. Stancik's office many times after I filed a lawsuit in New York State Court for fraud in the 1993 school-board election. His representatives said, "Thanks for calling us," talking about the information I got from Betty before the election. That, along with my lawsuit and various newspaper articles, started the investigation into the corruption and fraud in the 1993 school-board election and educational system.

I called Stancik's office, because I wondered if he'd be willing to testify at my trial. I told him I could guarantee the press would be there. His secretary said he'd testify at the trial if subpoenaed. "That's great," I said. "We can get the report, *From Chaos to Corruption: The 1993 School-board election* into the trial before the jury."

Since I was in court against the City of New York, however, Stancik's office refused to investigate my case in Staten Island. His investigator never officially interviewed me about the election fraud I uncovered. He only thanked me for the information on fraud and corruption in the board of education.

I was on my own. I didn't understand why Stancik's office refused to investigate my case, which was in federal court. It just didn't make sense. I respected him and his investigators for doing the best job I'd seen so far to fight for the education of New York City's children.

However, he did the biggest favor anyone could have done for my campaign when he released his report, *From Chaos to Corruption: The 1993 School-board election*.

I wondered what I needed to get a video of the perpetrators committing fraud into my trial. God must've heard me, because Stancik also released a video that was 67 minutes of proof of election fraud in different voting locations in the 1993 school-board election. Part of that video even aired on the TV news station in New York City.

I called Stancik's office to request a copy of their video. He said he'd send it to Jeff, my attorney, and he submitted the video as evidence.

I was getting so many calls with information about voting fraud in that election that my telephone answering machine was full for two weeks. That video apparently jarred plenty of people's memories. I used some of the information I received and passed the rest to Stancik's office.

One call came from Charlie Zappola, who worked in the State Island Board of Elections during the 1993 school-board election. He said he witnessed Kett going into sealed ballot boxes at the board-of-elections office. He had photographs of ballots on the floor and in garbage cans in the office. I called Charlie back to ask if he'd testify for us. He said yes.

I knew that meant that the case of Ladner v. City of New York was effectively won. Charlie Zappola kept his word and was deposited on June 11, 1996 by us and lawyers from the City of New York. He showed us pictures of thousands of 1993 school board ballots on the floor and in garbage cans before the count began. We filed Charlie's deposition as part of our evidence.

I felt certain the federal court would give me a trial. All the evidence in our report was correct. We had videos of election fraud, people stuffing ballots, Charlie's eyewitness report with accompanying photos, evidence of campaign workers counting ballots for the same candidates who they worked for, and unknown voters who actually lived in California and Hawaii.

Despite all that, it became apparent I had no chance of winning a seat on the school board during such a rigged election, even though criminals were convicted and put to death on less evidence than I had.

I hoped the judge would rule for summary judgment against the City of New York and recommend the U.S. Justice Department take over the city's board of education and order a new school-board election.

We returned to federal court a couple days after *From Chaos to Corruption: The 1993 School-board election* appeared on TV stations. The story was still buzzing in all the New York newspapers and TV shows. I met Jeff outside the courtroom and told him of my phone call with Stancik, who was willing to testify if we subpoenaed him. He said he would release the video to us to use. I was in a jovial mood, I said, "This case is over. It'll be a walk in the park."

"Not so fast. Let's see what happens when we're before the judge."

He was right. They called our case, and the judge acted like it was just another day. We tried to bring up Stancik's report, but the judge didn't want to hear about it. Instead, she granted the city more depositions.

Wow, I thought. *I'll be on this case until the day I die.*

Two years passed, with more evidence of a corrupt, rigged school-board elections piling up against the city. The legal papers soon filled fifteen large boxes. All I wanted was a trial, but all I got was a lesson in frustration.

Then the case became serious. I became angry while depositing Archibald F. Robertson of April 2, 1997, the chief operating office or Proportional Counts Association. Under oath, he testified, "The police officers called me about him as a reference. They told me of some trouble, deep trouble, with Mr. Hogenauer."

"What did the police officer tell you?" Ms. Le Goff, the New York City lawyer, asked.

"Do we have to go into that question?"

"Please. We need an answer for the record." "He [Hogenauer] molested some young people." "Was that in 1993 that you received the call?" "I think it was '94."

I became increasingly angry. It appeared that Hogenauer was molesting more young people one year after the school-board election! I didn't believe he molested any students in George Egbert Middle School while he was in the school for five days during the count, but we could have saved other children from being molested and the traumatic experience of losing their innocence and childhood. If only the city and the courts had done their job and acted upon my complaint.

Listening to Robertson's testimony about what Hogenauer was capable of turned my stomach. The City of New York was responsible for hiring him to work in a public school, which made me even more determined to make a better, safer life for the children in the city.

I did everything in my power as a father and citizen to prevent other children from being molested by Hogenauer to no avail. The City of New York hired a convicted kidnapper and child molester to be the count director in the George Egbert Middle School when it was open. He came into contact with over 2,000 children in the school for five days. The school sat at Midland Avenue, Staten Island. I told the reporter from the *Staten Island Advance* about Hogenauer's criminal record, so that parents could be warned and take action.

CHAPTER EIGHT
Let's Notify The Parents

I waited one week after calling the *Staten Island Advance* with important information on the issue, but nothing was published. Around eight o'clock one evening after work, I posted a handwritten flyer on a pole in front of the school with my phone number on it. I put down the information about Hogenauer and the dates and times he was in the school when children could have had contact with him.

The only call I received came from an official of the New York City Board of Education informing me that the poster was taken down that night before school opened. The person threatened to take me to court if I put up any more flyers. He never once asked if the story about Hogenauer was true. He seemed more concerned about the flyers.

"The students' safety is at risk with a convicted kidnapper and child molester roaming the school for five days!" I said. "No more flyers. Have you already informed the Board of Education about the information on the flyer?"

"The city knows about Hogenauer's criminal record."

"When we receive official information from the city, we'll take care of it and inform the parents."

"How long will that take?"

"I'm warning you, no more flyers. Got it?"

As far as I know, no parents for children attending George Egbert Middle School were ever notified.

That was why I felt the trial was so important. We had to shine a light on Hogenauer's criminal record. It seemed the city was more concerned about parents filing lawsuits against it for putting their children at risk. The Board of Education and the courts didn't care about the children's safety, and they did a good job of stopping my information from coming out. That was when I realized the effort to cover up the mess of the 1993 school-board election was a joint effort. The system was more concerned about losing money and the embarrassment of hiring a child molester and kidnapper than the safety of the children.

The only story that the *Staten Island Advance* was interested in was my stand on optional prayers in the school, one of my campaign issues.

I informed the *Staten Island Advance* as fast as I could when I found out Hogenauer's criminal record, so parents could have a talk with their children to find out if they came into contact with the man at school. If I were a parent of any child attending that school in May, 1993, I would have a careful conversation with my son (Hogenauer went after young boys) and daughters. If he tried to molest anyone, the parents could take action even many years later. My information was ignored. If the Staten Island public schools

could send letters requesting donations of toilet paper, surely they could send a letter telling parents that a kidnapper and child molester was at the school for five days while school was in session. I did all I could, but the information rested in the hands of the City of New York, and the Staten Island Advance.

Why was this information kept secret? Because it would change the educational system in the city. Parents would have been enraged to learn their children were in danger from a man like Hogenauer. Parents believe their children are safe in public school, and the education system wanted them to keep believing that. The truth was that all children are at risk, because there is no background check of school employees.

The more I learned about the Staten Island school system, the more shocked I felt. Members from a chapter of the North American Man/Boy Love Association were employed by the New York City Board of Education. NMBLA members were in the Staten Island schools in 1993 and had an open meeting! It was no secret to the Board of Education.

It might still be possible to file a lawsuit against the city for civil rights violations. Even if the federal courts and the U.S. Supreme Court ruled that it was just human error, the parents of the children who attended George Egbert Middle School in May, 1993, should ask a lawyer if they would have a civil rights case against the city.

When we were in court, the judge didn't mention anything about the possibility of children being molested by Hogenauer. We brought Robertson's testimony up and asked for a trial. We got the same response-more depositions. In 1998, five years after the rigged school-board election, the City of New

York made another motion that there wasn't enough evidence to proceed with a trial. We had witnesses under oath who admitted to fraud and stuffing ballot boxes against me. We had videos of election fraud. What more could they want? When I heard that motion, I had to hold onto the table in case the judge once again pulled the rug out from under me. She seemed relieved when the city made its motion.

I forgot exactly what she said, but instead of dismissing the motion out of hand, she said she'd take it under advisement.

One month later, she came up with a twenty-one-page decision-every criminal, corrupt, and fraudulent act against me was deemed human error. The case of Ladner v. City of New York was dismissed without a trial. How could I be awarded $76 million in a case that was dismissed?

Something very wrong here.

The part of Judge Gershone's decision that made my skin crawl was: Election irregularities that are fair and adequate human error in the conduct of an election do not rise to the level of a Fourteenth Amendment constitutional violation actionable under? 1983 in the absence of willful actions by state officials intended to deprive individuals of their constitutional right to vote. Short of that, human error is something we all have to live with.

Someone had to be on drugs to believe the 1993 school-board election was fair and adequate. How could she class committed crimes as irregularities? New York City was responsible for a rigged citywide election, and they are the responsibility of government officials. The city paid $4 million of taxpayer money to have that election by a shell corporation PCA without any assets or insurance bond, which were

required by the contract the officials signed with the city. The New York City Board of Elections was in charge of the citywide school-board election, yet they hired a count director with a criminal record that included fraud and kidnapping.

The twelve workers who did the actual count in the gym of the public schools turned out to be connected to various campaigns or to candidates who ran against me. A blind person could see that the evidence and testimony rose to the level to require a search for the truth and a trial.

I believe in truth, justice, and the American way, but after that court decision, I had my doubts. Had I been mistaken all those years?

It took me a couple of weeks after the decision to reset. I was back on track as pro-American. The United States of America is still the best country in the world. The district court had it wrong. However, there are checks and balances. The U.S. Court of Appeals would have the same laugh the traffic court did. Human error couldn't be allowed to stand as a defense against committing crimes.

CHAPTER NINE
All Aboard On The Way To The U.S. Court Of Appeals

After the decision was handed down, I went to Jeff's office at Moskowitz, Passman, and Edelman. I met Shelly, his partner, who wasn't happy with Jeff or me. He showed me boxes and boxes of legal documents and videos crowding their small office. I didn't have the heart to bring up my ideal of an appeal, but I had to.

I loved both of them, but they were right. The case had gotten too big. I was right about the corruption in the education and election system, because no one wanted the system to change.

"Mel, we're out of the case," Shelly said. "If you want to appeal, I'll give you the names of law firms that handle appeals. Frankly, I don't know any firm that handles election fraud."

I understood and couldn't argue with him. They did their best. The truth was, they were in over their heads.

"Mel, we have to get these fifteen boxes out of the office. I need the space." "Give me a couple days to see if I can find a lawyer who'll take on the appeal." "All right."

I walked into Jeff's office and told him about my conversation with Shelly. "I've taken our law firm to its limits," Jeff said. "It was quite an experience. Someday, you should write a book or think about making a movie about this."

"The book isn't finished yet. There's still the ending to be written." We laughed.

As we explored my options, I realized there weren't very many. "What's my next step?" I asked. "Nothing. End the case here and now."

"What are my only other options?" "You can appeal, taking it to the second circuit of the court of appeals, but you'll be hard-pressed to find a law firm who'll take the case. That's your only alternative."

If you can't find a law firm who'll will take your appeal, then you have two choices to quick the case and go on with your life and you will have a fantastic story to tell at party's about how you made into federal court on voter fraud or you can go Pro Se and appeal the case yourself. "But just remember anyone who has himself for a lawyer has a fool for a client."

I thought it over. "If that's my only choice, I'll go pro se."

"The only advice I can give you is when you stand in front of the three judges from the second circuit in the court of appeals, address them with, 'May it please the court.' That's traditional."

We shook hands. That was the last time I saw Jeff.

After I left his office, I was more determined than ever to bring the case before the court of appeals, and, if necessary to the U.S. Supreme Court .I kept on hearing the song by Tom Petty. The song was, I won't back down. I heard almost everywhere I went. The lyrics to the song reminded me that I made a promise to God and myself I'd do whatever it took to allow a safe education for our children.

Our forefathers did that, and it made our country great. I felt we were becoming like the latter days of the Roman Empire, when the average citizen was so lazy he rolled over when faced with the wrongs in society. What would our forefathers have done if they tried to raise the bridge tolls on the Staten Island Verrazano bridge to $17, which was what New York City did.

People frequently believe the proverb, "You can't fight city hall." You can. It's just very difficult. Civil rights are worth fighting for. If people won't fight for their rights, then they surrender the right to complain when those rights are lost.

When citizens stop fighting for their rights within the American system of justice, they would have no rights. That would mean the country was in decline. It would end up like the Roman Empire. The founding fathers signed the Declaration of Independence and knew it was signing their death warrant. Today's society lacks that kind of patriot.

I needed to make a lot of phone calls. I used a list of law firms Shelly gave me, which was only four. All turned me down. I kept calling other firms for three days to no avail.

I promised God and myself to go as far as I could to ensure our country's future. Soldiers give their lives for free and fair elections. I would go *pro* se and appeal the decision of human error. I looked forward to it. The appeal was a challenge, but the education and safety of our children were worth the effort. I would bring all the evidence of fraud and corruption against me in the election to the U.S. Court of Appeals. The depositions on their own would be enough for a trial and a search for the truth. The case wasn't about me. It was a way to improve the education of our children, a worthy cause.

I would put my faith in the hands of the Court of Appeals for the Second Circuit of the United States of America. I would stand with my head held high and without fear. If necessary, I would go to the United States Supreme Court.

I read the book I received at the U.S. Court of Appeals on how to file an appeal. Since the Court of Appeals made changes in December 1, 1998, to the rules, it felt like the Marx Brothers movie, *A Day at the Races*. I needed to get the changes to figure out what the first book on filing and appeal meant.

After reading through the legalese, I learned that the Court of Appeals limited the appeal to thirty pages or 14,000 words. It would cost $105.00. When I gave notice to the U.S. Court of Appeals and filed a fifty-five page brief on the facts and case law supporting why the court should grant me a trial, the clerk behind the counter looked at me.

"That's one long brief," he said. "The rules are thirty pages. Your brief is fifty-five. I have to ask my supervisor if I can docket the brief and accept your appeal."

I spoke to the supervisor and pleaded my case. We had a great argument. As I had been told, they didn't expect much of a case from a pro se lawyer. The clerk docketed my case, and I was assigned docket number 98-9285. The case was named Ladner v. New York City.

```
                    UNITED STATES COURT OF APPEALS
                         FOR THE SECOND CIRCUIT
                       UNITED STATES COURT HOUSE
                             40 FOLEY SQUARE
                            NEW YORK 10007

CAROLYN CLARK CAMPBELL
       CLERK

            Melvin Ladner
            60 Kenmore St.
            Staten Island, NY  10312


                                      NOTICE

                              Date: October 7, 1998
                              Docket No.: 98-9285
                              Re: Ladner v. New York City

            Dear Counsel:

                 Please be advised that the district court record on appeal in the
            above referenced case has been filed this date in the United States Court
            of Appeals for the Second Circuit.

                                       CAROLYN CLARK CAMPBELL, Clerk

                                       By:
                                           Natasha Godby
                                           Case Manager, USCA

            roantccnsl_frm
```

I was ready to begin the motions for the Court of Appeals to grant me a trial in a search for the truth.

After I struck out with the law firms to appeal my case, I knew I was on my own. I hoped that what Jeff told me, that I would have a fool for a client, wouldn't come true. I called the Federal Court and learned they had a *pro se* office. The best news for me was that the staff in the office was very helpful. They pointed me in the right direction, telling me what legal forms I needed to fill out and how to research for case law to bring my case before the court. I was advised that my chances of arguing in front of the three judges on the Court of Appeals was none. The court would most likely rely on the case law I submitted instead.

I was working a full-time job, caring for my sick wife who was battling cancer, and running a *pro se* law firm. Time passed quickly, until weeks seemed like days during the time between the ruling from the district court and the time it went before the Court of Appeals.

I started by researching case law. I found many case laws that proved that the traffic court judge was right. There was no such defense as human error. There was a degree of crime called criminal gross negligence, but it was still a crime. That meant a crime was a crime, and there was no way around it.

When they opened those sealed ballot boxes, they committed a crime. When they altered paper ballots that weren't counted, they committed a crime. The judge should have ruled it as criminal negligence to tamper with a voting machine and for Barbara Kett and her deputies to open the sealed ballot boxes without a court order. That was a serious crime.

Why were Barbara Kett and her employees being treated differently than other citizens? All I wanted was a trial to determine why they opened the sealed ballot boxes before the official count. The U.S. Court of Appeals should be able to decide on that in minutes, hopefully in my favor.

There was something that didn't make any sense. Though they testified that all three-Kett, Cominsky, and Jackson-opened sealed ballot boxes, only Kett's initials appeared on the paper ballots. If all three opened the boxes simultaneously, wouldn't it make sense that all three would place their initials on the paper ballots? Perhaps the other two weren't there when Kett opened the boxes. A trial would help me get to the facts to determine if Kett was working alone. I made motions that the city was forced to respond to. Their response was always the same. The city wanted a date as soon as possible in front of the Court of Appeals. My response was that I wanted a speedy trial. I was having too much fun with the City of New York, going back and forth with questions and motions asking for a speedy trial. They didn't expect me to be able to do much while operating pro se.

This is from the book furnished by the Court of Appeals with answers to most frequently asked questions:

Questions *Pro Se* Litigants Frequently Ask Below are some questions frequently asked by *pro se* appellants. The proposed responses do not have to be memorized but are provided as an example of the type of answer the litigant should receive. You may also want to refer the litigant to the appropriate rule, when applicable. A general principle is to not give too much information as that has a tendency to confuse the litigant.

I. GETTING THE APPEAL TO THIS COURT

Q: Where do I file the notice of appeal and how long do I have to do so?

A: In civil cases, a notice of appeal is to be filed with the district court and an appellant has 30 days from the entry of the order being appealed; but if the United States is a party to the suit then an appellant has 60 days in which to file a notice of appeal. See Fed. R. App. P. 3 and 4. (Note: You should not count out the period or tell the *pro se* litigant the date by when he must file an appeal.)

Q: How much does it cost and where do I pay?

A: It costs a total of $105 and the fee is paid in the district court clerk's office. Q: Do I have to fill out Forms C (Pre-Argument Statement) and D (Transcript Information) of C.A.M.P. or have the record below sent to this Court?

A: No, *pro se* appellants do not have to fill out forms C and D. However, you may want to make the litigant aware of Fed. R. App. 10(b), which requires that if a party wishes to urge on appeal that a finding

or conclusion is unsupported by or contrary to the evidence, then the party has to make sure that the record on appeal includes a transcript of all the evidence relevant to such a finding or conclusion. The record on appeal is compiled by the district court clerk's office for all cases in which a party in proceeding pro se. Therefore, the *pro se* litigant does not have to worry about compiling the record on appeal. The record can be corrected or supplemented by stipulation or motion made to the district Court or this Court. FRAP 10(e).

II. PRIOR TO ORAL ARGUMENT

A. BRIEFS AND MOTIONS

Q: What are the differences between briefs and motions?

A: A motion is an application for an order or other relief (e.g., assignment of counsel, in *forma pauperis*) relating to an appeal pending before this Court. See Fed. R. App. P. 27. A brief is a written argument as to why the appellant believes the court below made an error in judgment. See also Fed. R. App. 28.

Q: How many copies of the brief/motion do I have to file?

A: Motions: 4 copies plus the original. Briefs: 9 copies plus the original, for a total of 10. Pro se litigants are to be strongly encouraged to use a T-1080 form for their motions. T-1080 forms are available in the clerk's office. A *pro se* litigant may move to file fewer copies.

Q: How long can the brief be and does it have to be typewritten? Does the Court have samples?

A: Appellant's and appellee's briefs may be up to 50 pages long. (An appellant or appellee may choose to file a memo-brief, which is 10 pages or shorter.) Reply briefs may be up to 25 pages long. The Court prefers that briefs be typewritten. However, it will accept handwritten briefs, provided that the writing is legible. Under FRAP 30, appellant's brief should have a blue cover and the appendix should have a white cover. Reply brief is grey. Ramberto *(pro se* Unit Clerk's Office) keeps a set of sample briefs and appendices.

Q: How do I learn the schedule for my appeal?

A: The Clerk's Office will send you a scheduling order which will state when your brief and appendix are due, when your opponent's brief is due and the earliest week argument will be heard.

Under FRAP 31, a reply brief must be filed within 14 days of service of appellee's brief but at least 3 days before argument, except for good cause shown.

Q: How can I get more time in which to write the brief?

- A Motion for extension of time should be made at least 14 days before the brief is due. If the 14-day period has passed, then the litigant must file a motion for "leave to file a motion for extension of time out of time."
- APPENDIX

Q: What is an appendix and who has to file one?

A: The appendix is a set of the most important documents from the court below. The appendix should include, at the very least, a copy of the following items from the district court: the decision/order being appealed and the district court docket sheet. The appellant is required to file an appendix with the brief. See also Fed. R. App. 30. A litigant can move for leave to file a supplemental appendix.

C. WRIT OF MANDAMUS

Q: How do I file a petition for a writ of mandamus?

- The original and three copies of the petition for a writ of mandamus are to be filed in Room 1702 (at the front desk in the Clerk's Office). At the time of filing the petitioner must present either a check or money order for $100 or move for leave to proceed in *forma pauperis*. See Fed. R. App. P. 21.
- SERVICE

Q: Do I have to serve the other side?

A: Unless incarcerated, the pro se litigant has to serve the other side with a copy of motions, briefs and appendixes. The litigant must include an affidavit of service in the original copy of the brief or the motion that is filed with this Court.

E. ASSIGNMENT OF COUNSEL AND PROCEEDING IN *FORMA PAUPERIS*

Q: How can I get an attorney?

A: *Pro se* litigants may move for an assignment of counsel under 28 U.S.C. § 1915. However, you may want to advise the litigant that if her motion is denied, her appeal may be dismissed on the merits without the benefit of oral argument or the filing of briefs. A motion for the assignment of counsel suspends the scheduling order, if such an order has already been issued.

Q: If I do not have the money for the filing fee can I still appeal?

A: An appellant may move this Court for leave to proceed in *forma pauperis* by filing a notion and filling out a declaration that details the appellant's financial status. An appellant may fill out a Court-provided declaration or write one himself.

III. POST-APPELLATE RELIEF

Q: When does the mandate issue and what does that mean?

A: The mandate is issued to the lower court which closes the case here. In certain instances the mandate may be stayed, see Fed. R. App. P. 41.

Q: What do I do if I think this Court has made a mistake in the disposition of my appeal?

A: A. In this Court there are generally four types of relief.

1. Reinstatement the litigant may file such a notion when her appeal was dismissed for failure to file a brief or to pay the docketing fee.
2. Petition for Rehearing-to be filed within 14 days of the filing of the decision; litigant may file papers in support of the notion but they can be no longer than 15 pages. The movant must show some point of fact or law that the original panel overlooked. See Fed. R. App. P. 40.
3. Petition for Reconsideration—a litigant may file this motion if he is not satisfied with this Court's three-judge order. (Also the label used for petitions for rehearing filed after the 14-day period.)
4. Suggestion for rehearing en banc-same standard and rules for petition for rehearing. See also Fed. R. App. P. 35. The moving party has to file the original brief and 24 copies, for a total of 25.

B. Filing *a petition for a writ of certiorari* in the United States Supreme Court, You should point the pro se litigant to Supreme Court Rule 13, which, in addition to stating the time period for filing a petition for certiorari, also outlines the effect that filing a petition for rehearing in this Court has on the time period. (Note: You should not count out the period or tell the litigant the date by which she has to file her petition.)

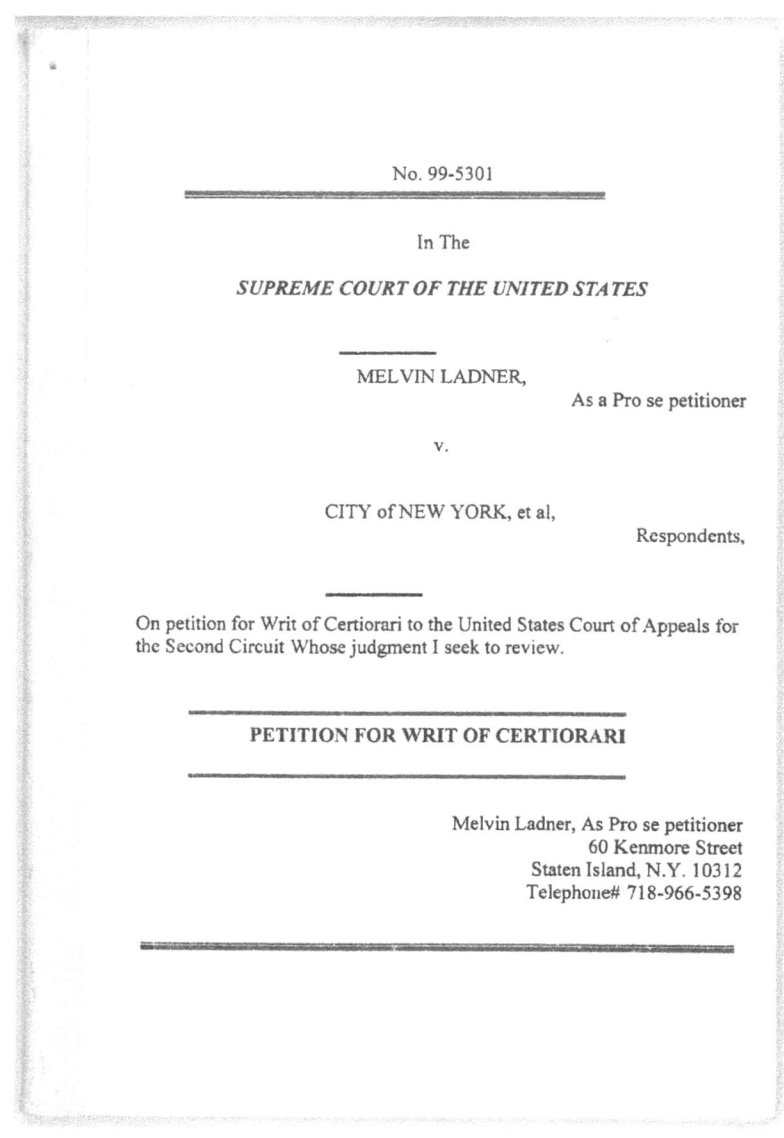

If a *pro se* litigant wishes to file a *petition for a writ of certiorari*, the Clerk of the United States Supreme Court will supply an informational packet. The address of the Clerk of the Supreme Court is: Clerk Supreme Court of the United States 1 First Street, N.E. Washington, D.C. 20543 (202) 479-3000.

Then came the day that Ladner v. City of New York was docketed on the calendar of the US Court of Appeals. To my surprise, the three-judge panel demanded and ordered me to appear in person and argue the case in front of the court.

DATE: April 7, 1999 NOTICE OF HEARING DATE SHORT TITLE: Ladner v. New York City DOCKET NUMBER: 98-9285 DATE OF HEARING: Tuesday, May 4, 1999 TIME

ALLOTTED FOR ORAL ARGUMENT: Ladner (5 mins); NYC (On Submission) The above referenced appeal is scheduled for oral argument on the day indicated in Courtroom 1705 (17th floor), United States Courthouse, 40 Centre Street (at Foley Square), Manhattan, New York City.

Court convenes promptly at 10:00 a.m. Counsel and *pro* se litigants must be present for argument unless earlier excused. Motions to adjourn argument must be promptly made and will be granted for grave reason only.

Counsel and *pro* se litigants presenting oral argument must register with the courtroom deputy no later than 9:45 am., either by appearance in the courtroom or by phone from the Video Argument Center, whichever applies.

Counsel and *pro* se litigants may seek the Court's permission to waive oral argument by submitting a letter request to the Office of Clerk (attention Calendar Deputy) not later than five days before the hearing week.

Counsel and *pro* se litigants **whose panel is sitting in courtroom 1705** may elect to present oral argument from any of the Second Circuit Video-Argument Centers by notifying the Calendar Deputy at 212-857-8595 any time before 9:30 a.m. on the day of argument. A notice regarding the Center is enclosed, and counsel are encouraged to call the Calendar Deputy for further details. Report all settlements to the Calendar Deputy as soon as effected. Ordinarily, and subject to the ruling of the presiding judge, motions or stipulations to withdraw with prejudice will be granted without appearance by counsel, but motions or stipulations to withdraw without prejudice filed within three business days of the argument will be considered at the time of argument, with counsel present and prepared to argue the merits.

CAROLYN CLARK CAMPBELL, Clerk COMPLETE ITEMS BELOW AND RETURN COPY OF ENTIRE FORM TO THE CLERK'S OFFICE NAME OF ATTORNEY/PRO SE PRESENTING ARGUMENT: FIRM NAME (IF APPLICABLE): CURRENT TELEPHONE NUMBER: THE ABOVE NAMED ATTORNEY REPRESENTS: ( ) APPELLANT- PETITIONER ( ) APPELLEE- RESPONDENT ( ) INTERVENOR ( ) AMICUS CURIAE DATE: SIGNATURE:

This is the United States Court of Appeals dated November 4, 1998.

It is very rare that a *pro* se person would argue in front of the U.S. Court of Appeals. The fifty-five-page motion I made for a trial laid out the whole case. It was all there, with evidence in case law from the federal courts. It wasn't a complicated issue to be given a trial to search for the truth. In my motion,

I argued for a trial to search for who, what, why, and how the election fraud occurred. There had to be another reason the appeals court wanted me to appear in person.

It told myself that whatever the court did, they weren't going to give me a trial. Why not? According to federal case law, the federal courts had the authority to hear criminal cases involving isolated incidents of elector fraud (see *Blitz v. United States*. 153 U.S. 308 [1894]).

As I wondered why the federal court wouldn't give me a trial, I concluded that they must have a gentleman's agreement not to prosecute voter fraud, even though free and fair elections were the foundation of our great country. Without free and fair elections, we wouldn't have a country.

I also knew that when someone stood before the three-judge panel, they would pepper the *pro* se lawyer with questions regarding the law and details about case law and the case itself. I had to be prepared.

The court of appeals sounded interesting. All I had to do was tell the truth. There was nothing to prepare for. If it was the real world, then I had the City of New York right where I wanted it.

I looked forward to testifying before the U.S. Court of Appeals. I wasn't nervous at all. I went to court with my wife and daughter, because I wanted my daughter to experience the U.S. justice system.

The Second Circuit Court of Appeals building was like something from a movie. "I think I hit the big time," I told my family.

I studied the granite columns and many long steps leading up. The steps were the width of the entire front of the building, which had to be a city block. It looked like something built in the 1930s, and I believe movies were made on those steps. It was very impressive.

We entered the anteroom, and the top lawyers were there. Six cases were to be heard that day, and the court allowed arguments for only five minutes.

A clerk of the court came up to me. "Are you Mel Ladner?" "Yes, I am." "I had a bet you wouldn't show up today."

We laughed. He and I hit it off. He told me I had five minutes to argue in front of the chief judge, the Honorable Ralph K. Winter, and two of the most senior judges, the Honorable Wilfred Feinberg and the Honorable Pierre N. Leval, on the court of appeals. I asked for more time to argue, because five minutes wasn't enough time to state all the facts.

"That's the rule of the court," the clerk said. "If they try to shut me up, I'll claim human error."

The clerk's mood turned serious. "Human error doesn't fly in the Court of Appeals."

"I agree."

My only preparation was to write down key words, which I planned to cross out one-by-one, as I argued my case. The most-important issue I wanted the U.S. Court of Appeals to do was issue an order that the parents of children attending George Egbert Middle School be notified that the count director was a child molester and kidnapper. After all, Hogenauer had roamed the halls of the school for five days and came into contact with students while school was in session. I hoped the court would also grant me a trial.

"Does Chief Judge Winter handle *pro se* cases?" I asked. "No, but we all know this is a special appeal. Since the chief judge assigned the cases on the court of appeals, he wanted to handle your case." I didn't know how to take that. Maybe he was kidding. I was a special case? Was that good or bad? I asked the clerk about it.

"It is what it is," he replied, leaving me to log in the other lawyers in the room.

I had the feeling I was about to be crucified like Jesus. I had the image of myself walking down the aisle carrying a large cross on my shoulder. When I stood before the chief judge and his two executioners, I could say, "Forgive them for they know not what they do."

I felt God was on my side. Though my mental image faded immediately, I had the feeling that the reason why the U.S. Court of Appeals wanted me to appear in person was to crucify me. Whatever I said or did before them, they wouldn't give me a trial. Well, two could play that game. *Mel, just tell the truth and be yourself, I thought. Let the chips fall where they may.*

I was at peace with myself, calm and filled with confidence. I was even in a good mood. Perhaps that's what happens when someone makes peace with God.

I could see how common sense could easily be lost in the U.S. Court of Appeals and why the court would be out of touch with average, middle-class citizens and their problems. The members of the court usually dealt with top law firms and the most- intelligent people in the country, which would shelter them from the real world, giving them the idea that such people were typical citizens. They would probably assume that children in New York City received a well- rounded education in the intercity schools. The members of the court would be insulated from the real problems of such children.

Fraud in an intercity school-board election wasn't that important in the world of ivory- league people. They should spend a day in such a school and find out it wasn't about education but surviving a day at school. The court lost its common sense when addressing education in the intercity school system. To the average citizens of such schools, it meant the difference between an excellent education for their children so they could escape poverty and lead fulfilling lives. Perhaps some would say I was blowing the situation out of proportion, but I wasn't. The candidates who won the election didn't represent the voters, so they didn't represent the education of the voters' children, either. I could see that clearly, as I mingled with those top lawyers waiting their turn before the court. The conversation I had with them made me feel badly out of place.

After I spoke with a few of them, they accepted me, because we were all in the same boat, waiting to appear before the court. I began to have fun with the situation.

"How do you feel about being the first *pro se* person to appear in person at this court in years?" one lawyer asked. "It's an honor to argue before the court for the education of my children. What can I expect when my case is called?" "You'll be asked many questions regarding the case law in your appeal." "My appeal is for the denial of a trial, which was based on human error."

More lawyers wandered over and joined the conversation. I felt I was the toast of the town. The more I explained the facts of the case, the more interested the lawyers became. They couldn't believe my case went that far without a trial.

When we were called into the courtroom, I filed in with the lawyers. I was impressed to see the room was decorated in early American furniture, with pictures of former judges of the court and Supreme Court judges past and present. The three judges already sat at the bench high above the audience. Court was already in session, as I was led into the room. I was ushered to a seat in the back, while the lawyers took the first two rows. I needed binoculars to see the judges from my position.

Standing before the judges, I wouldn't see any more than their heads. I'd have to look up to argue my case. A giant TV monitor sat on the judges' left side, facing the courtroom. Someone told me that the U.S. Court of Appeals was televised to all justice department officers and federal courthouses in the U.S. I looked around the room and thought, *the only one not being paid to stand in front of the judges is me, the pro se guy.*

I sat with my family, my only friends in that place. It was interesting listening to the arguments by the lawyers and the questions from the three judges.

The cases before the judges weren't very interesting. Most were boring contract law and corporate law. The lawyers for the case I witnessed, Chapin v. Giordano, were very nervous, which surprised me. The clerk called, *"Ladner v. the City of New York."*

I gave my wife and daughter a high-five, and they wished me luck. I stood and took my time approaching the bench. I wanted to savor the moment. Looking around, I saw everyone watching me, as I walked down the aisle. The judges gave me a stare that could kill.

"Will the court grant me more time to argue my case? Five minutes isn't enough to argue a case for the education and safety of our children. I would only be able to mention Count Director Bruce Hogenauer's criminal record and that he had the means and opportunity to commit fraud against me. Just his crimes alone would take more than five minutes of argument before the court."

"Mr. Ladner," Chief Judge Winter said, "that's all the court allows. You have five minutes to argue your case."

"I object!"

"On what grounds?"

"Since the court didn't allow me a trial to search for the truth about the election fraud against me in the 1993 school-board election, I would expect the common courtesy of hearing the evidence of the election fraud against me. If you look for a victim of election fraud and federal civil rights violations in the dictionary, you'll see my picture."

Dead silence filled the room.

"Motion denied," Chief Judge Winter said. "You have five minutes to argue your case, Mr. Ladner."

Since that was all I had, I would have to make the most of it. The case had been in New York state and federal courts for six years, with over 100 court appearances, depositions, and motions. It wasn't possible to condense all that into five minutes. I had to talk fast just like an auctioneer at an auction. "May it please the court," I began, remembering the only instruction Jeff Motelson gave me, "my name

is Melvin Ladner, and I am a pro se plaintiff in this action. I was a candidate in the fraudulent 1993 New York City school-board election. I ask the court to view the Stancik report and two videos that are in evidence. This will prove beyond a reasonable doubt that I am a victim of vote fraud and my civil rights were violated.

"Mr. Hogenauer is a very important witness in the action. He was the Staten Island count director for the 1993 school-board election. He had the means, opportunity, and motive to commit fraud in that election. He has information and is aware of the fraud against me. He was the perfect candidate to commit such fraud, but he has fled and refuses to testify. Hogenauer clearly has something to hide, which put my case to a disadvantage.

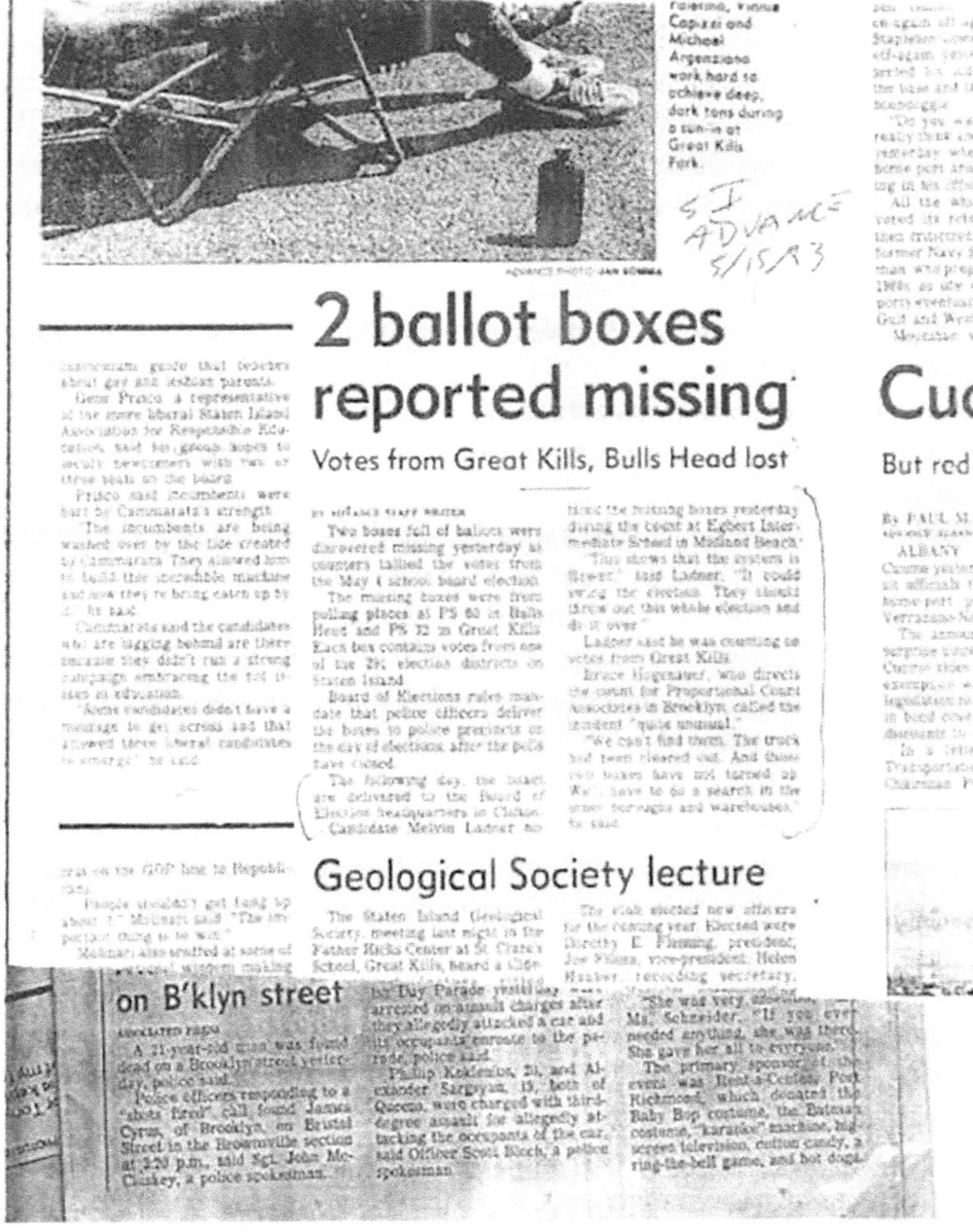

"When I called the New York City Police Department to the count site, Sergeant Garity arrived with two officers, and a NYCPD captain arrived later. When I made a police report for voter fraud and demanded the count be stopped, Hogenauer refused. I want a trial to put Hogenauer on the stand and ask who in the Staten Island Board of Elections gave him the order to continue the count and why?

"There are genuine issues of material facts in this case wherein a reasonable person would differ with the material facts. One example is when Kett, Cominsky, and Jackson of the Board of Election of Staten Island went into sealed ballot boxes and suspended the election while altering the ballots. No report was filed. The police were not notified.

Hogenauer didn't even know. Nobody at the count site knew that the initials BMK belonged to Kett. "In Robertson's deposition, he stated that if he knew there were initials on ballots, he would have stopped the count and disallowed the ballots. That's why I'm asking for a trial. The defendants in this case collectively altered ballots, scheduled, organized, administered, conducted, and operated the election and caused, manipulated, published, and tabulated a fraudulent vote count.

"I received information approximately three days before the count that I was intentionally excluded from the school-board election. The informant told me what ballot boxes to look for. When I went to the count site, I found out that the information about the intentional cheating was correct."

I paused and looked at the judges, expecting a question concerning who my informant was, but no one spoke.

I continued my argument. "Defendants admitted they tore open and entered sealed ballot boxes with voted ballots in them that weren't yet counted. They did this without a court order or by direction of a committee of the state senate or state assembly. This violates New York State election law sec. 3-222.2 as per Kett deposition on page 227, line eight. "Defendants admitted that they stuffed the ballot boxes with altered ballots not yet counted, violating New York State election law sec. 7-1096.5, see Kett deposition on page 229 line two.

"New York state election law sec. 8-310 statue provides as a safeguard that the number of ballots and stubs when issued to voters must be loudly announced, and the number of the ballots must be entered on the voter's registration card. The defendants completely ignored that procedure.

"New York State election law sec. 3-222.2 provides for the preservation of written ballots for six months. The defendants destroyed 24,000 ballet stubs and protest sheets, making it virtually impossible to defend this action and verify that the school-board election count was correct.

"When I was in law enforcement, and any person admitted to violating the law, we called that a confession, not human error. I'm asking the court to treat the defendants in the same manner as any other citizen in this great country of ours. When you intentionally violate the law, you should pay your debt to society. "Fifty thousand eligible parent voters, mostly poor, African-American, and other minorities, were intentionally denied the right to vote in the 1993 schoolboard election, thus violating the Fifteenth Amendment to the U.S. Constitution (see Stancik report of 190 schools that intentionally didn't forward parent voter lists). "While 50,000 hardworking parents voters who played by the rules were denied their right to vote in the 1993 school- board election, candidates received information from the New York

City Board of Elections and the New York Board of Education that they didn't verify the parent voter registration list and had their workers or friends vote as often as they wished, which they did. See the Stancik report and the video which is in evidence.

"Sample ballots were substituted for original ballots and counted.

Robertson's sworn testimony in evidence states that he had access to sample ballots for training purposes and still has sample ballots in his office. There were no controls on who had sample ballots before this election, which violates New York State election law sec. 7-106, 1, 2, and three. "Dead people were allowed to vote in the 1993 school-board election. Thomas Riley voted absentee after his death. In June, 1998, in open court, Kett stated that Thomas Riley was on the perpetual absentee list. My investigator, Bob Brull, interviewed Riley's wife, who stated he never voted absentee in his life or requested any absentee ballots.

"My lawyer asked the defendants to produce the notarized affidavit and letter filled out by Thomas Riley requesting an application for an absentee ballot. The defendants say they have it but never produced it.

"I ask the court for a summary judgment against the City of New York for failing to defend this action or for the court to grant me a trial." I intended to finish the argument with a strong statement. Federal courts have the authority to hear criminal cases involving isolated incidents of electoral fraud (*Blitz v. United States*, 153 U.S. 308 [1984]).

The case was decided, I believed, by the United States Supreme Court. My case had already been decided by a traffic court judge when he ruled against my motion of human error. He stated there was no such defense, which made the district court's ruling of human error and thus dismissing my case without a trial a travesty of justice.

Common sense should dictate that there's no such defense as human error, real or imaginary, and that anyone could see there was fraud committed during the 1993 school-board election, as well as at other New York elections. My federal civil rights were violated. It seemed a no-brainer that I deserved a trial to search for the truth, as well as a summary judgment against the City of New York, since Bruce Hogenauer fled and failed to defend his actions by refusing to testify.

Because the courts didn't act quickly concerning my complaint against Hogenauer, they missed their chance to prevent the 1994 rape and sodomizing of young boys. How could the court members sleep at night while condoning voter fraud and child molestation? In our evidence we had videos, pictures of ballots on the floor and in garbage cans before the count, and fifteen boxes of evidence supporting my claim of voter fraud against me.

Since I had five minutes, I figured I might as well get the best out of the situation before the Court of Appeals. None of the judges had any questions. They sat there, looking interested, but their expressions never changed. The only time one of them spoke was when Chief Judge Winter informed me my five minutes were up.

"I ask the court for more time," I said. "I deny the motion," he repeated. "Then I thank this court for hearing me. I remind the court that my case is for the education and safety of our children."

I turned with my head held high and walked back to my family. The courtroom erupted in applause and cheers. I told myself I was fighting for a good cause, something that was worth the effort. In the real world, I won the case for the education and safety for the children in New York City.

I began my appeal on December 7, 1998, and was assigned docket number 98-9285 on May 17, 1999. When the U.S. Court of Appeals came down with a court order and decision, it ruled that the U.S. district was right to claim it was all due to human error. I remembered what the clerk said, "Mr. Ladner, we all know this is a special case." I felt they deliberately ruined the chances for the children of New York City.

Without comment or ordering a trial, the U.S. Court of Appeals sealed the case of *Ladner v. the City of New York*.

All the evidence we collected meant nothing to the judges. The most important part of the sealing meant that Bruce Hogenauer's criminal record of child molestation and kidnapping would also be sealed. The parents of the children from George Egbert Middle School would never gain access to those records. Apparently, that was what the City of New York wanted, to keep the parents in the dark. City officials were willing to allow rape victims to live with being raped for the rest of their lives. In essence, the federal courts gave Hogenauer a free pass to rape more young boys. I believe even to this day, the parents of children who attended George Egbert Middle School on Staten Island don't know that Hogenauer was in their school for eight days. According to the court's order, the case I presented never happened.

The City, the Board of Elections, and Bruce Hogenauer won, as did the candidates who benefitted from the rigged election. The appeals court never ruled that human error was a legal defense, either. It seemed that it would be used only once, and no other court case would be allowed to cite it again. The biggest losers were the children of the New York education system, who would lose their innocence, safety, and security while attending public school in New York City. I was the top loser, because my hope and faith in the legal system died that day.

"Now Mel Ladner knows what the boy felt like when I molested him," Hogenauer shouted, when he attacked U.S. Marshal Bob Meltzer during Hogenauer's extradition back to the U.S.

The court did the same thing to the students of New York City and me with their decision of human error that Hogenauer did to the boys he molested.

```
                                                              13
    1                         Meltzer
    2      Q.    That was the duration of the time it
    3      would take to reach the coast of the United
    4      States?
    5      A.    Right.  It was approximately a six,
    6      seven-hour flight.
    7      Q.    Did Hogenauer strike you with one fist
    8      or with two?
    9      A.    He struck me about three or four
   10      times.  That's all I can tell you.  Whether
   11      it was both hands or one, I don't know.
   12      Q.    What part of your body did he strike?
   13      A.    He struck my head.
   14      Q.    Following that attack upon you, what
   15      did you do?
   16      A.    I restrained him, subdued him and he
   17      was handcuffed.
   18      Q.    Either immediately prior to, during,
   19      or immediately after the attack upon you, did
   20      Hogenauer say, shout, or otherwise
   21      communicate with you verbally?
   22      A.    Yes.  He said after the attack that he
   23      did it because he wanted me to know what the
   24      boy was going through, and I took that to
   25      mean the boy that he kidnapped.
```

Inmate Information and Status of Prisoner Bruce Hogenauer:

Inmate Information -Location/Status/Legal Dates/etc. Information/Error Message: Date of Information: DIN (Dept. Identif. Number) 87A4801 Inmate Name: Sex: Date of Birth: Race: Ethnic Origin: Custody Status: Housing/Releasing Facility: Date Received (Original): Date Received (Current): Admission Type: County of Commitment: Latest Release Date/Type: (Released Inmates Only) Crime 1, Description: IMPRISONMENT 1ST Crime 1, Crime Class: Crime 2, Description: Crime 2, Crime Class: Crime 3, Description: Crime 3, Crime Class: Crime 4, Description: Crime 4, Crime Class:

If all 4 crime fields contain data, there may be additional crimes not shown here. In this case, the crimes shown here are those with the longest sentences. Aggregate Minimum Sentence: 001 Years, 00Months, 00 Days Aggregate Maximum Sentence: 003 Years, 00Months, 00 Days Earliest Release Date: Under certain circumstances, an inmate may be released prior to serving his or her minimum term and before the earliest release date shown for the inmate.

U.S. Department of Justice Personal History of Defendant United States Marshals Service Name Hogenauer, Bruce William (Last) (First) (Middle) Business Name Bruce Anderson Criminal ID# 03263018 Race 7/24/44 W Sex M NYC Date & Place of Birth Citizenship U.S. How Acquired Birth

Height 5'9 Weight 155 Eyes Blue

Hair Brown Build Med. National Origin German Complexion Fair Scars None Deformities None Marks, Motes, Tattoos No Drug Addict (yes) (no) No Type Drug Peculiarities Address 37-52 64th St. Woodside Queens Basement Telephone Number None Date and Time of Arrest Place of Arrest Violation 18 USC 1201 Kidnapping Former Addresses 119 Frederica Clearwater, FL 03263-018

YAH

DOB 7/24/14 ADDRESS: 119 Fredica Ave, N Clearwater, FL BIRTHPLACE: NY, NY SEX; M COLOR HAIR Blu COLOR EYES Blu HEIGHT 5 09 OFFENSE Kidnapping S/NY INSTITUTION TO WHICH COMMITTED:

Arrested by FBI 10/24/83 Hillsborough Cnty Jail DATE COMMITTED 10/24/83 ACTION OR DISPOSITION $500,000 C/S COPY 1 TO ACCOMPANY PRISONER

Plaintiff's Exhibit 4

Date 8/6/97 Reporter MB

Prisoner's Name Hogenauer, Bruce William

Fingerprint No. 486105F Date Custody Assumed 11-04-83 Inst Abbr EDNY 2322 Prisoner Number 03263 018 Prisoner's Alias Bruce Anderson DOB 7-24-44 Age 39 Race W-1 Emergency Address 119 Fredireca, Clearwater 37-52 64th St. Woodside, NY Sex M Color Hair brn Color Eyes blu

Height 5'9 Weight 155

Offense Kidnapping 18 USC 1201 Institution to which committed MCC, NYD Date committed 11-04-83 Date released 1-23-84 Action or deposition Bail $500,000 remanded Released - Probation Prosecution deferred Plaintiff's Exhibit 3

Date 8/6/97 Reporter MB

UNITED STATES MARSHALS SERVICE FIREARM DISCHARGE/ ASSAULT REPORT INSTRUCTIONS:

1. Amember of the USMS shall prepare this report within 72 hours whenever he:

(a.) discharges a firearm other than at an authorized firearms range; or
(b.) Is the victim of a physical assault while performing a lawful duty.

1. Supervisory personnel shall review and sign she report prior to forwarding to the Chief of Internal Investigations.

2. Legibly complete all applicable items. USMS PERSONNEL INVOLVED: Name Robert A. Meltzer Title Supervisor DUSH Credentials No. 0659 Assigned District EDNY Date of incident January 9, 1987 Time 2:15 pm Location of Incident Aboard Pan Am Heathrow Airport London England Outdoors District Where Incident Occurred London England TYPE OF REPORT: Physical Assault Duty: On Duty Working with Partner Type of Assignment Transporting Prisoner Extradition Type of incident: Assault on Deputy by Prisoner REASON FOR DISCHARGING FIREARM WERE THE FOLLOWING NOTIFIED: FBI Yes Local Police No Lighting Conditions Good Artificial WEATHER CONDITIONS: Clear DID YOU HAVE PRIOR KNOWLEDGE THAT

THE SITUATION INVOLVED A PERSON WITH A DANGEROUS FIREARM? No TYPE OF PREMISES: Pan Am 747 DID YOU INITIALLY DRAW YOUR FIRE ARM: OFFICER'S WEAPON(S) (firearm) carried OPPONENTS WEAPON(s) Fist No of OPPONENTS Male 1 NO. ARRESTED Male 1 NO. OF SHOTS OPPONENT FIRED AT YOU: 0 NO. OF SHOTS YOU FIRED n/a DID YOU HAVE TIME TO AIM? n/a DID YOU HAVE TO

RELOAD? n/a INJURIES Opponent not wounded, Officer not wounded DISTANCE BETWEEN YOU AND OPPONENT WHEN FIRST SHOT WAS FIRED: n/a DESCRIBE PROTECTIVE COVER WHICH YOU USED n/a WERE IMPACT POINT(S) OF FIRED ROUND(S) DETERMINED? n/a DESCRIBE

THE INCIDENT IN DETAIL See Attached Memo REMARKS: (Include any information that may be used in training programs) PREPARED BY (Signature) TITLE Supervisor DUSM DISTRICT EDNY DATE January, 19 COPY 3-USMS EMPLOYEE'S COPY FORM USM.133 (Est. 0.23.70 No weapon

Plaintiff's Exhibit 2

Date 8/6/97 Reporter MB

CHAPTER TEN
Decisions Sealing My Case v City Of New York Forever By The United States Court Of Appeals For The Second Circuit.

```
                                              EDNY/bkny
                                              94-cv-2863
                                              Gershon
```

UNITED STATES COURT OF APPEALS

FOR THE SECOND CIRCUIT

S U M M A R Y   O R D E R

THIS SUMMARY ORDER WILL NOT BE PUBLISHED IN THE FEDERAL REPORTER AND MAY NOT BE CITED AS PRECEDENTIAL AUTHORITY TO THIS OR ANY OTHER COURT, BUT MAY BE CALLED TO THE ATTENTION OF THIS OR ANY OTHER COURT IN A SUBSEQUENT STAGE OF THIS CASE, IN A RELATED CASE, OR IN ANY CASE FOR PURPOSES OF COLLATERAL ESTOPPEL OR RES JUDICATA.

At a stated term of the United States Court of Appeals for the Second Circuit, held at the United States Courthouse, Foley Square, in the City of New York, on the 17th day of May, one thousand nine hundred and ninety-nine.

Present: HONORABLE RALPH K. WINTER,

        <u>Chief Judge</u>,

    HONORABLE WILFRED FEINBERG,

    HONORABLE PIERRE N. LEVAL,

        <u>Circuit Judges</u>.

- -

MELVIN LADNER,

    <u>Plaintiff-Appellant</u>,

TIMOTHY CARL,

    <u>Plaintiff</u>,

      - v. -   No. 98-9285

THE CITY OF NEW YORK, THE BOARD OF ELECTIONS OF THE CITY OF NEW YORK, THE POLICE DEPARTMENT OF THE CITY OF NEW YORK, THE BOARD OF EDUCATION OF THE CITY OF NEW YORK, BARBARA M. KETT, as Chief Clerk of Staten Island Board of Elections, THE STATEN ISLAND BOARD OF ELECTIONS, and THE RICHMOND COUNTY BOARD OF ELECTIONS,

    <u>Defendants-Third-Party Plaintiffs-Appellees</u>,

PROPORTIONAL COUNTS ASSOCIATES, INC.,

    <u>Third-Party Defendant-Appellee</u>.

```
Docket No. 98-9285
Page 2 of 2
- - - - - - - - - - - - - - - - - - - - - - - - - - - - - -
        Appearing for Appellant:  Melvin Ladner, pro se, Staten Island,
                                   New York.

        Appearing for Appellees:  Jane S. Earle, Corporation Counsel's
                                   Office, New York, New York.

                                   Archibald E. Robertson, Jr., Bronxville,
                                   New York.

             Appeal from the United States District Court for the Eastern
        District of New York (Gershon, Judge).

             UPON DUE CONSIDERATION, IT IS HEREBY ORDERED, ADJUDGED AND
        DECREED that the judgment of the District Court is hereby
        AFFIRMED.

             Melvin Ladner appeals from Judge Gershon's adverse grant of

        summary judgment. We affirm for substantially the reasons stated

        by the district court. See Ladner v. City of New York, 20 F.

        Supp.2d 509 (E.D.N.Y. 1998).


                                   FOR THE COURT:
                                   KAREN GREVE MILTON, Acting Clerk

                                   _Lucille Carr_     5/17/99
                                   By:                Date
```

I tried to figure out what the summary order from the court of appeals meant. After I did, I couldn't believe it. The appeals court ruled I was in the wrong court. Judge Glasser ruled I was in the correct court. Even Judge Gershon agreed. The City of New York brought me kicking and screaming into federal court from New York State court.

The city made a motion in New York State court that I should be in federal court, because there were federal issues involved in my case. When the City made the motion, we argued to remain in New York State court. Two federal judges agreed there were federal laws that were violated in *Ladner v. the City of New York*. Was I missing something?

The case was sealed as tight as a mummy's tomb, because the moving party forced the case to go to federal court, and the federal court accepted. That didn't make any sense. That rewarded the City of New York for moving the case into federal court, only to have the federal court declare we were in the wrong court. To top it off, the appeals court denied me a trial and sealed the records of the case.

The U.S.Court of Appeals' decision was even more surprising. It appeared that human error was allowed as a defense, and human error was committed by the defendants who committed crimes during the 1993 schoolboard elections. However, that defense was used only in my case, and it would never be allowed in another case.

As if adding insult to injury, the appeals court gave me a court order informing me that I had ten days to refile the appeal. If the appeal ruled against me, I would be fined. What judge would rule against the chief judge in the same court? None.

I kept thinking about the appeals court ruling and the Staten Island traffic court judge's comments. He said there was no such thing as human error. Could it be that the Staten Island traffic court judge refused to play politics, or was he smarter than the judges in the court of appeals? If the U.S. Court of Appeals was right, I should have won my parking ticket case by using the defense of human error.

One of the many complains I made to the Appellate Court was that 50,000 eligible parent voters, mostly poor, African Americans. and minorities, were intentionally denied their right to vote in the 1993 school-board election. That violated the Fifteenth Amendment to the Constitution. I asked the court of appeals to read the Stancik report, which spelled out the details regarding denials with intent to prevent minorities their right to vote in that election. There were video tapes of minorities being denied their right to vote. That violated the federal law of the Voting Rights Act of 1965. What more did I need to get a trial? I asked myself if the City of New York violated the civil rights of voters in the 1993 school-board election. By reading the Voting Rights Act of 1965, I believe they did.

The Voting rights act of 1965:

The **Voting Rights Act of 1965** (42 USC §§ 1973-1973aa-6)[1] is a landmark piece of national legislation in the United States that outlawed discriminatory voting practices that had been responsible for the widespread disenfranchisment of African Americans in the U.S. [2] Echoing the language of the 15th Amendment, the Act prohibits states from imposing any "voting qualification or prerequisite to voting, or standard, practice, or procedure...to deny or abridge the right of any citizen of the United Sates to vote on account of race or color."[3] Specifically, Congress intended the Act to outlaw the practice of requiring otherwise qualified voters to pass literacy tests in order to register to vote, a principal means by which Southern states had prevented African Americans from exercising the franchise. [2] The Act was signed into law by President Lyndon B. Johnson, a Democrat, who had earlier signed the landmark Civil Rights Act of 1984 into law.[2][4]

The other complaint I made to the court of appeals was that 50,000 hardworking parent voters who played by the rules were denied their right to vote in the 1993 school- board election. Some candidates knew before the election that the board of elections hadn't verified the parent voter registration list. The

candidates with that information had their workers and friends vote as many times as they wanted. Video evidence of that was given to the court of appeals and was also in the Stancik report. The case was getting personal. The appeals court order told the students of Staten Island that they didn't care about their safety or education. Fraud in citywide or national elections didn't matter. I thought of all our young, brave soldiers who, from the beginning of our country, gave their lives so we could have free and fair elections. What a shame that our great country came to that point. I had two choices after the district court decision of human error. I could quit and walk away and have great stories to tell at parties, or I could go to the final appeal before the U.S. Supreme Court. That would be my last strike at the bottom of the ninth inning.

I realized that the case was more than the education and safety of children in New York City. It had become political and could change the way the U.S. held elections.

I also had learned that the court system wasn't honest once it became involved in politics. Facts and evidence were like smoke and mirrors when brought to court. It turned out that the court system depended more on who someone knew than the facts and evidence he might have. The reason we had great lawyers wasn't dependent on the fact that they were highly intelligent or the best speakers in the world. To win a political case, they had to win motions before a trial. In my case, I couldn't even win a single motion for a trial. If the court wanted to change the fraud and corruption in the U.S. elections, my case would have been the vehicle for that change. The court clearly had its own political agenda. I would go to the U.S. Supreme Court with my eyes wide open. If I were in Las Vegas, I wouldn't have taken on the odds for my chances of winning a case before the Supreme Court. However, I learned in school that Americans stood for truth, justice, and the American way. I decided to take the bet and try to win before the Supreme Court.

After the U.S. Court of Appeals denied me a trial and sealed my case, I kept thinking about what the traffic court judge told me. Saying there was no such defense as human error in the real world, he was right. How could a simple ruling for a trial get so complicated? I must've touched a nerve. As far as election fraud went there was only one court left to try, the Supreme Court, my place of last resort.

I called the top ten law firms in the country and told them about the election fraud and how the future of all our children was at stake. I asked for pro bono work on my case. All of them turned me down. If I wanted to hire someone, it would cost over $200,000 to bring a case before the Supreme Court. Even if I had the money, none of the law firms would take the case.

After striking out with the law firms, I became my own pro se lawyer again. I decided to call the New York City corporation counsel. I tried to negotiate a deal to settle the case, asking the city to change the educational system.

I told the council that it would save the city billions of dollars in tax money by reducing administrative staff in the Board of Education. If they did that, I'd go away and drop all criminal charges and lawsuits. I added I wanted our agreement in writing. When they refused, I said, "I'll see you in U.S. Supreme Court." New York City knew the courts wouldn't change the corrupt election system, and no law firm would take such a case. The city could stall with motions that I was forced to respond to, which would cost time, effort, and money. I was in a hard place, but who was the worst person in the world to deal

with? It was me. I knew I was right about the rigged election in 1993. The case had become my hobby, and I would give my best effort to win it. The case had become personal. I promised myself and God I wouldn't quit, even if that meant going to the Supreme Court. The education and safety of our children and the future of our country was at stake. I would do whatever it took. It was like kayaking down the dangerous Hillsborough River, with snakes and alligators, not knowing what was around the next bend.

I researched the subject on the Internet and found a lot of information about the Supreme Court. The rules and regulations were mind-boggling. However, there was one way to avoid all the regulations- make a motion for *forma pauperis*, which meant pauper status. If the Supreme Court granted my motion the proper status, I could handwrite the case on regular paper. The Supreme Court would also appoint a lawyer to *try Ladner v. the City of New York*. Rule 39 on page 49 of the rules of the U.S. Supreme Court stated how to proceed in *forma pauperis.*

1. A party seeking to proceed in *forma pauperis* shall file a motion for leave to do so, together with the party's notarized affidavit or declaration (in compliance with 28 USC. 1746) in the form prescribed by the Federal rules of Appellate Procedure, Form 4. The motion shall state whether leave to proceed in *forma pauperis* was sought in any other court and, if so, whether leave was granted.

CHAPTER ELEVEN
The U.S. Supreme Court.
The Court Of Last Resort!

I filled out all the legal forms for forma pauperis and sent them in on June 14, 1999, with a check for the filing fee of $300 to the U.S. Supreme Court and hoped for the best.

No.

In The

SUPREME COURT OF THE UNITED STATES

MELVIN LADNER, As a *pro se* petitioner

TIMOTHY CARL,

V.

NEW YORK CITY, BOARD OF ELECTIONS OF THE CITY OF NEW YORK, NEW YORK CITY POLICE DEPARTMENT, NEW YORK CITY BOARD OF EDUCATION, BARBARA M. KETT, as CHIEF CLERK OF THE STATEN ISLAND BOARD OF ELECTIONS; STATEN ISLAND BOARD OF ELECTIONS, RICHMOND COUNTY BOARD OF ELECTIONS,

Defendants,

PROPORTIONAL COUNTS ASSOCIATES, INC.

Third-Party Defendant,

MOTION FOR LEAVE TO PROCEED IN *FORMA PAUPERIS*

The petitioner asks leave to file the attached petition for a writ of certiorari without prepayment of costs and to proceed *in forma pauperis*.

Petitioner has **not** previously been granted leave to proceed in *forma pauperis* in any other court.

Petitioner's affidavit or declaration is support of this motion is attached hereto.

Melvin Ladner, As Pro se petitioner
60 KENMORE STREET
STATEN ISLAND, N.Y. 10312
TELEPHONE# 718-966-5398

```
SUPREME COURT OF THE UNITED STATES
        OFFICE OF THE CLERK
        WASHINGTON, D. C. 20543


                    July 20, 1999


Mr. Melvin Ladner
60 Kenmore Street
Staten Island, NY 10312

            Re:  Melvin Ladner
                 v. City of New York, et al.
                 No. 99-5301

Dear Mr. Ladner:

    The petition for a writ of certiorari in the above
entitled case was filed July 19, 1999 and placed on the
docket July 19, 1999 as No. 99-5301.

    A form is enclosed for notifying opposing counsel that
the case was docketed.

                         Sincerely,

                         William K. Suter, Clerk
                         by
                         Gail B. Johnson
                         Assistant


Enclosures
```

The problem was that the Supreme Court had detailed forms to fill out for *pauperis* status. I had a major problem. I was awarded $76 million against Proportional Account Associates that I couldn't collect, and I was required to include that on the assets form I sent in. I laughed out loud when I filled in the sum and thought *When the U.S. Supreme Court reads the form and sees $76 million in assets, I'll bet they rule I'm the wealthiest pauper in the U.S.*

I had no chance of being granted forma pauperis status, but I was stalling for time to get myself organized. I filled out the motion and hoped the Supreme Court would take time to deny me that status. That would give me the time I needed to publish the forty-one books that adhered to the rules of the court. I didn't wait for an answer. I started writing a brief entitled *A Petition for a Writ of Certiorari*, which meant I was asking the Supreme Court to take my appeal and decide my case.

It was weird that when I ran for the school board, one of my campaign promises were to have optional prayer in school. I took a lot of flak over that. The tradition in the Supreme Court was that the brief of the *writ of certiorari* started with a prayer. The petitioner respectfully prays that a *writ of certiorari* be issued to review the judgment below. I agreed with putting prayers into the brief, because I said many prayers during my other dealings with the federal courts.

It was easy to complete the motion for a *writ of certiorari*. I had all the information right in front of me. The most-important goal I wanted to accomplish was to be given a trial. I also wanted to know if the State Island traffic court judge's decision was right when he said there was no such defense as human error. I hoped to have the U.S. Supreme Court if there was such a defense. I wrote down fifteen questions I wanted the court to rule on. As per the rules of the Supreme Court, I put the whole case into legal question. My case was simple for a trial. I had all the evidence before the federal court. Convicted murderers were put to death with less evidence than I had.

Then I thought what the clerk of the Court of Appeals told me, that I was a special case. I never heard that there was such a decision of *collateral estoppel* or *res judicata*, which sealed my case forever. Maybe the clerk was right, and I was a special case. One case law that would be a no-brainer to give me a trial was the federal courts did have authority to hear criminal cases involving isolated incidents of electoral fraud. See *Blitz* v. U.S. 153 U.S. 308 (1894).

Tradition as per rules of the US Supreme the questions start: with: QUESTIONS PRESENTED

1. I RESPECTFULLY REQUEST that the Supreme Court of the United States question the election fraud violations of the democratic process during the New York City 1993 School-Board election as cited by evidence, two videotapes and internal school report, see exhibit L.
1. I REPECTFULLY REQUEST the Supreme Court to question the ruling of the United States district court for the Eastern District of New York, Judge Nina Gershon ruling dated September 14, 1998 and United States Court of Appeals for the Second Circuit dated May 17,1999. The ruling that denies this case a trial or summary judgment is preference on two points 1. That this was human error (HUMAN ERROR is not an affirmative defense) 2. This case does not belong in Federal Court. I cite cases of Federal Law violations and Judge I. Leo Glasser Court ruling that the federal court is indeed in its jurisdiction to hear this case. That the defendants did violate the 14th and 15th Amendment to the United States Constitution. I ask the court to dismiss these two arguments, which provide a cloud of smoke to hide the grim truth of the corruption and intentional fraud that plagued the New York City 1993 School-Board Election.
2. The record shows that evidence was destroyed. I request the court question whether the defendants should be sanctioned for destruction and spoliation of irreplaceable physical evidence? Defendants admitted that they intentionally destroyed evidence of over 24,000 ballots stubs and protest sheets INTER ALIA (which means among other things. violating New York State Election Law sec.3222.2, making it virtually impossible to defend this action and verify that the 1993 School-Board election was correct. Is this Spoliation of Physical evidence or just human error?
3. As cited in the Stancik report, it has been proven that defendants did intentionally prevent and denied over 50,000 parent voters mostly poor, African-Americans, and other minority from voting in the 1993 New York City School-Board election, thus violating the 14th and 15th Amendment to the United States Lots Constitution. Does this violate any Federal Law? Is this just human error?

Candidates received information from the New York City Board of election and the New York City Board of education that they did not verify the parent voters' registration list, had their workers and friends commit intentional voter fraud by voting as many times as they want to, which they did. See the

Stancik report (exhibit L) and two videotapes that are in the record. Does this violate Federal Law? Is this just human error?

1. Employees of the New York City Board of Education public school principals forwarded parent voter registration forms to selected parent voters that would vote for their candidates. The New York City school principals intentionally prevented other parent voters from voting in the 1993 school-board election. Does this violate federal law? Is this just human error?
2. Defendant Chief Clerk of Staten Island Board Election Barbara Kett and other officials of the New York Board of election admitted and did intentionally violate election laws by ripping open and entering sealed ballot boxes containing voter ballots not yet counted. The defendants did this to prevent me and other candidates from winning an elected office, thus violating my 14th amendment rights. The defendants did this without a court order or by direction of a committee of the New York State Senate or State Assembly, violating New York State election law Sec.3-222.2 Is this an affirmative defense of just human error? As per opinion and order of Judge Gershon on page 11 and 12 this is just human error and does not violate any federal law. Does this violate the 14th amendment? Does the above action by the defendants violate any Federal Law?
3. Defendants admit through sworn testimony that they stuffed the ballot boxes with a ton of altered ballots not counted. Defendants admit that they violated election laws and committed crimes and misdemeanors. I received information 3 days before the vote count that certain ballots and ballot boxes were altered to prevent other candidates and me from winning the election, thus violating my 14th Amendment rights and violating New York State Election law sec.7-106.5. Judge Gershon in her opinion and order ruled that this is just human error. Does this violate Federal law? Is this just human error?
4. The defendants initiated the adjudication of this case from New York State Court to Federal Court. Further Judge I. Leo Glasser ruled that we were indeed in the proper court. It is disingenuous to bring my case to Federal Court, and argue successfully a summary judgment that his case is now in the wrong court.

1. I respectfully request the court to consider if dead people voting absentee and filing notarized applications and using the U.S. mail to send fraudulent voter absentee forms to the New York City Board of Election violates Federal Law. Does this violate U.S. mail fraud laws? Is this just human error?
2. I respectfully ask the court to consider if changing the ballot total and official tally wrappers from red marker to pen and pencil, not at the count site but at another location, changed the outcome of the election, preventing other candidates and me from elected office. See the two videotapes in the record. Does this violate any Federal Law? Is this just human error?
3. Sample ballots were substituted for original ballots and counted. Robertson's sworn testimony states that he had access to sample ballots for training purposes before the election and still has many sample ballots in his office. There was no safeguard to insure that fraudulent sample ballots replaced real ballots. Do fraudulent sample ballots that are counted violate any Federal Law?

4. The defendant Proportional Count Associates is in default in this action. The defendants kept on accepting all motions for Proportional Count Associates. Defendants as far as I know did not inform Judge Gershon about Proportional Count Associates' default. Does this violate my civil rights?

This was Staten Island Count Director Bruce Hogenauer's first job out of prison for child molestation and being a fugitive from justice. Hogenauer has a very lengthy arrest record, which includes forgery. He was in charge of paper ballots, written in pencil and stored in cardboard ballot boxes. I received information that Mr. Hogenauer committed voter fraud against me in the 1993 school- board election.

Are there genuine issues of material facts in this case, that reasonable minds would differ with the genuine issues of material facts? Should I be given a chance to search for the truth and be granted a trial?

The next part of the petition for the *writ of certiorari* was the case laws that would argue the facts of the case. I had enough case laws to fill a law library. The hard part would be to publish forty-one booklets with seventy-four pages of rules of the Supreme Court of the United States. I started to get advertising sent to my home from printers who worked for big law firms that argued before the U.S. Supreme Court. It was funny that the advertising was addressed to me, as if I were a lawyer.

When I called the printers, one of the first subjects I raised was that I was be *pro* se in the case before the Supreme Court. They asked about the case, and I replied, "It's about election fraud. I'm trying to get a trial."

"What's the big deal about going to a trial?" "I don't have a clue why the court wouldn't give me a trial."

The conversation continued for five minutes. "How much does it cost to print the forty-one books?""Around eight thousand dollars." "Is there any way to get them printed for less?" "I'm the cheapest firm that does Supreme Court work."

He was right, too. I received bids from other printers asking twice as much.

I worked for a union doing security work. I spoke to the president of the union and said, "I hit a brick wall regarding printing the booklet for the Supreme Court."

"Why don't you go to Staples?" he asked in jest. "They do printing." "That's a good idea." I was serious about visiting Staples.

I did my rounds supervising the security staff on other sites when I saw a Staples, though it later became an Office Depot, on Seventh Avenue and Fortieth Street in Manhattan. I spoke to the man behind the counter and explained I needed forty-one books to be printed for the Supreme Court. I gave him the book of seventy-four pages of rules for the court, and he thumbed through it.

"Give me a week, and it'll be done," he said. "How much will it cost?"

"A nickel a page. We have sixty-pound paper in the store. We also might have cover paper. Let me check." He came back in five minutes. "Yes, we have the right weight and color paper for the cover in stock. Binding is also available."

I found all the supplies I needed to file the *writ of certiorari* with the U.S. Supreme Court at Staples. When I calculated the price in my mind, it came to less than two dollars per booklet.

"My name's Mel Ladner. What's yours? Can I have your phone number?" "My name's Dan." He gave me the number. "I'm attending law school.

This would be a great experience for me. If it's OK with you, may I bring the Supreme Court rulebook and motion of the *writ of certiorari* to class?

Maybe I can get my classmates and professor to help us do the project."" That would be a great class project. Could I grade the booklet? If the U.S. Supreme Court accepts booklets; you'll earn an A." "Sure. Can I use this project on my résumé?" "Whoever works on it will get a recommendation letter from me for his or her résumé."

I added I wouldn't hold him, the store, or anyone who works on the booklets responsible if the Supreme Court rejected the booklets. I wrote it on a piece of paper and had it notarized while I was there. To me, it was like winning the lottery. To Dan, it was a great opportunity to advance his law career. It was a win-win situation. I knew I had the right person when he pronounced *writ of certiorari* correctly.

That was a lesson for me. For every situation or big problem, there's a perfect match to fix it.

Dan and I had many phone conversations about the legal system. I got the impression from him he would've paid me to print the booklets for the Supreme Court. The college professor never went to the Supreme Court before. I had the impression that the professor and his fifteen students got a kick out of doing the project. It was fun, and I offered to send pizza to the class and have a post-project party.

Three weeks after I met and made the deal with Dan, the U.S. Supreme Court booklets were finished. They looked perfect in every way. They could have been used as samples for how the booklets should be done. I was impressed with the detailed work the law students and professor did. With the discount Staples gave on large orders, I paid $2.95 for each booklet. I was ready to go before the court.

I returned to Staples with a commendation letter for the students. It had the heading of *Ladner v. the City of New York*, U.S. Supreme Court case 99-5301. I thanked them for helping me with the case.

"How many recommendation letters do you need for the students and professor?" I asked. "Just make the copies here, and I'll pay for them."

"They're five cents a page."

I handed him a twenty. "Keep the change."

My case was docketed on June 16, 1999, with docket number 99-5301 in the U.S. Supreme Court.

Then I received a letter from Mr. William K. Suter, the clerk, telling me I had sixty days to correct my writ to petition the Supreme Court for *forma pauperis*. I had apparently violated rule 14.5, rule 33.2, rule 39, and rule 29.5. *Wow, they're strict*, I thought, thinking how tough it would be to comply with all the rules for the forty booklets.

I did what the Marx Brothers did in the movie *Day at the Races*. I looked up the rules and saw I really had violated them. It took two days to fix the problem, then I sent my motion of *forma pauperis* back to the Supreme Court.

SUPREME COURT OF THE UNITED STATES
OFFICE OF THE CLERK
WASHINGTON, DC 20543-0001

WILLIAM K. SUTER
CLERK OF THE COURT

July 8, 1999

Melvin Ladner
40 Kenmore St.
Staten Island, NY 10312

RE: Ladner v. New York City, Board of Elections

Dear Mr. Ladner:

The above-entitled petition for writ of certiorari was postmarked June 14, 1999 and received June 14, 1999. The papers are returned for the following reason(s):

No motion for leave to proceed in forma pauperis, signed by the petitioner or by counsel, is attached. Rules 39.2 and 39. The motion must be signed.

No notarized affidavit or declaration of indigency is attached. Rule 39. You may use the enclosed form.

No affidavit or declaration of service, specifying the names and addresses of those served, was received. Rule 29.5.

Please correct and resubmit as soon as possible. Unless the petition is received by this Office in corrected form within 60 days of the date of this letter, the petition will not be filed. Rule 14.5.

Sincerely,
William K. Suter, Clerk
By:
Jeff Johnson
(202) 479-3034

Enclosures

I waited on the forty-one booklets until I received a decision. If the Supreme Court granted my motion for pauper status, I would send just one booklet to the Supreme Court, as per their rules. The other thirty-nine would become Christmas gifts. If they denied my motion for pauper status, I would send in all forty books. I had everything covered. The case was a lock. How could the Supreme Court rule that human error was a defense for committing crimes?

All I had to do was wait for their ruling on my pauper status. How would they notify me? I never did anything like that before, and I didn't know anyone who appeared before the Supreme Court. How long would it take them to decide? I called the U.S. Supreme Court to find out the answers. All I got about my motion for pauper status was that it would be answered in writing, and they could take as long as they wanted.

I waited. Every day I went to work and called my wife to ask if any mail came from the Supreme Court. She always said, "No." When I arrived at work, my fellow workers asked, "Any news from the Supreme Court yet?" "None."

Summer turned into fall. The Supreme Court's next session would open on October 4, 1999. I wondered if the court could issue an order for pauper status on their opening day. A couple days after the Supreme Court opened, I received a letter dated October 4, 1999 in my mailbox from the Supreme Court of the United States, Office of the Clerk, informing me that the motion of petitioner for leave to proceed in *forma pauperis* was denied.

Petitioner is allowed until October 25, 1999, within which to pay the docketing fee required by rule 38(a) and to submit a petition in compliance with rule 33.1 or the rules of this court.

In layman's terms, I was done. The court wanted the forty booklets made and mailed to the court in less than three weeks. It would've been impossible if I hadn't already made the booklets. I was born in Brooklyn, and I knew that the court simply wanted to get rid of me. If they had granted me a reasonable time, like ninety days, to print the forty booklets, I would've had a fifty-fifty chance of the court accepting my appeal.

The Supreme Court had assumed I'd been waiting for them to rule and was sitting on my hands all that time. If I didn't send in the forty booklets, I would have given them a free pass to ignore me. Then they wouldn't have needed to reject my appeal of *Ladner v. City of New York*.

They would have said, "We would've taken the appeal if only Ladner had sent in the forty booklets."

If the media had the printed details of my case, or if the story got out on TV showing the details of the rigged election, I felt that would have pressured the federal courts to give me a trial.

I finally knew that I had no chance of the U.S. Supreme Court taking my case. The case was over, but I would send in the forty booklets. If anything, they would embarrass the court when they rejected my case. When they received my petition for a *writ of certiorari*, the Supreme Court would have to decide my case. If they rejected it, with its defense of human error, then election fraud was accepted, child molesters and kidnappers were OK in schools, parents didn't have to be notified that their children came into contact with Hogenauer, opening sealed ballot boxes and altering ballots was standard procedure,

videos and photographs in evidence of election fraud meant nothing, and the investigation by Stancik's office and the report of election fraud were meaningless.

The 50,000 African Americans and other minorities being denied their right to vote in the 1993 school-board election brought us back to the old days of poll taxes in the 1950s, where the states prevented African Americans and other minorities from voting. That, too, would be acceptable as far as the federal courts were concerned. We should also remember the dead people who voted in that election. If and when *Ladner v. New York City* was rejected, all those issues would be allowed.

I didn't have to wait long for a decision. On November 15, 1999, the U.S. Supreme Court rejected my appeal for a trial. They sealed my case forever, *and Ladner v. New York City* would never be cited in any action in the United States of America again. If it weren't for my writing this book, my case for a trial would be held in complete secrecy in the federal court system. The case was over, and the city of New York won.

CHAPTER TWELVE
My Conclusions

What did New York City really win in my federal court case? Nothing, because statistics found in USA Today show only 38.9% of the students in the New York City school system graduate from high school. The system has a budget of over $20 billion per year. Yet it has failed, and who suffered? Is it the employer who can't find a qualified person to fill a technical position, or a taxpayer who has real-estate taxes for school taxes that are so high they look like a telephone number? Most of the budget is wasted on administrative cost and basic school materials and not on teachers' salaries.

God bless all the teachers who put up with the crap in the education system. I tried to fix it to no avail.

When I ran as a candidate in the 1993 citywide school board election one of my main issues was parents could not opt out of controversial subjects taught in schools. All parents should have a choice about what their young children are taught about sexual issues in public school. If the policy does not change providing an opt out clause on controversial issues, then this will be the end of public education. Maybe that's the plan to get rid of public education and replace it with private/charter schools. Parents, politicians and teachers must wake up and smell the roses, because the future of our great public education system is in jeopardy.

My campaign platform from 1993 is still a good educational policy today.

Would it be a good optional policy to saluting the American flag, Pledge of Allegiance prayer at the beginning of the school day?

How about an Accredited optional class in worshiping of God, taught by Religious leaders. What I learned from my experience with America's legal system is that The federal courts are just gatekeepers to stop anyone from changing the country's fraudulent election system. The system accepts a certain level of fraud in elections, but the 1993 citywide school-board election was way over the top even for such a corrupt system. That's why the federal courts refused to give me a trial. At a trial, it would have been revealed exactly who, when, why, and how election fraud was committed. The public would demand that the courts go after the bastards who committed the election fraud. We could have shone a light on all the problems in U.S. elections.

Mr. Mel Ladner

Chairman, President, and CEO.

c/o The Trump Organization

725 Fifth Avenue,

New York, NY 10022

Telephone# 212-832-2000

Fax: 212-935-0141

Feb. 3, 2016

Dear Mr. Donald Trump:

I am enclosing my book HUMAN ERROR it's a non-fiction book about election fraud.

Hopefully what happen to me when I ran in a rig election will not happen to you. If there is lessons to be learn is that the federal courts do not get involved in the election process. You can see what you will be up against if and when you feel that you have been cheated in the election.

Mr. Trump, I am and adherent supporter of your candidacy for president of the United States. And if there is anything I could do to help you win in the election in FL. Please contact me.

Please enjoy my book HUMAN ERRROR.

Very truly yours;

Mr. Mel Ladner

I am respectfully requesting that the U.S. Supreme Court:

1. The U.S. Supreme court Officially notify all the parents of George L. Egbert intermediate junior high school, 333 Midland Avenue, Staten Island New York who attended the school in May of 1993. That their children were at risk when they came in contacts with Bruce Hogenauer, a child molester. During the election count in May, 1993. while school was it was in session.

2. The U.S. Supreme court reopen and unseal my case of Melvin *Ladner v. the City of New York*, #99-5301. So my case can be studied in law schools. I want the public to witness how the courts react and handle political criminal cases. 3. I am requesting the U.S. Supreme court grant my

summary judgement of $76,000,000 dollars plus interest, against Proportional Counts Associates and the City of New York. who were responsible for the rigged school broad election and hiring the count director, a child molester and forger to be in charge of counting the votes.

3. I want the U.S. Supreme court to explain how with so much evidence of voter fraud and rigged election could in God's name not grant me a trial to search for the truth. How could the people that are responsible for the rigged school broad election not be punished?

4. I respectfully request that the U. S. Supreme court issue an official apology to voters of New York City and especially the parents of the children that were at risk of being molested while attending George L. Egbert intermediate Junior high school and me, Mel Ladner for the courts not doing their job of protecting our basic rights for free and fair elections and protecting the safety of our children!

We must clean up our own election system. after investigating the New York City election system, I found out that there is election fraud that happen in most elections that can change the outcome of close elections.

I have watched the 2020 Donald Trump v. Joe Biden Presidential election coverage on television. I wish I could have been part of the investigation into the allegations of election fraud. But I was not given the opportunity to investigate the election. I can only speculate that with the tens of thousands of drop-off ballots boxes on street not being monitored and mail in ballots that were counted: the officials of the department of elections failed to check the drop-off ballots and the mail in ballots for accuracy, who filled the mail in ballots out or where the drop-off ballots came from?

If I told you that in some states in our country you don't have to show identification to vote you would think I was joking! This only creates more speculation that the 2020 Presidential election was rigged?

I can assure you that no state agency is assigned to investigate voter fraud. The courts turn their backs and do not get involved in voter fraud. It's a free pass to commit voter fraud. Our great country, the good old U.S.A. deserves free and fair elections! The courts and states must take voter fraud seriously for the good of our country!

I hope and pray to God that our country's future is better for the next generation than ours. Maybe we could have changed the election system to become fair and honest, and maybe we would then have more citizens running for office instead of career politicians.

I feel sorry for the students and the educational system I failed to help. No one likes to lose, and I lost big, but it wasn't for lack of trying. As an individual, I fought and did everything I could for the education and safety of the children of the City of New York. I would do it again in a heartbeat, because I believe it was the right thing to do. God bless the United States of America. Mel Ladner

President Donald J. Trump has the book you just read "Human Error" first edition in his campaign office at Trump Tower.

February 29, 2016

Mel Ladner

Dear Mel,

Thank you for sending us the book "Human Error." It will remain in our campaign office so visitors are able to appreciate the thoughtful generosity of our supporters, like you.

America needs reform and a President with the ability to bring about real, positive, economic change. Mr. Trump's experience as a business executive, employing thousands, maintaining balanced budgets and winning at negotiations all over the world makes him the most qualified candidate to restore American greatness. Together we will re-energize the spirit of the American people.

Mel, we are honored to call you a valuable member of Team Trump. Supporters like you, sharing your passion and excitement for a new candidate - highly qualified and unconventional- are the best way to spread the values, ideals, and principles of Mr. Trump's Presidential Campaign.

Together we will Make America Great Again!

Sincerely,

Team Trump

725 Fifth Avenue · New York · New York · 10022 · www.DonaldJTrump.com

Paid for by Donald J. Trump for President, Inc.

ABC News 20/20 147 Columbus Avenue New York NY 10023 (212) 456 2020

Dear 20/20 Viewer:

Thank you for your recent letter suggesting a story for 20/20. Given the high volume of letters we receive daily, we regret that we cannot contact you personally.

As you know, each 20/20 broadcast features only three subjects which we must select from hundreds of ideas. Due to our schedule, we are not able to look into your suggestion at this time.

Thank you for being in touch with 20/20. We appreciate your thinking of us.

Sincerely,

The Senior Producers
ABC News 20/20

back the in-

...en

...e most neglected ...on. We make the ... next year will be ...is year. The tech-...pared children for ...the same as those ...e year 2000. This ...wrong. The future ...derstanding of the ...ed for success. Suc-...hildren's world will ...rent base of knowl-...e currently possess. ... being satisfied with ...d school system and ...great school system. ...of comparison is no ... we compare with ... districts in New York ... point of comparison ... with the best school ... the country. Tell me ...compare to Scarsdale, ...nceton, N.J., or Short ... Tell me we are as good ... than they are, and I will ...fied.

...Brennan

...orical funding and similar ...nents have clearly identi-...d benefited the differing ...tions of children who have ... needs and circumstances. ...ere are a vast number of ...tional funding for materials and equipment.

■ Geography instruction must be an integral part of social-studies programs.

■ Even more emphasis on improved technological skills in keyboarding, computer literacy and an investment in equipment, supplies and materials for our middle schools Career Education programs.

Needless to say, although our district children do well, we must continue to motivate and challenge all pupils to fully develop their potential.

Timothy Carl

Our school system is failing to teach the students what it was originally created to teach — the basics. We need only look at some of our graduates to realize the students are not adequately educated in reading, writing and mathematics. In addition, we are failing them and the nation as a whole by almost completely neglecting American history and government, geography, science and the arts. One need only view our nation's decreased standing in the world to prove this point.

We must produce graduates who can read, write and calculate as well as understand the workings of their own government and ...dent. This should be one of the top priorities of the Second District when dealing with the Division of School Facilities.

Melvin Ladner

One of many neglected areas of education is our school budget of $7.5 billion. If this was a corporation it would be the 10th largest in the world. I believe the $7.5 billion budget is being wasted, mismanaged or even stolen. I am announcing a S.O.S. (Save Our Schools) from waste, mismanagement, smoke screens and possible thievery. Only 33 percent of the school budget reaches the classroom. This means more than $5 billion is missing every year. This must change. By focusing on social issues the school system is creating smokescreen that keeps everyone's attention off the real problem of where the money from the budget is going. I propose an independent audit of the budget to get a grasp of where all of the $5 billion that is missing every year is going. The monies found will be used strictly for our children's education.

Betty Martinucci

The most neglected area of education on Staten Island is the largest segment of our school population — the average child. We have ...sizes teachers cannot nurture the students appetite for these skills.

As important as communication skills are, the school system does not have laboratory facilities available for its students and faculty. Therefore, as students advance the system's capacity to promote and improve skills diminish.

I think it is imperative to upgrade the teaching facilities within school system and that a literacy coordinator should be hired by the Board of Education to organize a far-reaching program to raise the reading and writing levels of Staten Island students.

Tottenville PTA has recognition day

The Tottenville High School PTA hosted its annual teacher recognition day in the school cafeteria yesterday.

The yearly event was arranged and chaired by executive member Angie Frele and other PTA executives. The PTA highlighted the afternoon festivities with a raffle and many prizes for teachers and staff. The next meeting will be May 25 at 8 p.m.

E
95
5

...nnoying for the great majority of ...our children.

CHAPTER THIRTEEN
"The Smoking Gun" The Official Stancik Report: From Chaos to Corruption, proofs Election Fraud

Executive Summary

Our ten month investigation closely examined the integrity of the May 1993 New York City Community School Board Election. School board elections are at the heart of decentralization, which should enable local communities to exercise control over the education of their children. Local board members have a direct impact on the quality of education in the district. The thirty two boards elected last May set policy for their districts and control budgets in excess of $100 million, as well as thousands of educational jobs.

We found widespread fraud and corruption as well as administrative mismanagement in many areas of the election process. Both of these present serious dangers because, when they flourish, parents and community members are denied the voice decentralization was designed to give them. A brief summary of our most illustrative findings follows.

Parent voter registration

Poor planning and coordination by the Board of Elections and the Board of Education once again had a disastrous impact on the registering of parent voters. While in Manhattan anyone could pretend to be a parent and cast as many votes as names he or she could make up, duly registered parents lost their votes through administrative fumbling.

- In Community School District 2, one undercover investigator voted fifteen times under fifteen different fictitious names. He even voted twice in front of the same poll inspector. Another investigator voted ten times in District 6 using fictitious names.

- Due to administrative errors, each of the 25 fictitious "parents" had valid voter registration cards waiting for them at the polling sites.

- Parent voters from 190 schools, who had legally registered in and before 1989, lost their right to vote in 1993 when principals at those schools failed to return their certification lists. The Board of Education did not ensure that the lists were completed and returned.

Election Day

School board elections should be conducted with a seriousness and integrity that reflect their importance to the community. The chaotic conditions that reigned in New York City this year instead reflect the Board of Elections' disinterested attitude toward an election it plainly sees as unimportant.

- Parents and other registered voters lost their votes in a host of ways. Parent voters were turned away because the Board of Elections had sent their cards to the wrong sites, or because the inspectors did not know to look for them in a separate roll book ade up for parent voters.

- When two school districts shared one voting site -- these sites were known as "split district" sites -- voters from one district were often given the ballots for the other. On some occasions, the ballots for only one district were available.

- Sample ballots virtually identical to the real thing were not marked as samples, with the result that many wound up filled out and dropped into the ballot boxes. Once again, disenfranchisement could be avoided only by sacrificing integrity concerns, and the Board of Elections was forced to count the sample ballots as valid.

- Voters were afforded little dignity or privacy. At best the voting "booth" was a small cardboard divider. At worst, it was a bench shared with other voters. Often, voters had to fight off candidates or their supporters telling them how to vote.

- The most basic security precautions, such as sealed ballot boxes, were ignored. One of our investigators actually lifted the top off the box to insert his ballot inside. The attending inspector just laughed.

- Widespread electioneering was tolerated. One candidate approached voters at the Ramirez Senior Citizens Home in District 7 as they were voting and repeated her slogan, "Carmen Arroyo #1." As our investigator was marking his ballot in another district, a woman approached him with a list of candidates and said, "these ten here…it's a good decision." Similar scenes were witnessed throughout the city.

- Essential materials such as rollbooks, ballots, and ballot boxes were often hours late in arriving at their sites. At one site, voting commenced only after a voter found the ballots in a corner of the gymnasium.

The Vote Count

Despite widespread irregularities cited by investigators and journalists in the 1989 vote count, the Board of Elections seemed disinterested in improving the integrity of the 1993 count. Two means of getting a more honest count were obvious: attract new contractors to perform the count, and automate the count to reduce opportunities for fraud. The Board of Elections did neither. With almost no effort to find new contractors, the Board awarded the job to the <u>only</u> bidder, Proportional Count Associates (PCA), who had won the contract for three of the last four elections. Predictably, PCA delivered a far from satisfactory performance.

- Though automation was recognized as an important tool to improve integrity, the Board of Elections did not explain what automation meant either in its contract or in the pre-bid conference.
- The Board of Elections did not consult with its own computer unit on the software PCA wanted to use. The software was only tested once, with no Board of Elections personnel present.
- In District 11, PCA hired candidate Rodney Saunders' son Keith to count ballots. In District 13, PCA hired Candidate Marilyn Mosely's campaign workers to count ballots.
- In District 13, PCA lost a ballot box containing at least thirteen ballots. The ballots were never recovered.
- Tally sheets and vote stubs, mechanisms designed to guard against ballot stuffing, were routinely ignored.

The Cost

What the School Board Election lacks in integrity and decorum, it makes up for in cost. The price, both in dollars and in police manpower, is staggering. The police cost is particularly troubling, since it is directly attributable to the paper ballots and complex ballot counting system used only in the School Board Election.

- The Board of Elections spends approximately $4 million on the Community School Board Election, about the same as it does on a general election.
- For each of the eight days between Election Day and the start of the count, a total of thirty police officers and three sergeants spent full eight-hour shifts guarding the cardboard ballot boxes in warehouses.
- For each day of the counting, a total of ninety six police officers and nine sergeants spent full shifts guarding the count sites.
- Thus, at a time when New Yorkers are increasingly concerned about their safety, the School Board Election required that the police spend almost 10,000 crime fighting hours watching boxes.

○ ○ ○

In addition to the gross mismanagement described above, our investigation also uncovered cases of deliberate fraud and misconduct.

Voter Fraud

In possibly the most egregious fraud perpetrated in an election already riddled with improprieties, unsuspecting Fordham University students were duped into participating in the Community School Board Election in the Bronx. Two Fordham seniors who worked part-time in the District 10 office cast more than one hundred votes in the names of their fellow students to help a District 10 candidate get elected.

- Nicole Avallone and Jean Marie Gildea, two Resident Advisors at Fordham, filled out absentee ballot applications for their fellow students, obtained the ballots, and cast them -- all without the consent and knowledge of their unsuspecting classmates.

- Students from as far away as Hawaii and California were surprised to find themselves registered to vote in the Bronx.

- James Sullivan, director of Pupil Personnel in District 10, orchestrated Avallone and Gildea's efforts.

Undue Political Influence

Our investigation revealed that the pressure suffered by educators to get involved in political campaigns is not limited to any one district. To the contrary, we found that teachers and school staff in District 21 in Brooklyn were pressured to participate in political campaigns. In District 9 in the Bronx, school employees were tapped to throw a fundraiser. School employees feel that they have no choice but to pay their political dues.

- Stuart Possner, principal of PS 100 in District 21, used certain staff members to pressure his teachers to join a local Democratic Club. He stacked the Club's membership so that it would vote to endorse one of his supporters on the School Board, Sheldon Plotnick. Many of the teachers do not live in the neighborhood of the Club, let alone in Brooklyn.

- Possner had his henchmen collect Club dues from teachers while they were in the classroom. Other allies made sure that the staff would be at the important Club meetings to vote for Plotnick.

- Teachers who did not attend Club meetings were punished in school the next day.

- PS 100 teachers reported being the victims of Possner's graphic and aggressive sexual harassment. One teacher likened the staff to "battered women" who see no way out of their destructive environment.

- In District 9, School Board Member Carmelo Saez coordinated efforts for a fundraiser which was attended by almost every principal in the District and many other District employees. Virtually every task needed to pull off the fundraiser was accomplished using District personnel and resources. Although many thousands of dollars were raised, the distribution of the proceeds remains a mystery.

Petition Review

The petition review process is replete with arcane rules and secrecy that give political insiders an advantage over parents and community members without political clout. The secretive process makes it easy for politicians and commissioners to cut deals behind the scenes to favor certain candidates.

- The manner in which the Commissioners of the Board of Elections held the hearings to review the challenges to candidates' petitions raised serious questions about the integrity of the process.

- In closed door meetings, Board of Elections commissioners voted to place District 12 candidates Randy Glenn and Ed Cain and District 8 candidates Ciro Guerra and Steven Eskow on the ballot,

despite the fact that all four candidates fell short of the requisite two hunderd nominating signatures. No record of the vote or proceedings was made.

- Bronx Republican District Leader Fred Brown was captured on tape saying that "it cost a helluva chip" to get State Senator Guy Velella to contact his father, Elections Commissioner Vincent Velella, to restore Glenn and Cain to the ballot. The integrity of the petition review process was further compromised by the fact that Elections Commissioner Paul Mejias had business interests in both districts.

- At the same time, District 10 Candidate Herbert Suss was excluded from the ballot for a technical violation. A political outsider, Suss was not given the same consideration afforded to the well-connected candidates in Districts 12 and 8.

Petitions

Community School Board candidates violated petition rules in a variety of ways for a variety of reasons. Our investigation revealed that for whatever reason, candidates largely disregarded the rules, opening the door to forgeries.

- Sister Elizabeth Kelliher, a long time Board member in Community School District 1, broke the law to secure the requisite number of nominating signatures. Kelliher used one set of volunteers to collect nominating signatures on her petitions, then asked others who were not present when the signatures were obtained to falsely swear that they had witnessed them.

- Forged signatures appear on several pages of Kelliher's petitions.

- Kenneth Drummond and Veronica James, candidates in District 12, used school employees to collect signatures and then had others sign as the witness. Drummond and James were indicted by a New York County Grand Jury as a result of their petition scheme and their cases are pending.

- In District 10, candidate Marvin Kamiel obtained and circulated petition pages before the official start of the petition period. Kamiel's wife, Harriet, signed as the subscribing witness for signatures which she did not collect.

- Many signature collectors left the date blank so they could "backdate" petition pages. Others left the candidate's name blank so that the pages could be distributed to fellow candidates in need of nominating signatures.

Residency Fraud

Candidates all too often ignored or circumvented the requirement that they live in the district they seek to serve as school board members. People with minimal, if any, ties to the local school district create sham addresses or otherwise misrepresent their true homes in order to get elected to the school boards. As a result, genuinely concerned parents and community members are denied that opportunity.

- Kenneth Drummond, who was already removed from School Board 12 once before for not living in District 12, still lives in a luxury highrise in Riverdale. In a secretly recorded conversation, he

admitted that he installed a telephone in a South Bronx apartment to convince investigators that he lives there.

- School Board 9 member Benjamin Ramos claimed to live in an apartment within the confines of that District for the purpose of running for the school board. We found substantial evidence indicating that Ramos lives in South Plainfield, New Jersey.

Campaign Advertising

Even campaign advertising was infiltrated by fraud. In one district, when genuine endorsements were not forthcoming, a candidate's supporter brazenly enacted a fraudulent advertising scheme.

- In Community School District 27, it seemed that Candidate Geraldine Chapey was the lucky recipient of endorsements by the Gateway Republican Club and a junior high school parents association. In fact, William Sampol, who was implicated in a 1989 report on corruption in District 27, circulated phony flyers. He signed them as "president emeritus," but he has never been the president of either organization and both groups said they deliberately decided not to endorse any school board candidates this year.

Financial Disclosure

Surprisingly few candidates disclose their finances as is required by law. Leaving the public without this information makes it easier for candidates to pressure school employees to contribute to their campaigns.

- The financial disclosure rules were routinely violated but no one enforced a penalty. More than twenty five percent of the candidates ignored the financial disclosure requirements altogether.

- The CSA Pic 10, a political action committee supporting candidates in District 10, raised over ten thousand dollars, but inaccurately and falsely reported how they spent the money.

Recommendations

The events chronicled in this report make it clear that the present system of electing representatives to the local school boards must be changed dramatically. In addition to systemic recommendations, we have made disciplinary recommendations to the Chancellor and we have referred evidence of criminal activity and conflict of interest to the appropriate adjudicating agencies.

- Proportional voting should be eliminated.

- Votes should be cast on the voting machines used in the general elections.

- The impact and advantages of moving the election to coincide with the general election should be evaluated.

- The Board of Education should immediately begin planning a complete overhaul of the parent voter registration process. The current contradictory mandates of the Education and Election Laws with respect to parent voter certification should be reconciled.

- All decisions made by the Board of Elections regarding candidates for Community School Boards must be made in public and on the record.

- The financial disclosure requirements for Community School Board candidates should be tightened, clarified, and enforced. Candidates who fail to comply should not be sworn in as board members.

- The Board of Education should require more detailed disclosure of residency status from Community School Board candidates.

- The Board of Education should extend "whistleblower" protection to the students of the New York City Public Schools and their parents.

CITY OF NEW YORK
THE SPECIAL COMMISSIONER OF INVESTIGATION
FOR THE NEW YORK CITY SCHOOL DISTRICT

EDWARD F. STANCIK
SPECIAL COMMISSIONER

FROM CHAOS TO CORRUPTION:
AN INVESTIGATION INTO THE 1993
COMMUNITY SCHOOL BOARD ELECTION

By: ROBERT M. BRENNER, Deputy Commissioner
REGINA A. LOUGHRAN, Special Counsel
THOMAS COMISKEY, Supervising Investigator
TRACY KRAMER, Intelligence Analyst

December 1993

This case was primarily investigated by a Task Force under the direction of Supervising Investigator Thomas Comiskey who was assisted by Senior Investigator Thomas Fennell. Senior Investigators James Skennion and Larry Kendricks, and Financial Investigator Penni Rose completed the team. The intake of complaints was handled by Investigator Jacob Deutsch.

At times, the Task Force was assisted by the entire Investigation Division under the supervision of Chief Investigator Ernest Mahone and Deputy Chief Investigators Anthony Jacaruso and Michael Gallaro.

ACKNOWLEDGEMENTS

This office gratefully acknowledges the assistance provided to this investigation by outside agencies and individuals.

Special thanks to James F. Gill, Austin Campriello, and Amyjane Rettew for their guidance and support.

We thank the Office of Mary Jo White, United States Attorney for the Southern District of New York, especially Michele Hirschman, Chief of the Public Corruption Unit and Assistant United States Attorney Susan Brune.

We also thank the Office of Robert M. Morgenthau, District Attorney of New York County, especially Daniel Castleman, Chief of the Investigations Division; Roslyn Mauskopf, Chief of the Frauds Bureau; Assistant District Attorney Sheryl Robinson, and Detective Rosalind Lunetta of the District Attorney's Squad.

We thank the Office of Charles J. Hynes, District Attorney of Kings County, especially Dennis Hawkins, Deputy District Attorney, Chief of the Corruption Investigation Division, and Anne Seely, Deputy Chief of that Division.

We also thank the Office of Robert T. Johnson, District Attorney of Bronx County, especially Stephen Bookin, Chief of the Investigation Division.

The New York City Conflict of Interest Board was particularly helpful and we thank former Executive Director Mark D. Hoffer and Acting Director Jo-Antoinette Frey.

We thank First Deputy Police Commissioner John Pritchard.

While in the course of reporting the results of this investigation we are sometimes critical of the New York City Board of Elections, nevertheless, we are grateful to Administrative Manager Jon Del Giorno for his patience.

Last, but certainly not least, we thank law student interns Sari Granat, Alison Geneen, Jason Fruhschein, and college intern Jennifer Vacchio for their invaluable assistance in this investigation.

From Chaos To Corruption:
An Investigation Into The 1993 Community School Board Election

The Election Process: A Recipe for Disaster

If the purpose of the decentralization of the New York City Schools is to empower local communities and encourage parental involvement in the education of their children, then the manner by which the decentralized Boards elect their representatives is a recipe for disaster.[1] The Community School Board election process, complete with paper ballots and proportional representation, is archaic and easily manipulated even when everyone plays by the rules. However, as our investigation reveals, the situation is aggravated every step of the way by practices which defy oversight and diffuse responsibility for enforcement. In the current system, rules are ignored with impunity and the fear of penalty for one's transgression is virtually nonexistent.

The result is an election that is too often the captive of a select group of political insiders who know when and where the rules can be used or abused for their benefit. At the same time, parents and teachers in the classroom, the intended beneficiaries of decentralization, are discouraged, disenfranchised, and often outright coerced. Deals to determine who should count the votes or remain on the ballot are shrouded in secrecy while ordinary voters are forced to vote in open-air "booths" and teachers are forced to publicly pledge and demonstrate their allegiance to candidates holding power. In this atmosphere, the appearance of impropriety is inevitable and destructive even where corruption does not exist. Well-meaning parents and teachers either leave the system or, in the words of one candidate, "do what they have to do to survive."

Over the course of our ten month investigation, we received scores of complaints from virtually every district in the city. This report includes only the most illustrative examples of the failed electoral process. Many other complaints have been and continue to be investigated and may be the subject of future reports or will be referred to the appropriate adjudicating agencies. However, what is clear is that the problems are not isolated or divorced from the educational process. They directly impact on the teachers' ability to teach and on the students' ability to learn throughout this city.

ADMINISTRATION OF THE ELECTION

On May 4, 1993, James Skennion, a resident of Stuyvesant Town with no children in the public schools, voted fifteen times as a "parent voter" in District 2. Likewise, Santiago Martinez, a resident of Queens with no children in the schools, voted ten times in Manhattan's District 6.[2] At the same time,

---

[1] When the New York City school system was decentralized in 1970, community school boards were created to govern the City's thirty two local school districts. Each local board, made up of nine elected members of the community, sets policy for the schools in its district and hires the district's school administrators. Each board controls a budget of $60-125 million.

[2] Skennion and Martinez are investigators working for the Special Commissioner. Though between them they "voted" twenty-five times, they did so in such a way that their ballots would not ultimately be counted. In that way, the system could be tested without actually affecting the outcome of any race.

parents of children at **190** schools who registered prior to January 1993 were removed from the rolls without any warning and without any recourse.

Meanwhile, throughout the system, voters acknowledged as duly registered faced other indignities on Election Day. They were forced to vote without even a modicum of privacy. Handed a ballot and shown a seat at a table, voters penciled in their choices with elections officials, or worse, school officials looking over their shoulders. And even then, they were not assured that their vote would count. Sample ballots, designed to look exactly like the real thing, fooled the Board of Elections' own inspectors, leading them to erroneously provide the invalid replicas to voters seeking to actually cast their vote.

Voters overcoming all these obstacles had no assurance that the ballot they cast would actually end up at the proper count site nine days hence. Split election districts, unsealed boxes, and sloppy paperwork, if not outright corruption, led to wayward ballots turning up at count sites bearing no relation to the district where the vote was cast.

Finally, even where voters were able to vote and Board of Elections officials got the ballots to the proper count sites, observers were given ample reason to question whether the final tally truly reflected the will of the people. In one district, the son of a candidate was hired to count votes cast in his father's race. In another, campaign workers for one candidate were hired to count votes in the very race in which they participated. In still another race, a candidate was credited with first choice votes from ballots which did not even include him among any of the voter's preferences.

The explanation for these and other horror stories at the polls lies, in part, with the all but orphaned status of the Community School Board Election within the electoral system. The Community School Board Election is governed by two statutes with conflicting goals and administered by two bureaucracies with different priorities and expertise.

Under the current statutory scheme, the Board of Elections is charged with administering an election whose ground rules are largely set by the school decentralization laws, a statute with which it is unfamiliar. The decentralization laws provide that the Election Law applies except where specifically modified by the Education Law. However, such modifications have changed most everything except the agency ultimately responsible for collecting and counting the ballots. The Education Law calls for proportional voting, paper ballots, and a two-tiered registration process, all procedures foreign to the Elections Board. To make matters worse, the Board of Elections must rely on the Board of Education to perform crucial tasks such as the registration and certification of parent voters, and chooses to contract out the actual counting of the ballots to a private entity wholly unaccountable to the public.

Though this scheme has been in place since the inception of decentralization, the two city agencies and the private entity most often chosen to complete the process have yet to devise a way to properly coordinate their activities so that voters are registered and paper ballots are properly collected and counted. It is clear that the Board of Elections treats the Community School Board vote as a recurring nuisance it must deal with but need not master, while the Board of Education, for its part, points its finger at election officials as the source of its recurring nightmare.

PARENT VOTER REGISTRATION

Nowhere is the lack of coordination between the Board of Education and Board of Elections more clearly revealed than in the process of registering parent voters. Under the Education Law, all registered voters and all parents of children enrolled in schools under the jurisdiction of the Community School Boards are eligible to vote.[3] However, parents not otherwise registered to vote must register as parents and be certified as such by the Board of Education in order to be allowed to cast a ballot.[4] Thus, the statute mandates that the Board of Elections and Board of Education work together to produce an overall list of eligible voters from a pool of registered voters and parents. However, despite the legislative directive, effective coordination continues to elude the Boards with disastrous results.

A History of Problems

Producing a list such as the legislature requires would seem to be a simple task. However, even the first step, identifying eligible parents, has been historically problematic for the Board of Education. Prior to 1989, the Board left the responsibility for registration and certification up to the individual principals. Under that system, the principals were responsible for confirming that each person who claimed to be a parent voter did indeed have a child enrolled in the school. They sent a list of the voters they deemed valid to the Board of Elections, who then entered the names onto the voter rolls. That system was a failure because some principals proved incapable or unwilling to register and certify parents who were in fact eligible. Moreover, many parents believed that principals were tempted, if not outright motivated, to register and certify only those who would support candidates the principal favored.[5]

Parent Voter Registration: Vintage 1989

In 1989, at the insistence of the Board of Elections, the Board of Education divested the principals of their certifying authority. Instead, the Board of Elections sent to the Board of Education lists of approximately 50,000 people who were registering as parent voters for the 1989 election or who had registered for prior elections. Incredibly, the coordinators of the registration effort did not realize until receiving the 50,000 names that they could not verify whether the people on the list were eligible parent voters. The lists the Board of Elections sent did not contain sufficient biographical information about the registrants to do the necessary cross-checking with the Board of Education's central files.

Lawrence Becker, Counsel to the Chancellor, recognized that the Board would be held responsible if a list of eligible voters was not forwarded to the Board of Elections. However, the Board of Education's operations staff made clear that verifying parent eligibility through field checks would be a practical

---

[3] The New York City High Schools are administered by a division of the central Board. Therefore, parents of students in high school are not eligible to vote as parents but may vote if validly registered for the general elections.
[4] See Education Law, Section 2590
[5] In fact, we have reported that at least in District 12, community school board members appoint principals who can "deliver the vote." Principals are expected to register parents who will vote for the board members who helped secure the principals' appointments (*Power, Politics, and Patronage: Education in Community School District 12*, April 1993, page 11).

impossibility. Thus, Becker directed Doreen DeMartini, the coordinator of the registration effort, to merely declare all the names on the list "certified" without attempting any verification.

Thus, in 1989, all those who sent in registration forms, regardless of their status as parents, were allowed to vote. Moreover, they could vote as many times, under as many different names, as they wished. Just such a scenario was demonstrated by an investigator from the Gill Commission who "voted" thirty three times despite having no children in the schools.[6]

Trying to Get it Right

In preparation for this election, the Board of Education and Board of Elections did attempt to learn from their mistakes. Once again, however, the efforts of the two agencies fell short and produced disastrous results. Parents at over 190 schools, all of whom had previously registered, were disenfranchised while large numbers of new registrants whose status as parents had yet to be verified were entered onto the rolls and allowed to vote. Still other parents were misinformed, misdirected, or otherwise discouraged from casting their ballot.

How did the system break down yet again? In searching for the answer, this office received conflicting testimony from representatives of both agencies. The fingerpointing itself was indicative of the lack of cooperation and communication that has plagued this process from the beginning. Nevertheless, certain truths emerged.

Repeating Old Mistakes

In preparing for the election, the first issue that the two agencies had to resolve was how to treat those 50,000 parents who became voters without any verification. Both agencies agreed that those parents could not remain on the rolls without verification this time. Not only was there the possibility that many of those on the list were ineligible to begin with, but those who were determined valid in 1989 may well have lost their eligibility in the ensuing four years. However, the same problem that the Board of Education faced in 1989, namely the incompatibility of the Board of Elections data and the Board of Education's central filing system, remained. The Board of Elections had obtained significant information about the voter, as it did in its regular registration process, but little about the prospective voter's child. On the other hand, the school system's data base is organized according to its primary clients, the children. Thus, the Board of Education had two options: require all those who wished to vote as parents to register anew or develop some way to verify parental status at the local level. The Board chose the latter option.

Once again, the fate of prospective parent voters was left to the individual principals. In January, the central Board of Education began sending print-outs to each principal containing the names of all individuals who claimed to have a child in the principal's school. The principal was required to perform a simple task, merely to check "Yes" or "No" next to the parent's name, indicating whether the parent

---

[6] The Gill Commission, formally known as "The Joint Commission on Integrity in the Public Schools," had an investigator cast ballots in two districts in Manhattan. In order not to influence the vote, the investigator intentionally voted in a manner that invalidated the ballot.

had a particular child in the school, and then send the list to the Board of Education, who forwarded it to the Board of Elections. According to the plan, the Board of Elections would only reenter onto the rolls those whom the principal "certified" with a "Yes." Those who received "No" classifications or whose child happened to attend a school where the principal did not respond would not be reentered.

This plan totally ignored the lessons the Board of Education had presumably learned in past elections. Once again, nothing prevented the principals from playing favorites with their certifications. In fact, the central Board of Education did little to ensure that the principals participated at all. The result was predictable and alarming. As of Election Day in May, 190 principals had failed to fill out the forms and return them to the Board of Elections. Since no action at the local level meant decertification by the Board of Elections, any parent of a child at one of those 190 schools who had registered prior to 1993 was doomed to be turned away at the polls. According to Jon Del Giorno, the administrative manager at the Board of Elections, he repeatedly voiced his concerns about the lack of response from principals to Doreen DeMartini, from the Office of Monitoring and School Improvement. However, the Board of Education's efforts to compel compliance after being alerted to the problem were half-hearted at best. DeMartini made follow-up telephone calls to the principals but made no other effort to induce compliance. Moreover, no disciplinary measures were imposed or even considered against those who ignored the directive entirely. Finally, neither Doreen DeMartini nor Jon Del Giorno notified those in danger of being disenfranchised by the principal's failure to act. If either one had done so, those parents in danger of being knocked off the list may have been able to reregister in time.

Trying Something New

Though the Board of Education reverted to its old ways in handling the old registrants, it did develop a new form and a new certification process for those registering in 1993. Unfortunately, in the implementation, time pressures and a total lack of coordination with the Board of Elections doomed this process as they had those that came before it.

This new system did have significant advantages over the old one. Most importantly, it allowed for a centralized certification process. This time, Doreen DeMartini and the Board of Education's Director of Data Services, Wayne Trigg, made sure that the Parent Voter Registration Form prepared by the Board of Elections required the parent to include sufficient biographical information about the child to allow data entry staff at 110 Livingston Street to cross-check against the Board's central files. Further, Trigg developed a system where at least some of the registration forms were pre-labeled with the student's name and a code identifying his or her parent or guardian. In this way, those involved in the certification process could quickly compare the information filled out by the registrant with the data maintained at Board Headquarters.

Finally, the two agencies agreed to a two-step process requiring each agency to perform only those tasks within its own area of expertise. The forms were sent directly to 110 Livingston Street, where the Board of Education would use its central files to verify the registrant's parental status. Then, and only then, the verified forms would be forwarded to the Board of Elections for entry on their eligible voter rolls. This approach would allow Wayne Trigg's group to utilize its extensive data on students and its knowledge of

the various programs and special schools in the community school system as a whole to resolve minor discrepancies in the forms that might otherwise lead to disqualification.[7] At the same time, the Board of Elections could limit its operation to its traditional methods of compiling voter lists and buff cards.

Despite the good intentions in the general planning stages, problems arose in implementation. As a first step in the process, DeMartini and Trigg compiled a list of the 700,000 students enrolled in schools under the jurisdiction of the thirty two Community School Boards. From that list, they created a label with each child's name on it and affixed the label to a blue Parent Voter Registration Form. DeMartini then arranged for the forms to be sent to the districts, where superintendents were to distribute them to principals who were to distribute them to students who were expected to bring them home.

Even a casual observer of the history of certification must be struck by the inherent problems in this system. The first obvious flaw was the allocation of only one pre-labeled and coded form per student. Providing forms for each parent in a given household would have served two purposes: it would have encouraged the participation of all parents and enhanced the Board of Education's ability to quickly certify applicants. Providing only one form meant that the traditional two parent household was left to fend for itself and obtain a second, unlabeled form, which could not as easily be cross-checked at 110 Livingston Street. However, despite the obvious logic of such an approach, DeMartini and Trigg made no attempt to utilize their central data base to determine which students lived with one parent and which lived with two.

Next, this plan reintroduced the principals as essential cogs in the distribution process. Incredibly, DeMartini brought the principals back into the system without providing enhanced supervision of their activities. In testimony before this office, she was asked:

Q: Were principals given a date by which they should have the forms distributed?
A: No. They were just told to do it...
Q: Does the principal have to notify either the superintendent's office or your office that they have complied with their obligation?
A: No. They were not asked to do that.

Furthermore, her explanation for not bypassing the principals and mailing registration forms directly to parents was altogether unconvincing:

> One [reason] is cost. Because then we would be paying to mail them plus paying for the return mail on them and then we had considered the possibility at one point and attempted to look at a design and it was a very cumbersome design and we felt it would be very difficult to put instructions in multiple languages. . . . Perhaps it could be done.

Given the principals' track record with respect to parent voters and the central Board of Education's cavalier attitude towards compliance, it is not surprising that this office received numerous complaints from parents who did not receive forms of any kind until after the registration deadline. For example, in District 2, parents at PS 6 did not receive forms until well past the deadline. Dr. Richard Gold and his wife,

---

[7] For example, problems arose when the Board of Elections failed to realize that more than one school could have the same number or name in different boroughs.

registered voters in District 3, wished to vote in District 2 where their son attends PS 6. However, they did not receive any forms until April 15, almost a week after the April 9 deadline. As a result, the Golds did not vote. Likewise, Shana Zaflow, another resident of District 3 who preferred to vote in District 2 as a parent, received nothing from her child's school until a week after the deadline. Thus she had to vote in District 3, where she was a registered voter. These were not isolated incidents. Rather, they reflect but one principal's failure to carry out even the most basic administrative tasks associated with the election. Indeed, Carmen Fariña, the Principal at PS 6 admitted that through an administrative error, she failed to send the forms out on time. According to her, the forms arrived at her school without "a dated material warning." Thus, she had no idea that it had to be opened immediately. As a result, the package intended for immediate distribution languished in the mailroom. If this situation could occur at PS 6, a school that parents aspire to send their children to, one wonders how often the scenario was repeated city-wide in schools receiving less attention.[8]

In April, the Mayor directed that the City expend substantial extra funds to publicize the upcoming election and encourage parent voter participation. Perhaps the Board of Education should have taken advantage of available funds to ensure that the most useful registration forms reached parents at the appropriate time.

Changing Plans on the Run

To make matters worse, the logical division of labor that the Board of Education and Board of Elections had arrived at in January broke down in April. The system whereby Wayne Trigg's unit reviewed all registration forms and sent only the valid ones on to the Board of Elections for inclusion on their rolls was scrapped at the insistence of election officials.[9] By the beginning of April, Daniel DeFrancesco, Executive Director of the Board of Elections and Jon Del Giorno, the Administrative Manager, were concerned that their staff would not have time to enter all the new registrants onto their rolls if they waited for the Board of Education to pre-certify them. Their concern was fueled by the Board of Education's failure to comply with the statutory timetable for providing a list of certified voters. Thus, they insisted that DeMartini and Trigg send all the forms to them prior to performing any checks.[10]

---

[8] The Board of Education labeled approximately 700,000 Parent Voter Registration Forms and distributed them to the Districts. However, by April 5, only 22,313 had been returned for verification.

[9] Board of Elections and Board of Education officials gave sharply conflicting testimony with respect to whether the change in procedure had been planned all along. Doreen DeMartini testified that on April 5, she was told by Daniel DeFrancesco, Executive Director of the Board of Elections, that contrary to original plans, his agency needed to immediately receive all the registration forms in order to prepare their rolls in time. Wayne Trigg, also from 110 Livingston Street, corroborated DeMartini's version. However, Jon Del Giorno claimed that the change should have come as no surprise to DeMartini. He insisted that "she knew how the system was going to be designed because that was our whole discussion between my staff and her…my staff said there would come a point where we had to cut off them doing the precertification and we would take over that role." However, Lonnie Ranghelli, the head of Del Giorno's Data Entry Unit, had yet a third version of events. According to Ranghelli, the Board of Education deviated from the original plan from the beginning and without any request from him. He claimed that even "the first couple of batches of forms [he] got were not certified." Whatever the actual original understanding was, there can be no dispute that the Education Law required the Board of Education to provide a list of "certified voters" by April 4, something they were unable to accomplish.

[10] DeFrancesco and Del Giorno's concerns regarding the timely receipt of certified parent voter registration forms turned out to be well-founded. Despite their request that the Board of Education immediately send them all forms, the Board of Education held onto scores of forms until well after the Election. To this day, according to Kathy King, counsel to the Board of Elections, the Board of Education continues to forward uncertified forms.

Under this new plan, the Board of Elections could not avoid injecting itself into the certification process. In doing so, the whole system became more cumbersome and more prone to error. First, the Board of Education had to send those forms it received to the Board of Elections. Elections personnel then logged in all the forms including those not yet verified. Then, they sent a list of the newly logged in names back to the Board of Education for certification. Once there, Wayne Trigg and his staff attempted to match registrant to student. When and if that was accomplished, a new list was produced and delivered to the Board of Elections. Finally, Board of Elections officials who had previously logged all applicants onto their database had to weed out those who remained uncertified before creating the rolls that would be sent to the polling places.

In this manner, what began as a two-step process, with the Board of Education certifying and the Board of Elections registering, became a relay race with each agency passing lists of prospective voters back and forth before either could accomplish their goals.[11] And as with any relay, each time the handoff occurred the likelihood that one agency would fumble it increased substantially.

The System Breaks Down Again

And fumble it they did. In the most significant miscue, Board of Elections clerks in the Manhattan Borough Office were apparently not made aware of the change in procedure. They continued entering the blue parent voter cards in the official voter books after April 5, as if the Board of Education was still "pre-certifying" them. Moreover, when the Board of Education did send subsequent lists of valid parent voters, the election clerks did nothing to weed out those cards already entered without the Board of Education's stamp of approval.

Thus, at least in Manhattan, history repeated itself. While, this time, the Board of Education did not merely "deem" all applicants "certified," the clerical error made at the Manhattan Board of Elections had the same effect. Our experience suggests that anyone who sent in a card could vote. Indeed, a person could vote as many times as he or she applied. Though no one at either agency has admitted to this faux pas, its occurrence was graphically confirmed on Election Day by investigators from this office.

James Skennion and Santiago Martinez, neither of whom are parents of students in the New York City Public Schools, submitted numerous Parent Voter Registration Forms using fictitious parents and students names. None of the cards they submitted were "certified" by the Board of Education.[12] Yet, on Election Day, those same cards were in the parent voter registration books at every location they visited. With their registration cards in place, Skennion and Martinez "voted" twenty-five times between them.

---

[11] The Board of Education was required by Education Law Section 2590 to provide the Board of Elections with a list of certified voters by April 4. However, meeting that deadline was impossible since under the election laws voters, including parent voters, could register up until April 9. Thus, the Board of Education was rushing to certify all valid applicants right up until Election Day and beyond. The Board of Elections, for its part, was racing to complete their voter rolls before they were due at the poll sites.

[12] On May 7, 1993, Doreen DeMartini delivered to this office the final list of "certified" parent voters. She indicated that she was delivering an identical list to the Board of Elections. None of Skennion and Martinez's fictitious names appeared on that list or on the earlier lists that had been provided by the Board of Education.

Our investigators were not the only ones affected by what became a de facto open-door policy in Manhattan. The spouse of an employee of this office submitted a Parent Voter Registration Form in order to vote where his child was enrolled in District 2. His form was filled out completely and accurately and was submitted to the Board of Education well within the time period for registration. Yet, he did not appear on the Board of Education's certification list. Nevertheless, his card miraculously appeared at the polls on Election Day.

Again, Board of Education and Board of Elections officials were at a loss to explain how the card appeared at the polls. However, there are only a few possible explanations. For the card to end up at the polls, Board of Elections clerks had to enter some cards into the books without even bothering to send the names to 110 Livingston Street. For it to fail the initial certification hurdle, either the Board of Elections clerks failed to include sufficient information when they sent lists to the Board of Education or Board of Education officials failed to review or were unable to certify even those forms containing completely accurate information. Whichever scenario explains what happened, it is clear that the process was in a shambles by Election Day.

Indeed, the variety of ways in which the certification system broke down on Election Day was almost limitless. While certain parent voters in Manhattan were allowed to vote even without certification, others were turned away even after receiving the Board of Education's approval. This office received numerous complaints from Brooklyn residents who sought to vote in the Manhattan district where their children went to school. Despite accurately and promptly applying to vote as parents and being so certified by the Board of Education, many were denied their right to do so. Time and time again, Board of Elections clerks sorted the registration forms according to the parent's home address rather than the child's school. Thus, even after being certified, some parents were not recognized as parents in the very schools that their children attended. They were free to vote as parents in boroughs where they had no children in school, but were denied the same right in the districts where they had a vested interest.

Finally, in the most absurd example of certification run amok, former Chancellor Anthony Alvarado, now Superintendent of District 2, found his certified parent voter card in Brooklyn, where he lives, but his name was nowhere to be found in District 2, where his children go to school and where he is the chief administrator.[13]

The problems with the 1993 parent voter registration and certification effort cannot be understated. Thousands of parents never received registration forms. Thousands more who registered prior to 1990 were disenfranchised without warning. Still others were not "certified" despite meeting all the requirements and following all the rules. At the same time, others lacking any standing to vote were given free reign to cast ballots as often as time and stamina allowed. Yet, Board of Education officials claim that this year, the effort ran more smoothly than the last.[14] If that is the case, the rate of improvement is far from satisfactory. Before the 1996 election, nothing short of a complete overhaul of the process is in order.

---

[13] Alvarado ultimately was able to vote in District 2 because, before the election, Deputy Superintendent Andrew Lachman discovered that Alvarado's card was in Brooklyn. Lachman convinced the Board of Elections to transfer Alvarado's parent voter card to Manhattan where it belonged.

[14] Both Doreen DeMartini and Wayne Trigg claimed that the certification process went more smoothly in 1993 than in 1989.

ELECTION DAY

The chaos, confusion and mismanagement that characterized the administration of the parent voter registration process was inevitably felt on May 4. This office received dozens of allegations of election day improprieties, ranging from Board of Elections poll site inspectors directing people to vote for specific candidates to a candidate rifling through ballot boxes. Just as disturbing as the individual illicit acts, though, is the picture that emerges of the day itself. The complaints reflect, and our undercover investigators confirmed, that May 4th was a day of rampant chaos when ballot boxes were unsealed and sometimes open; ballots, roll books, and even inspectors showed up at the polls hours late; voters were forced to cast their votes without a modicum of privacy; candidates openly campaigned at the polls; and voters were shuttled to and from different poll sites as time and time again, their voter registration cards did not appear in the proper roll books. The confusion was so pervasive that one undercover investigator voted twice at the very same poll site, each time before the eyes of the same inspector. On May 4th, voters were faced with a daunting obstacle course, and only those with the most persistence, endurance, or luck succeeded in casting a ballot that, in the end, was counted.

The Election Day experience of Investigator Santiago Martinez exemplifies the chaos and confusion that characterized Election Day. A Queens resident, Martinez has no children attending New York City schools. Yet he voted ten times in the 1993 Community School Board elections. Martinez used fictitious names to register multiple times as a parent voter. Each time he voted, Martinez encountered an incident that mirrored the complaints we received and typified the problems that occurred on Election Day.

Two Pools of Voters

The Board of Elections demonstrated its inability to efficiently manage the two pools of eligible voters: duly registered voters and those who registered as parent voters. Some people who registered as parent voters -- such as PS 130 Principal Lily Woo -- were either disenfranchised or forced to vote by affidavit ballot[15] because their parent voter cards were sent to the district in which they live, rather than to the district in which their children attend school. Even in those cases in which registration went smoothly and the cards were sent to the proper places, other voters were disenfranchised or, at best, forced to vote by affidavit ballot, because of obstacles they faced at the local level. At the Community School Board Election in Manhattan and Queens this year, each poll site should have had a book containing a buff-colored registration card for each duly registered voter and a book of blue cards for parent voters.[16] Despite this clear distinction between the two pools of voters, poll site inspectors -- often accustomed to working at a general election -- assumed that all voters were duly registered citizen voters, or "buff card voters." For instance, when Claudette Bryant, who registered through the Board of Education as a parent voter in District 11, went to vote at her child's school, the inspector asked for her name, then searched for her buff card. Bryant does not have a buff card, of course, because she is not registered to vote in the

---

[15] Voting by affidavit ballot increases the chances that the voter will be disenfranchised, because the affidavit ballots can be challenged and because there is a complex form to fill out which can, especially for voters with limited English proficiency, be difficult. If the form is filled out wrong, the ballot is invalidated.

[16] In the other boroughs, the voter registration books were replaced by computer generated lists.

general election. Upon not seeing her card, the inspector asked Bryant her address. When he heard that she lived in another part of town, he informed her that she was at the wrong poll site. Uncertain of where to go, Bryant did not vote.

Denise Charles, another parent voter, was more persistent, and thus in the end she succeeded in casting a ballot. Having registered as a parent voter in District 29, Charles went to PS 156, where her child attends school. The inspector did not find a buff card for Charles, and told her that she was not registered to vote there. Confident that she was in the right place, Charles went home to get the parent voter confirmation card she had received from the Board of Elections. Only when she came back to the school with the card did the inspector realize that Charles was a parent voter, whose name should appear in the book of blue cards, not the book of buff cards.

Investigator Martinez was also prevented from voting by misinformed inspectors who guided him off course. When Martinez went to vote at PS 145 as "George Greene," the inspector asked him his address. When he heard that "Mr. Greene" did not live in the area, he told him that he was in the wrong place. Like the inspectors whom our complainants encountered, the inspector at PS 145 turned "Mr. Greene" away without considering the possibility that he was a parent voter.

Similarly, Investigator Martinez had registered to vote at PS 152 as a parent voter named "Vicente Quintana." When he arrived at the school on Election Day, he told the inspector that he has never been a registered voter, and that to register for the Community School Board Election, he filled out a blue card. Despite these clues that "Mr. Quintana" had registered as a parent voter, the inspector nevertheless looked for "Quintana" in the book of buff cards. Having already voted eight times that day, Martinez knew to persist. He told the inspector that he would not have a buff card because he was a parent voter, not a duly registered voter. When the inspector found "Quintana" in the book of parent voters, she exclaimed, "I got another live one, thank God!" How ironic that Vicente Quintana was not "a live one" at all, but a fictional name made up by our investigator. Unfortunately, many parents did not clear the hurdle that arose because Board of Elections employees failed to distinguish between buff card voters and blue card voters.

Split Districts

The poor training of the inspectors extended beyond their failure to comprehend the basic structure of the Community School Board Election: voters either voted as parent voters or as duly registered voters. Parents who voted at poll sites that served as voting places for two community school districts -- known as "split district sites" -- were not even assured that they would be given the proper ballot. Thomas Edison High School in Queens served as a poll site for Districts 28 and 29. But at 8:30 a.m., when James Kennedy, a registered voter in District 29, went to vote, only District 28 ballots were available. The inspector gave Mr. Kennedy a District 28 ballot and told him to write the names of his choice District 29 candidates on the bottom of the ballot. The inspector then put Mr. Kennedy's ballot in the District 28 ballot box, practically ensuring that his vote would not be counted.

When Mr. Kennedy's son Chris went to vote about 45 minutes later, he was given the same instructions. But Chris Kennedy, understandably afraid that his vote would not count if he used a District 28 ballot, preferred to wait to cast his vote until the District 29 ballots arrived. He was finally able to vote

at 10 a.m., four hours after the poll site was scheduled to open. Concerned as well that his father's vote would not be counted, Chris Kennedy complained to the director that his father had voted for District 29 candidates, but that his ballot had been placed in the District 28 box. The director told Kennedy not to worry. He had opened the ballot box and shuffled through the ballots to find the ones that did not belong there. He assured the concerned Kennedy that he took those ballots out and put them in the District 29 box. As we discuss elsewhere, the regulation that boxes be sealed was routinely ignored citywide.

When the District 29 ballots finally arrived at Thomas Edison High, confusion persisted. Cynthia Clandenine, a registered voter in District 29, was given a District 28 ballot because, the elections worker explained, "your last name begins with C." For reasons known only to them, the inspectors gave District 28 ballots to those voters whose last names begin with the letters A through L, and District 29 ballots to those whose last names begin with the letters M through Z. When Ms. Clandenine arrived at the polls, she complained to the site coordinator, who finally explained to the inspectors what they were doing wrong.

What happened at Thomas Edison was representative of the disorganization that prevailed at split district sites throughout the City. At PS 130, a split district site for Districts 25 and 26, only District 26 ballots were available. The coordinator notified the Board of Elections at 6 a.m. that District 25 voters would not be able to vote, but by 1 p.m. she still had not received the District 25 ballots. At August Martin High School in Queens -- another split district site for Districts 28 and 29 -- the coordinator did not provide District 28 ballots until 9:30 a.m., when a *voter* found them, unopened, in a corner of the gymnasium. The coordinator of that poll site admitted that she did not know that her site was a split district site until late in the morning. "I don't think they elaborated sufficiently on the split district aspect of the election," she said of the training provided for poll site inspectors.

Late Arrivals

Even voters who were not at split district sites were prevented from voting because ballots, roll books, and other crucial materials arrived at the poll sites late. Ballots did not arrive until 11 a.m at PS 36 in Manhattan. At a Brooklyn poll site, the parent voter book did not arrive until 9 a.m., three hours after the polls were scheduled to open. At a District 24 site in Queens, the key to the voter registration books was not located until a half hour into the morning. And on Staten Island, two inspectors did not show up at PS 8 until 9 a.m. When they finally arrived, they found the register books and ballots on the floor behind the table. Voters who came to vote before 9 a.m. had to find their way to another voting table and vote by affidavit ballot.

No Controls On Voting Twice, or Three Times, or...

While obstacle after obstacle blocked legitimately registered parent voters, cheaters were not pulled out of the race. To vote at PS 192, Investigator Martinez used the name "Alejandro Brito," and claimed that his child attended the school. Despite the Board of Education's elaborate system for rooting out such fraud, "Mr. Brito's" parent voter card arrived at PS 192 on Election Day. Even if the Board of Education had successfully completed its certification process and disposed of the fraudulent card, an imposter like "Mr. Brito" still could have cast a ballot. At the poll site, the inspectors simply asked "Mr. Brito" his

name and had him fill out a ballot and stuff it in the box. The inspector did not even confirm that "Mr. Brito" had a blue card, let alone require him to sign it. We will never know how many people walked in off the street, claimed to be parent voters, and voted at that poll site.

Opened Boxes

The official rules of the Community School Board Election specify that all ballot boxes should be sealed shut until the ballot count begins.[17] This crucial rule safeguards against fraud and errors that could affect the election's outcome. But we found that sealed boxes were the exception, not the rule, on Election Day.

The inspector at Thomas Edison High School who moved James Kennedy's ballot from one box to another was only one of many people who reached into the ballot boxes and accessed the ballots. At PS 165 in Manhattan, one of our investigators, working undercover as an inspector, witnessed a Board of Elections official remove the lid from a ballot box and rifle through the ballots. And Lorraine Lurie, an inspector at PS 44 in Manhattan, told us that whenever an inspector realized that a ballot had been placed in the wrong box, he or she simply opened the box, removed the ballot, and placed it in the correct box. When the polls closed, the PS 44 inspectors opened the boxes and proceeded to count the ballots.[18]

The complaints we received parallel our investigators' experiences. Ballot boxes were unsealed at most of the polling sites where our undercover investigators voted. Investigator James Skennion, who voted 15 times, encountered unsealed boxes at several locations. When he asked an inspector at PS 33 in District 2 why the boxes were unsealed, she replied that she and her coworkers did not tape the box because they were "lazy." She assured Skennion that he need not worry; the inspectors would see to it that no one tampered with the boxes. Later in the day at PS 158, as Skennion went to vote for the eleventh time, he noted yet another unsealed box. He casually lifted the lid off the ballot box and placed his ballot in the box. The inspector just laughed.[19]

Local Rules

Throughout the day, "local rules" governed the election because misinformed inspectors were not aware of the official rules. For example, in addition to the names on the ballot, a voter may vote for an unlimited number of "write-in" candidates by writing the candidates' names on the bottom of the ballot. However, this information was news to many inspectors. One voter complained to this office that the inspector told her she could only vote for three people. Investigator Martinez got first-hand experience of this confusion. An inspector at PS 189 told Martinez -- this time voting as "Frank Ocacio" -- that he could vote for only ten candidates. And at PS 52, an inspector told Martinez (a.k.a "Albert Feliciano")

---

[17] *The Election Officers' School Board Manual, Training Edition*, p.4. See also Election Law section 8-102.
[18] At the end of the day, inspectors are required to record the number of ballots cast in each box. To figure out how many ballots were cast, the inspector is supposed to check the number of the next ballot that was available for use. This is supposed to obviate the need to open the box and count the ballots.
[19] Both Investigators Skennion and Martinez wore concealed recording devices when voting. In addition, for much of the day, they were followed by another investigator carrying a concealed video camera.

that he must limit his choices to nine. One District 13 voter complained that the inspectors instructed him to put an "X" next to his candidates of choice, an error that would invalidate his ballot.

Another rule that was at the mercy of local employees was that regarding sample ballots. Except for a slight difference in color, the sample ballots for the Community School Board Election were identical to the official ballots. In fact, even the sample ballots read "Official Ballot for Community School Board Members." Nowhere were they marked "Sample Ballot." Not surprisingly, many of these ballots ended up marked, in the boxes. In one district in Chinatown, sample ballots ended up in the ballot box. The Board of Elections realized that for a good portion of the day, the inspectors were giving out the cream-colored sample ballots, rather than the official white ballots. So as not to disenfranchise voters, the Board of Elections decided to count the sample ballots from that election district.

Other makeshift rules at certain poll sites did nothing to infuse the election with a sense of uniformity, professionalism, or integrity. According to New York State Election Law, voters are permitted to mark their paper ballots with pen or pencil. Given the fact that a large number of boxes were left unsealed, many voters who were provided with pencils were understandably wary that their ballots would be erased and renumbered. To add to the confusion, many inspectors and police officers on duty did not know if voters were supposed to use pen or pencil.

The voting procedure varied from district to district. The official Inspector's Handbook clearly states that the voter should hand his or her ballot to the inspector, who should place the ballot in the ballot box. Yet, our undercover investigators were sometimes told to place the ballot in the box and sometimes told to hand the ballot to the inspector. The lack of uniformity increased the appearance of, if not actual, impropriety. Voters reported that they felt the election was shoddily run and that they doubted the integrity of the process.

Voting in Public

Even if the Board of Elections inspectors guided voters to a successful finish with correct information, the voters were forced to exercise their franchise in public. The "voting booth" provided for privacy was, at best, a cardboard divider. At worst, it was a bench with three other people huddled next to the voter. While Investigator Skennion voted at PS 158, another investigator walked up behind him -- uninterrupted -- and took a photograph of Skennion marking his ballot.

Bad Training

Poll site inspectors were clearly unaccustomed to working at an election with paper ballots, proportional representation, and two pools of eligible voters. They were misinformed about many rules, from small but significant details like whether one should vote in pen or pencil, to elements crucial to the election's integrity, such as how many candidates a voter can vote for and how and when to count the ballots.

Some of this confusion no doubt resulted from the fact that inspectors are expected, but not required, to attend a training class to prepare for the Community School Board Election. Those who do not attend are still permitted to work. Not surprisingly, about 25% of the poll workers who worked on Election Day did not attend a training session. Even those who do attend the training session are not likely to retain

everything they need to know to be efficient workers. "Many inspectors forget the procedures or the biggest problem is many inspectors don't show up to training. And an untrained poll worker will make mistakes...," Jon Del Giorno said.

Electioneering at the Polls

The chaotic atmosphere at the polls was not solely the product of incompetent inspectors. Candidates and their supporters played their role in the circus-like elections, campaigning in the polling places, approaching voters to "suggest" candidates, and even using schoolchildren to electioneer for them.

Throughout the day, people electioneered at the poll sites, an activity that violates both the New York State Election Law and the Chancellor's Regulations. One poll site inspector watched a District 7 candidate approach voters as they were voting at the Gilbert Ramirez Senior Citizens Home and repeat her slogan, "Carmen Arroyo #1." She even leaned over the shoulder of one voter and pointed to her name on the ballot. When voter Robert Weiner went to vote at PS 105 in District 11, a woman offered him an "approved" list of candidates.

Candidates and their supporters took advantage of the chaotic atmosphere by trying to pass themselves off as Elections officials. In District 32, supporters of candidate Tito Velez set up a table outside the school to look like an official elections table. They posted official Board of Elections signs that read "Vote Aquí," and juxtaposed them with posters proclaiming Tito Velez as the number one choice. In District 24 in Queens, supporters of candidate Daek Lee Pak accompanied Korean voters into the polls and walked them through the voting process, translating for them as they went along. At PS 52, Investigator Martinez went through the entire voting process without interacting with an inspector. A woman with no Board of Elections identification handed him a ballot and explained to him how to vote. She took the opportunity to include some extra advice. "Well, we as parents of this school we are supporting Mrs. Jackson," she said. She also suggested that Candidate Lisando would be a good choice. She then instructed Martinez to place his ballot in the box.

When he voted at PS 189, a woman who identified herself as a PTA member approached Investigator Martinez, who was posing as "Frank Ocacio." Enjoying free access to the polling area, the PTA mother went right up to him as he was marking his ballot and offered her assistance. She showed him a list of candidates on a yellow piece of paper and advised, "These ten here, from the yellow one, it's a very good decision." The woman's words of wisdom to our undercover investigator at PS 189 capture the essence of the Community School Board Election. "Be careful with your vote, because that vote is worth a lot of money," she warned him. "Look, power and everything. So then, be very careful."

In District 21, an undercover investigator observed as the Education Slate's attorney, Robert Muir, injected himself into the process. As a voter was about to cast her ballot, Muir purposefully created a commotion, complaining loudly that the inspectors were favoring certain candidates. When the argument that ensued diverted everyone's attention, Muir took the opportunity to tell the voter for whom to vote.

Even Board of Elections officials offered their advice as to who were the best candidates. As Investigator Martinez voted at PS 192, a poll site inspector directed him to "vote for the Hispanics, my

son." Given this active campaigning on the part of Board of Elections inspectors, it is easy to imagine how voters had so little confidence in the integrity of the election. What voter wouldn't hesitate to hand a paper ballot to an inspector who actively supported certain candidates?

The examples we cite in this report are not the isolated mishaps of an otherwise orderly day. Rather, these stories illustrate the patterns of confusion and ineptitude that characterized Election Day. The complaints we received from voters, inspectors, candidates, and other involved parties indicate that the same problems were repeated again and again throughout the City. Perhaps the election is best seen through the eyes of Elliot Miller, a new Staten Island resident who voted this year for the first time in the New York City Community School Board Election. "I was appalled by what I saw," Miller said, noting the absurd lack of privacy and the fact that he was given a pencil to mark his ballot. "Where is the integrity of the election here?"

COUNTING THE BALLOTS

When the last School Board Election was completed in 1989, observers reported irregularities in the counting of the ballots. Specifically, investigators and journalists noted that ballots had disappeared, ballot boxes seemed to have been tampered with, and ballot counters appeared incompetent at best and, at worst, under the influence of drugs or alcohol.

Dissatisfaction with the process led the State Legislature to consider several bills that would have radically altered the present system. In fact, to allow time to accomplish that task, the election was moved from 1992 to 1993. However, no reform legislation passed. Thus, it was up to the Board of Elections to work within the existing framework to come up with a more professional, efficient count for 1993. But, despite the horror stories reported in 1989, the Board of Elections exerted little effort to ensure a more satisfactory result this year. Indeed, as they carried out the task of organizing and overseeing the ballot count, the Board demonstrated an attitude of indifference toward the Community School Board Election.

There was general agreement that some sort of automation should be used to minimize human error in 1993.[20] Nevertheless, the Board waited until December 1992 -- less than six months before the election -- to solicit information about ways to automate the counting of the ballots.[21] Even then, the Board made no real effort to search for organizations with experience in running automated elections. To aggravate matters, the Board distributed a confusing, uninformative contract. In its request for bids, the Board of Elections made no attempt to define what they meant by "automation." The Board even asked potential contractors to provide "computer illiterate employees."[22]

---

[20] According to former Board of Elections Commissioner Alice Sachs, the members of the Board of Elections had agreed that an election utilizing machines would be more efficient and more accurate.
[21] Board of Elections Administrative Manager Jon Del Giorno claims that the Board got such a late start because they expected legislative action.
[22] See Conducting The May 4th Community School Board Election Count By Automation and Proportional Representation, The City of New York Board of Elections Contract, page 9.

Once the Board of Elections awarded the contract, they left responsibility for ensuring the integrity of the count to the winning bidder. However, the company that the Board of Elections hired to run the count, Proportional Count Associates (PCA), exhibited little interest in ensuring that the ballots were counted properly and that fraud, or the appearance thereof, did not taint the process. PCA employed candidates' relatives and friends to count ballots, used untested computer software, shuffled ballots from district to district, and handled key items with the utmost carelessness. The existence of these appalling conditions would cause anyone to question the election's results. Indeed, we found that the problems with the ballot count did not end with the appearance of impropriety. Confirming voters' fears, the one pile of ballots we spot-checked contained votes that were credited to the wrong candidate.

Contracting Out

As it has done every three years since the school system was decentralized, the Board of Elections contracted with an outside firm to count ballots. But, despite public dissatisfaction with the 1989 count, the Board exerted minimal effort to reach out to new firms. In December 1992, Jon Del Giorno, the Board of Elections Administrative Manager, met with the two agencies who had manually counted the ballots in the past, Honest Ballot Association (HBA)[23] and Proportional Count Associates (PCA).[24] Then, after the two meetings, the Board of Elections advertised the contract for only one day -- February 25, 1993 -- in the *City Record*. In fact, neither HBA nor PCA, the only two agencies who showed up at the pre-bid conference the next month, learned of the contract through the advertisement. Rather, they relied on their contacts within the Board to learn of the timetable and requirements.

The Pre-bid Conference

As they went through the motions of recruiting vendors, it became increasingly clear that the Board of Elections was investing minimal time and effort into setting up the 1993 election. The Board exhibited its indifferent and careless attitude at a pre-bid conference in March, when potential bidders presented the Board with their questions about the contract. For starters, a potential bidder who attended the conference pointed out that even the most basic information, such as when the bid was due, was left out of the contract proposal.

Further confusing vendors, the contract called for an "automated" count, but the Board of Elections left the bidders to define that key term. Rather than explain how they wanted the vendor to automate the process, the Board merely passed along a request by people who were concerned that the election be conducted efficiently. "We don't specify the automation, type of programming," Del Giorno told potential bidders, "but we're requesting that it be in an automated fashion, which is a request by the School Board Coalition members." Even when the potential bidders repeatedly attempted to narrow the request so they

---

[23] HBA performed the count in 1986. They had earned the contract in 1986 as the lowest bidder, but their competency was challenged by Archibald Robertson of PCA. After a hearing, HBA retained the contract, however the Board of Elections had sided with Robertson at the hearing. As a result, HBA remains suspicious of the relationship between PCA and the Board of Elections.

[24] PCA performed the count in 1980, 1983 and 1989.

could evaluate whether they were equipped to do the job, the Board declined to specify what they meant by "automation."

Throughout the conference, the Board provided vendors with vague or, equally as frustrating, conflicting information. The lengthy contract specified that the vendor *would not* have to post a performance bond, an expensive requisite that, if required, could turn away a vendor. At the conference, however, Del Giorno -- either not anxious to attract new bidders or just unfamiliar with the contract -- said that the vendor *would* have to pay for the bond. He added that the Board would evaluate requests to waive the bond on an individual basis. Whether the failure to point out the waiver provision was deliberate, negligent or accidental, HBA President Murray Schwartz reported to us that his uncertainty over whether the bond would be waived was instrumental in HBA's decision not to submit a bid for the contract.[25]

Board of Elections representatives had trouble answering a variety of other inquiries, from questions about the escrow account which would hold the vendor's computer software to the simple question of whether the Board would provide tables and chairs for the count. Del Giorno's comments at the pre-bid conference in part explain why participants were left without more guidance:

> You know, from the Board's position -- I think part of the problem is that we're trying to -- we're running -- we're administrating an election for another group -- trying to satisfy their needs...

Awarding The Contract

As a result of the Board's lax attitude and poor planning, only one vendor -- the one who performed three of the last four counts -- submitted a bid for the contract. Unchecked by the regulatory forces of competition or effective supervision, PCA delivered a performance that was far from satisfactory.

The Software

As we have stated, one of the Board of Elections' main objectives for the 1993 election was to contract the count to a company that would automate the tally. But PCA -- the vendor they secured to do the job -- had no definitive computer plans or equipment when they won the contract. As of March 12th, when the bid was filed, PCA President Archibald Robertson had no binding contract with Jamie Darnow, the computer consultant he eventually hired to create a software program and to supply computer equipment for the count.[26] When they finally did agree on a plan, PCA decided to fully computerize only one district. The program determined how many of the paper ballot votes went to each candidate, obviating the need for a manual count. The other thirty one districts only used a computer to record and add figures the tally clerks had already counted by hand. It also randomized the draw of ballot boxes. Though Robertson professed amazement at the program, Darnow described it as strictly "Computer 101."

---

[25] In 1986, HBA was forced to obtain a bond. However, the bond was waived for PCA in 1989 and again this year.
[26] Robertson and PCA did not posses any automation equipment, nor did they have the capacity to computerize. They had never performed anything but a manual count.

Perhaps one of the reasons the Board of Elections had to settle for such a basic computer program is that they never even consulted with their own computer unit about the software, either before or after they awarded the contract. Lonnie Ranghelli, the Board's Manager of Systems Programming and Operations, had no input into the contract. He was not present at the pre-bid conference, where he could have answered questions about the request for an "automated" system. Before the contract was awarded, no one asked his opinion on PCA's program. After the contract was awarded, Ranghelli was asked to look at the software, but he never did. Nor did he check on the count as it was proceeding. When we asked Ranghelli if he had seen District 32, Robertson's "experimental" site which might have served as a model for future School Board elections, Ranghelli replied, "I wouldn't know where District 32 is."

Even though the computer program was hardly state-of-the-art, the Board of Elections would never know how extensive or effective the system they paid for was, because they never tested it. Originally, they had planned to test the software after they awarded the contract because they did not have time to evaluate the potential programs before choosing one. But apparently by the time the vendor was chosen, the Board of Elections lost interest, for no one from the Board evaluated the program. "We demonstrated it, but I don't believe anyone from the Board came," Robertson told us. "I have found that out to be true," Del Giorno confirmed. "There was testing done by the vendor, but not with any of my people supposedly present."

The Count

The Board of Elections, clearly annoyed that they were stuck with administering this election for "another group," did not seem to care whether the count was done properly. Thus, the public's last hope for quality control was PCA. This hope was slim, however, given that organization's past performance. True to form, PCA did not ensure the public that the ballots were counted impartially and honestly. As a result, the count as it was conducted left many people doubting the accuracy and integrity of the results. We focus on some of the more illustrative occurrences that characterized the circus-like counting of the ballots.

When the last ballot and stub were placed in the respective boxes on Election Day, the boxes were sealed and taken by the police to the local precincts. The next day, the boxes were grouped by borough and transported to five warehouses. The boxes remained there, under police guard, while Board of Elections officials examined affidavit and absentee ballots. PCA was scheduled to begin the count at 9:00 a.m. on May 13, 1993. They would work every day until they counted all of the votes and determined the results.

Hiring

The lack of quality control began right at the beginning, when PCA geared up to hire a work force. A shell organization, PCA hires a full "count force" each time it contracts to run an election. In this case, Robertson hired his friends and relatives and political referrals without questioning potential employees to determine if they had an undue interest in the election's outcome. As site directors and assistant site directors, Robertson hired his son Randy, Randy's fiancée Elizabeth Siemsen, Robertson's associates Enrique Ramos and Kevin Hanlon, Diane Hanlon, Richard Hanlon, Sara Hanlon, and Kevin Hanlon's brother-in-law, Al Virgo. The tally clerks, who actually count the ballots, were not interviewed.

PCA's staff training was no more scrupulous than its hiring procedure. Robertson boasted of an exacting training program for site directors. He arranged three training sessions that were held in April and May. In actuality, however, few if any directors attended more than one session. One of the training directors (Robertson's son Randy) had never before participated in a count. Robertson also made sure there was a "computer training" requirement. But all participants had to do was read a manual and watch a sample count. No substantial efforts were made to ensure that the site directors, who would be supervising all of the workers at the count sites, were well prepared. PCA arranged no training at all for tally clerks before the day of the count. Instead, the counters received "on site" training from the directors the day they arrived on the job.

All In The Family

It was not long before PCA's failure to properly screen its employees resulted in an absurd situation. The count agency hired Keith Saunders, the son of District 11 candidate Rodney Saunders, to count District 11 ballots. An investigator from this office went to the site and informed site director Joe Ortiz of this blatant conflict of interest.[27] Ortiz did not seem particularly concerned about the information, but at the insistence of our investigators, he removed Keith from the count tables and assigned him to move boxes. Nevertheless, within a few minutes, Keith made his way back to the counting tables. Again Ortiz did not seem concerned. Even after Robertson -- who learned of the situation from our investigators -- told Ortiz to dismiss Keith immediately, it was well over an hour before Ortiz got around to carrying out the command.[28] Ortiz later explained his delay by saying, "I was too busy."

After the count, in testimony before this office, Ortiz explained how he came to hire a candidate's son to count ballots. Ortiz recalled that on the morning of the count, he was complaining about his lack of staff when a woman named Mrs. Saunders, who introduced herself as the district leader of Coop City, said her son was available to be hired. "I looked at him, he looked like an intelligent young man, we spoke a few minutes and I said, yea sure, why not," Ortiz testified.[29] When he found out that Keith was the son of a candidate, Ortiz said, he saw no reason to remove him. Demonstrating PCA's failure to institute quality control checks, Ortiz testified that in all his years as a site director he never once inquired about relationships between his employees and candidates.

In fact, the Board of Elections' contract forbids PCA from hiring any member of a candidate's immediate family to count ballots in that candidate's district. But, like so many other rules governing the count, lack of oversight or enforcement rendered the regulation virtually useless.

---

[27] Ortiz, a veteran of Community School Board Election counts, first became a site director in 1980. According to Ortiz, he was referred to Robertson by the Bronx Democratic Club run by Stanley Friedman. Assemblyman Hector Diaz, who was then district leader, asked Ortiz to apply for the job. In 1980, 1983, and 1989, Ortiz handled the count in District 12. Ortiz was not involved in 1986.

[28] When first challenged by this office, Robertson assured us that it was impossible that Keith Saunders could be working at the District 11 count site. Only when confronted a second time did Robertson acknowledge the truth and agree to order Saunders' dismissal.

[29] Ortiz had two other last minute hires as well. Diane and Sal D'Ambrosio appeared at the count site and said they had been referred by Bronx County Democratic Chairman George Friedman. They were hired on the spot.

You've Got A Friend

In other districts as well, those who were hired to count ballots had close relationships with candidates. In District 13, several candidates and their representatives complained that individuals who had worked actively on candidate Marilyn Mosely's campaign were working as tally clerks at the site. When the site director, Bernice McCallum, discovered that the allegation was true, she promptly dismissed the clerks in question. Though the site director acted appropriately, the situation should have been avoided by quality control checks, such as employee screening.

Instead, PCA relied upon the judgement of the individual site directors to ensure integrity. McCallum took immediate action upon learning about the relationships because, she explained, she "thought it was appropriate," not because she had been trained to do so or because of any rule. One can only guess how many other relationships simply went undetected, were deliberately kept quiet, or were considered "irrelevant" by a site director.

Public Skepticism

One of the inherent problems in counting paper ballots on which voters list numerous choices is that two competing interests need to be satisfied. On the one hand, the complexity of the count and sheer volume of paper to be sorted necessitates some extra measures to ensure accuracy. At the same time, those very factors, by themselves, invite greater skepticism and greater scrutiny by the public. This dilemma was dealt with differently at each count site. Site directors tried to strike a balance between the absolute right of the candidates' representatives under the Election Law to observe every aspect of the count and the need to prevent undue interference. The results of their efforts were mixed at best. In the end, the lack of uniformity aggravated the public's perception that certain candidates were receiving preferential treatment.

Though candidates are entitled to have two representatives and two observers at the count site who are entitled to move anywhere within the count area,[30] PCA's interpretation of this rule varied from site to site. In Staten Island's District 31, the site director strictly enforced a rule created by Robertson that mandated that observers stay three feet away from the counters because, he explained, the count is "not a spectator sport." The District 11 site director waived the rule when he felt it was appropriate. District 13 observers were even more frustrated, when the site director, attempting to enforce the "three foot rule," apparently had trouble distinguishing between a foot and a yard, and made everyone stand back nine feet.

At many districts, the observers' view of the counting process was further obscured because the computer screen faced away from onlookers. Thus, even when a counter entered data correctly, observers denied access had reason to doubt the honesty and accuracy of the operation.

---

[30] Representatives have "full authority to move anywhere within the central counting quarters for the district, to inspect all activities of the count without interfering therewith and to exercise all rights conferred on watchers under the election law." Observers "shall be given facilities for keeping in full view all ballots outside of containers and all containers of ballots at all times when such ballots are not being sorted or counted, from the time when the ballots first arrive until all ballots have been placed in containers and removed for safe-keeping at the end of the count." Education Law Section 2590-c(6)(c)(2)(3). The law also provides for attendance by candidates, the media and the public. See Education Law Section 2590-c(7)(27).

Mishandled Items

PCA's careless handling of items such as ballots and computer diskettes containing election results only aggravated public suspicions about the integrity of the process. During the count at District 10, an unidentified person appeared at the count site with several District 10 ballots. Site Director Albert Virgo[31] took the ballots and gave the stranger approximately thirty District 11 absentee ballots that he had come across earlier in the day. When we questioned Virgo later, he said that he thought the man to whom he gave the ballots worked for PCA, but he admitted that he could not be sure. "But, um, he told me his name. I, I really don't know what it is. It was Vinny something, I'm not really sure. Um, I do not know," Virgo explained. Even if Virgo had thought to ask for identification, the inquiry would have been pointless. PCA does not provide any of its employees with identification -- another example of lack of quality control.

When the District 4 count ended, site director Enrique Ramos lost the computer diskette containing the results. Without the diskette or a backup on the computer hard drive, the ballots would have had to be recounted. As it turned out, the tabulations had been saved on the hard drive and were ultimately retrieved. Yet, what was most alarming was Ramos' blasé reaction to his blunder. Jamie Darnow, who had been summoned to retrieve the lost information from the computer's hard drive, reported that Ramos "thought it was very funny" that the disk was gone. "Ricky was running around talking about it being no big deal and laughing about it," Darnow said. The diskette was found on Thursday behind the back seat of Ramos' brother's car.

PCA even failed to carefully track the locations of boxes full of ballots. A preliminary count of boxes at the District 13 site indicated that three boxes were missing. Robertson was not concerned about reports of missing boxes, he said later, because one of his employees at his headquarters was charged with the responsibility of locating them. "In most cases they were found, so I didn't get involved in worrying about which boxes were missing," he said. The boxes were not found by the third day of the count, so Robertson went to District 13 and tried -- to no avail -- to find them. The three boxes were never found.

According to Robertson, the Board of Elections later explained that two of the three boxes never existed. No ballots were cast in those two election districts, so ballot boxes were never assembled. The third box, they said, did exist and contained 13 ballots.[32] In testimony before this office, Robertson, who said he was "proud of the fact that we found almost all of [the missing boxes]," demonstrated his lack of regard for each and every vote.

Q: The District 13 count went on as if those thirteen people had never voted?
A: Had to.
Q: And so those thirteen people voted for nothing, in effect?
A: Their ballots never came to me to be counted.

In District 31, a useless hunt was conducted for two missing boxes, which actually never existed. In fact, the two election districts represented by the "missing boxes" were disbanded before November

---

[31] Virgo is the brother-in-law of Kevin Hanlon of PCA. This was his first count.
[32] Robertson testified that 13 ballots disappeared. A candidate's representative reported that the missing box actually contained 16 ballots.

1992, months before the Community School Board Election.[33] But because PCA used an old list of election districts, which included the two defunct districts, they expected the boxes to arrive at the count. Board of Elections officials told Robertson before the count began that the two boxes would not be sent to the count site. But Site Director Bruce Hogenauer still initiated a search when he did not see the two boxes. "I am not sure I fully appreciated the significance of the information I passed along myself," Robertson said later in an attempt to explain the mixup.

White Sheets/Green Sheets/Stubs: What Are They For?

Public suspicions about the integrity of the process were heightened further when some of the institutional safeguards against ballot loss and or ballot stuffing were ignored. When the polls closed at 9:00 p.m. on May 4, each Board of Elections inspector was supposed to determine the number of votes cast at his or her poll and record it on a green certificate and a white certificate, which were sent along with the box to the count site.[34] Each box was also accompanied by a "stub box" containing a ballot stub to correspond with each ballot cast. The purpose of the certificate process and of the ballot stubs is to guard against ballot stuffing or ballot stealing. If the number on the certificates and the number of stubs do not match the number of ballots in the box, officials would be alerted that something is amiss.

However, many PCA counters failed to heed such warnings. Those who chose to check the certificates or stubs at all often discovered that the number on the certificate did not match the number of ballots in the box. Nevertheless, Robertson instructed his employees to continue counting.[35] In fact, the director of the District 11 count, Joe Ortiz, testified that the counters would continue counting even if it appeared that a substantial number of ballots had been added to or removed from the box:

Q: Do you care what numbers are placed on the green certificates?
A: No...It doesn't concern the fact that I'm going to count what's there. My job is only that. It's not to reflect upon whether there are too many ballots in there or not enough ballots....
Q: So, if the green certificate in the box said 12,000 votes, and you opened the box and there were twelve votes in there -- you would not be concerned by that?
A: That's correct.
Q: You would not go searching for where those 11,988 other ballots were?
A: You're right.

Even the Board of Elections agreed that the sheets should not be looked at unless someone submits an official challenge to the number of ballots in the box. "The count company is responsible to tell us how many ballots are in [the box], and we would go off that count number, not what is on the canvass sheet," Del Giorno explained. The ballot stubs, another intended safeguard, are also ignored. In fact, although Board of Elections inspectors were required to collect the stubs, even Del Giorno did not know why. "I am not absolutely positive," he said. "It is probably outdated and should be taken out of the law."

---

[33] This according to Barbara Kett, Chief Clerk of the Board of Elections Staten Island Borough office.
[34] The inspectors are not supposed to actually count the ballots cast, although in some cases they did, as we described earlier in this report. Instead, the total is determined by looking at the number of the next unused ballot.
[35] Robertson testified that he instructed his employees to make note of the number on the certificate, "but to disregard it otherwise."

Even if the carelessness and disregard for safeguards and procedure did not in fact affect the outcomes in the thirty two districts, they did have a detrimental impact. The manner in which apparent safeguards were ignored reinforced the belief that the process was not fair and impartial.

THE COST: TOO HIGH A PRICE?

As one might expect, the cost of conducting the 1993 Community School Board Election was substantial. The price paid might have been acceptable had the operation run smoothly. As we illustrate in this report, however, just the opposite occurred.

The Breakdown

The Board of Elections expended approximately four million dollars on the 1993 Community School Board election -- roughly the same cost as a general election in November.[36] This figure included printing the ballots, transporting materials such as boxes and ballots, inspector fees, the fee charged by the independent contractor who counted the ballots, and a $25 payment to police officers who used their own vehicles to open and close the polls on election day.[37] The count contract alone cost the Board of Elections almost half a million dollars this time.[38]

In addition to the costs borne by the Board of Elections, other city agencies incurred significant expenses. The cost of police manpower came out of the pocket of the New York City Police Department. While in a general election police officers are assigned to the polls from 6:00 a.m. to 9:00 p.m. on Election Day, the Community School Board Election, as it is currently conducted, requires police guards from the moment the polls open on Election Day until the count is finished weeks later.[39] The resulting cost -- for merely watching boxes -- is staggering.

Until the start of the count, the ballots were stored at five locations -- one in each borough.[40] It took thirty officers per day to guard the boxes, plus three sergeants per day to supervise the assignment.[41] Thus in the eight days before the start of the count alone, the Police Department paid 240 police officers and twenty four sergeants to watch boxes.

---

[36] This is according to Jon Del Giorno, Administrative Manager of the New York City Board of Elections.
[37] The printing of ballots for the Community School Board election is particularly expensive, in part because there are 32 different ballots and within each the candidate names must be rotated so that each has a turn at the top. This is done in case a significant number of voters merely write one through nine for the first candidates. Despite the fact that this is a non-partisan election, the same number of inspectors are employed -- two democrats and two republicans per table.
[38] The actual contract bid was $423,585.00. Archibald Robertson testified that he would be submitting a bill requesting ten percent above the contract price -- which he did -- as is permissible under New York City guidelines. Thus he was paid $473,385.00. Again this might be acceptable had Robertson actually paid his site directors the $2,900 budgeted in his bid. Site directors testified, however, and Robertson admitted, that most directors contracted for and were paid $1,000 for their services at the count.
[39] This is prescribed by law.
[40] Ballots are cast on Election Day, May 4th, but are not counted until May 13th. During this period, the Board of Elections validates affidavit ballots and accumulates absentee ballots.
[41] Figures were provided by the New York City Police Department. The Police Department regulations prescribe the assignment of one sergeant for every ten officers on duty.

Once the count began on May 13th, one police officer was on guard at each of the thirty two count sites. Since there were three shifts per day, the Police Department paid for ninety six police officers and nine sergeants per day.[42] What this means to the average New Yorker is that from the time the polls closed to the time the count was completed, almost 10,000 crime-fighting police hours were spent watching boxes. And the cost to the Police Department? More than a quarter of a million dollars.

One final cost was paid by the Board of Education. While so many police officers were guarding the boxes, the school custodian or one of his assistants, at each of the thirty two school buildings where the count was taking place, had to be on duty because technically their schools were in use twenty four hours per day, every day, until the process was completed.[43] Assuming the custodian assigned a cleaner to keep the building open around the clock, the worker received his usual $12 per hour plus overtime and night differential.[44] The total cost was hundreds of dollars per day per school.

FRAUD and MISCONDUCT

As we have demonstrated, the agencies charged with administering and governing the Community School Board Election failed miserably to plan and to coordinate their efforts. In addition, the Board of Elections, an agency that is intentionally comprised of an equal number of Democrats and Republicans monitoring each others' actions, proved to be ill-equipped to serve as a watchdog for a non-partisan election. These factors in effect gave the candidates license to break the laws and rules governing the election. The lack of accountability also enabled everyone involved -- including elections officials, candidates, and their supporters -- to engage in questionable activities without having to explain themselves.

This investigation found widespread disregard for the rules with respect to campaigning, petitioning, residency, advertising, fundraising, and even voting. Ultimately, this contempt for the rules led to outright fraud. Just as disturbing, it enabled politics to infiltrate the school system, and educators were once again demeaned by the undue pressures put on them to participate in political campaigns.

VOTING

In possibly the most egregious fraud perpetrated in an election already riddled with improprieties, unsuspecting Fordham University students from as far away as California and Hawaii were duped into participating in the Community School Board Election. Our investigation reveals that the turnout from the Bronx campus was not a spontaneous outpouring of civic pride or awareness. Rather, it was the direct result of a fraudulent voting scheme perpetrated by fellow students working part time for District 10.

---

[42] We were told that even in those districts where the count was finished within a few days, the officers continued to be assigned to watch the empty ballot boxes and stubs until the count was finished city-wide. Presumably this is done in case there is a court challenge.
[43] Schools that were used as polling places were also kept open by custodial staff until 9:00 p.m. on Election Day
[44] This is the lowest estimate. Obviously the cost would be much higher if the custodian or fireman kept the building open.

The "Electoral College"

When all the votes were counted in District 10, Edward McCarthy received 154 "number one" votes culled from absentee ballots. Of those, 117 absentee ballots were "cast" by Fordham University students. With this support, he gained a seat on the Board. The only problem is, most of the students there never knew they were exercising their franchise for McCarthy or for any other candidate.

During the 1992-1993 school year, Nicole Avallone and Jean Marie Gildea, then both Juniors at Fordham University, were hired as temporary workers in the district office of Community School Board 10. Early in 1993, they began taking advantage of their positions as Resident Advisors (commonly known as RAs) in Fordham dormitories to assist in the reelection campaigns of Ed McCarthy and his slate. At the urging and direction of one of their employers in the district, Avallone and Gildea canvassed their dorms, registered their classmates to vote, induced them to request absentee ballots, obtained the ballots intended for the students themselves, and cast them without their classmates' knowledge or consent.

In April, Avallone and Gildea set the scheme in motion. As a first step, they approached students under their supervision in the dorms. They attempted to register any students not yet registered in the Bronx regardless of their ties to District 10. It did not matter where their charges lived when not attending classes because, as matriculating students temporarily living on campus, they would be entitled to vote in the district encompassing the University.

While one may question why freshmen students from across the country would be interested in voting in a local school board election, the initial registration drive broke no rules and, alone, would not be subject to scrutiny. However, the events that followed make clear that, in fact, the registration drive was nothing more than a necessary prelude to the fraudulent scheme.[45]

The second stage of the plan required the wholesale application for absentee ballots for all the newly minted registered voters. To orchestrate this, Avallone and Gildea obtained an absentee ballot application from the Board of Elections for each voter they registered. They then filled out the forms completely before bringing them to the students for their signatures.[46] Avallone and Gildea indicated on the applications that each student would need an absentee ballot because they would be "home" on May 4, 1993, rather than on the Fordham campus.[47] They did not tell their fellow students, nor did the students realize, that by signing the absentee ballot application filled out in that manner, they were swearing falsely that they would be at home and not on the Fordham campus on Election Day. In fact, all of the newly registered voters contacted by this office were on campus on May 4 After learning that he had unwittingly sworn

---

[45] In fact, the RAs' deceptive practices began even in the registration phase. Most students were not apprised of the significance of what they were signing. Two students who signed registration forms thought they were signing petitions. One student thought it was some kind of evaluation. One thought it was a credit card application. And still another told Avallone that she was already registered in Staten Island, to which she was told: "It doesn't matter, you can vote in two places."

[46] Only one of the more than twenty students we spoke to recalls filling out any portion of the document filed in his name.

[47] One of the other Resident Advisors who assisted Avallone and Gildea described how Gildea used the Fordham University student directory to fill in student address information, including home addresses, on the registration forms and absentee ballot forms before getting the students to sign. On some of the forms the fact that someone other than the applicant filled out the body is clear by the mistakes that were made. On one, the applicant's last name was misspelled and on another, the hometown was misspelled.

falsely, one student confronted Avallone. "If anyone asks, just tell them you were home on May 4 and the absentee ballot will count," she told him.

To ensure the scheme's success, Avallone and Gildea "authorized" themselves to pick up the ballots from the Board of Elections on the students' behalf.[48] None of the students we spoke to noticed or understood the significance of Avallone's or Gildea's name appearing on their application forms. None wrote their RA's name there themselves.

Once the RAs got their fellow students to sign off on the absentee ballot applications, filled out by them in advance, everything was in place for the final phase of the scheme. Avallone admitted to investigators that she picked up the ballots from the Bronx Board of Elections and brought them to the District 10 office rather than to the voters. There, she and Gildea filled them all out, placing a "1" next to Ed McCarthy's name and the numbers "2" through "9" next to other candidates' names.

There was but one final hurdle to overcome. Absentee ballots must be placed in sealed envelopes and the voter must sign the outside, swearing that he or she has voted once and only once by way of the enclosed ballot. Thus, before the ballots could be cast, Avallone and Gildea needed to get signatures on the envelopes.

At first, Avallone showed students the ballots already filled out and sought their signatures on the envelopes. However, she found that the students were less pliant when votes were being cast for them than they were during the earlier registration drive. One student, Lisa Cali, recalled a floor meeting that Avallone called during which she displayed absentee ballots already filled out and sought to get the students' signatures. According to Cali, several students balked at the idea and the RA backed down.[29]

Undeterred, Avallone and Gildea next tried to get the signatures on the envelopes without telling the signers that a ballot was enclosed. They enlisted another RA, Tracy Pertusiello, to accomplish this. Gildea brought ballot envelopes to her and asked her to get the students in her dorm to sign them, Pertusiello told investigators. Gildea never told her that ballots were inside. Eventually, however, a student opened the envelope before signing it and found an absentee ballot inside, already completed. Taken aback, the student asked Pertusiello "who am I voting for?" Not knowing herself, Pertusiello replied: "I don't know; ask Jean."

Finally, it appears that Avallone and Gildea dispensed with the approaches to students altogether. They merely sealed the envelopes with the ballots inside, signed the voter's name on the outside themselves, and returned them to the Board of Elections where they were counted. Twenty one of the students we talked to, all of whom had votes cast in their names, stated categorically that they did not vote.

Why would two resident advisors at Fordham University go to such lengths for a candidate for a local community school board? And even if motivated to do so, where would two political neophytes such as Avallone and Gildea obtain the means and know-how to pull off such a scheme?

---

[48] Section F of the absentee ballot application gives the voter the opportunity to specify the means by which he will obtain the ballot. For example, the voter can indicate that he or she will pick it up from the Board of Elections, can request it be mailed to a specified address, or can designate an agent to retrieve it for him. If a voter chooses the last option, his agent is merely authorized to pick up the ballot, not cast it for the voter.

When confronted by investigators from this office, Nicole Avallone provided an answer. She said that Jim Sullivan had orchestrated their efforts. Sullivan, the Director of Pupil Personnel in District 10, recruited her and Gildea while they were working in the district office, Avallone said. He instructed the two students to canvass their dorms, register classmates, induce those classmates to request absentee ballots, obtain the absentee ballots themselves, and cast them all for Sullivan's preferred candidates. It was Sullivan who provided the registration forms and applications for absentee ballots and who directed the coeds on exactly how to fill out the ballots, Avallone said.

Avallone's claims are consistent with the explanations she and Gildea gave to students they approached. One student recalled that Avallone and Gildea told him that "they were working for their boss who works for the Board of Education and they had to do it [sign up students] to keep their jobs." Several others recalled being told that the RAs were working for their boss at the Board of Education. Still others who were recruited to help in the "registration process" were told that they could get a job registering students to vote for Avallone and Gildea's boss, whom they said was a candidate in the local school board election.[49]

Avallone's claims are also consistent with Sullivan's involvement in this year's election in District 10. Principal Gerald Friedlander testified that Sullivan, a long time political operative in the district and active member of the Ben Franklin Club in Riverdale, was the "political director" for the slate supported by the Council of Supervisors and Administrators (CSA). Ed McCarthy was a member of the slate. Moreover, Sullivan himself was the designated agent to receive the absentee ballots of other voters who cast their votes for Ed McCarthy.[50] Thus, it makes perfect sense that Jim Sullivan would recognize Fordham University as a potential source of votes, enlist the students working in his office, and provide them with the means and know-how to tap into that source.

With the help of Fordham's unsuspecting students, Ed McCarthy was reelected, Jim Sullivan retained his position in the district office, and Nicole Avallone and Jean Marie Gildea received a civics lesson they would never find in their college textbooks.

UNDUE POLITICAL INFLUENCE

In our report entitled *Power, Politics and Patronage: Education in Community School District 12*, released in April 1993, we chronicled the ways in which a local political machine influenced the inner workings of a school district. Through our investigation of the election process we have confirmed that the experience in District 12 was not aberrant nor limited to a poor district in the South Bronx. Indeed, we found that the pressure exerted on Jean Marie Gildea and Nicole Avallone is familiar to school employees across the City. In an election year particularly, political considerations repeatedly

---

[49] One of those recruited, Resident Advisor Peter Fowkes, was paid $100. Gildea told him the money came from her boss. She told another RA, Tracy Pertusiello, that her boss was pushing her to do it and paying her $100 off the books to get student signatures.

[50] Sullivan was the designated recipient of absentee ballots for two applicants. One, an employee of Fordham University, wrote that he had work commitments on May 4; the other indicated that he expected to be in the hospital on Election Day.

take precedence over educational concerns. This year, teachers, administrators and paraprofessionals in several districts faced varying degrees of pressure to actively campaign for candidates running for community school boards. The political chores solicited ranged from small favors like cooking food for a fundraiser to more active involvement such as carrying nominating petitions, contributing to campaign committees, and actually joining political clubs. The pressure exerted varied as well from overt arm-twisting to subtle coercion.

District 21: From Schoolhouse to Clubhouse

The experience of teachers in District 21 during this election demonstrates the way local politics can infiltrate and infect the local school system. An overwhelming number of teachers and support personnel were drawn into a political feud having nothing to do with the functioning of the school district. In the process, many expressed the firm belief that they had no choice but to participate.

In December 1992, Sheldon Plotnick, the incumbent president of the Board, announced his intention to run first for reelection to the School Board and later in the year for the City Council seat held by Sam Horwitz. Plotnick expected that Horwitz, who was retiring, would endorse him as his successor. When that did not occur, a very public feud broke out between Plotnick and Horwitz's ally and chosen successor, Assemblyman Howard Lasher. The first salvo was thrown by Lasher when he denied an application by Plotnick and his school board slate to rent the Community Democratic Club as its headquarters.[51] Plotnick took this as a sign that the Club, as then constituted, was not going to back him in either of his election bids. To counter the Lasher gambit, he would need to delay in order to enlist reinforcements.

To delay the process, Plotnick challenged the legitimacy of the Lasher-Horwitz faction's control of the Club, claiming that they had gained control of the executive board through an illegal vote. To enlist reinforcements, he turned to those who owed their livelihood to him: the supervisory staff of the school district. The supervisors, in turn, pressured their staff in a myriad of subtle and not so subtle ways.

Once Plotnick succeeded in getting the Club to hold a new vote and had mobilized the district staff, he could put his plan into action. At the direction of many District 21 supervisors, large numbers of faculty and staff joined the Club and paid the membership fee. Then, once the new vote was held on April 1, the regular Democratic Club members were overwhelmed and Plotnick gained control. What followed was a fait accompli. The newly constituted membership voted to endorse the Education Slate in the School Board Election and Sheldon Plotnick for both the School Board and City Council. In the process, teachers were forced to make political contributions and participate in political activity in violation of the City Charter.[52]

---

[51] Lasher, the Club leader, announced that renting the club to Plotnick would violate the spirit, if not the letter of the Serrano Law. In his view, which he imparted to the members, it was mixing school business with politics.

[52] Under City Charter section 2604(b)(11)(c), no city officer or employee may compel, induce or request any subordinate officer or employee to make a political contribution. Furthermore, no city officer or employee may request any subordinate to participate in a political campaign. See Charter Section 2604(b)(9)(b).

Solicitation in the School

The logical point man in Plotnick's strategy to take control of the local Democratic Club was Stuart Possner. Possner, the Principal at PS 100 in the Brighton Beach section of Brooklyn in District 21, was already a member of the Community Democratic Club and a Plotnick supporter. Better yet, he was indebted to Plotnick for years of support despite the principal's past outrageous conduct.[53] With Possner spearheading the operation, the faculty and staff at PS 100 started joining the Club in record numbers in January 1993.

Just as Plotnick knew he could rely on Possner, Possner had his political loyalists whom he enlisted to clarify his wishes to staff members. Myra Abramowitz, the UFT representative, whom witnesses describe as the de facto Assistant Principal; Michele "Micki" Davis, the library teacher; Naomi Fritz, a paraprofessional; Elyse Schneider, the computer teacher; and Randee Bleiberg, who is assigned to the language arts "cluster" position, participated to varying degrees in the politicizing of PS 100.[54] Each of these staff members held non-classroom positions which gave them ample time to circulate among the staff and pass the word that the Principal wanted everyone to join and participate in the local democratic club's affairs.

During January, Possner had these individuals enroll the PS 100 staff in the Club and collect the ten dollar political contribution. They accosted teachers in the school office, in the auditorium as their students practiced for a play, and in the classroom during teaching hours in front of the children. In doing so, the recruiters told the faculty that it would be a good idea to attend.[55] If a teacher initially responded "no," she was told to think it over. That teacher was approached again and again -- in the classroom -- until she joined the Club. One teacher who continued to hold out finally learned why she was repeatedly pestered to join the Club. "[Possner] wants me to talk to all you girls about the Club," Micki Davis explained to her.

When that teacher learned that her principal was interested in who joined, she agreed to pay the membership fee. Most of the teachers we interviewed said that they paid the ten dollar Club fee because they felt that it was a small price to pay to be left alone. One teacher said that she believed that if she did not pay the fee, "I would have a difficult time getting along in this school." As our investigation progressed, it became clear that her fear was well-founded, and that to be "left alone" by Possner was a coveted, but fleeting status.

The April 1st Meeting

The majority of the PS 100 staff were signed up as members of the Club in January. Then, a few months later, just before the Club's scheduled vote to determine control of the executive committee, the

---

[53] Possner was arrested and indicted in 1986 for charges of Grand Larceny, Filing False Documents and Tampering with a Witness for crimes he committed while running a summer camp at PS 188 in Brooklyn. Possner submitted fraudulent time sheets so he could receive a salary check made out to a person who never worked at the camp. He also charged parents tuition, even though it was paid for by government funds. Possner pleaded guilty to a misdemeanor. Despite these school related crimes, the District 21 School Board and Superintendent Donald Weber took no disciplinary action against Possner.

[54] Bleiberg's mother is Marcey Feigenbaum, one of Plotnick's officers at the Club.

[55] Elyse Schneider told one teacher that it was "a good idea to show her face" because, as a Special Education teacher, she works "for a lady named Laurie Plotnick." Laura Plotnick is the head of Special Education in District 21 and the wife of Sheldon Plotnick.

teachers were again approached. This time, they could not buy peace by making a contribution. They were expected to attend the meeting after hours. On the day of the meeting, a PS 100 student circulated a staff organization sheet with the question "Are You Going?" printed at the top. Each staff member was expected to sign "Yes" or "No" next to her name on the sheet and initial it.[56] Many of the teachers who thought their association with the Club had ended when they paid their monetary dues wrote "No." But, at 3:00 p.m., as those teachers were leaving for the day, Naomi Fritz stood in the school office with the sign-up sheet on a clipboard and gathered the teachers around her. She repeatedly asked: "Are you going? Are you going?" Several teachers remained steadfast in their decision not to attend. According to the teachers, Fritz responded, "he says no is not good enough." Upon hearing that, teacher after teacher took the clipboard from Fritz and changed her "No" to a "Yes."

Many of the teachers who committed to attend the meeting had no idea what it was all about. Some of the teachers who were aware that they were expected to vote that night joked that they would vote against Possner's people to "get back" at him. As they arrived at the meeting, however, they learned that steps had been taken to make sure that Possner's plan did not backfire. To begin with, the "secret ballot" would not be so secret, as the ballot number for each member was placed next to her name in the sign-in book. In addition, the teachers had the palm cards they had been given to remind them why they were there. In one case, Possner went so far as to lean over the shoulder of a teacher to make sure she was following the "suggestions." With the help of Possner and PS 100, Plotnick easily gained control of the Club, the first step toward winning the endorsements he had sought.[57]

Those Who Stayed Behind

Although the vast majority of the faculty and staff at PS 100 went to the April 1st meeting, a few teachers either could not go or simply did not want to go, even when pressured to do so by Possner. The day after the meeting, Possner announced that a movie would be shown in the auditorium and that certain teachers would supervise all the students while the remainder of the faculty would enjoy extra preparation time, a cherished commodity for classroom teachers. It was immediately obvious to the entire staff that those teachers assigned to the movie had not attended the meeting the night before. As witnesses explained, usually when students watch a movie, all classroom teachers receive "prep" time, while paraprofessionals and "cluster" and Special Education teachers supervise the children. But this time, Possner directed particular classroom teachers to report to the auditorium while Micki Davis, Naomi Fritz, Elyse Schneider, Randee Bleiberg and others who had paid their dues enjoyed some free time.

Though this "punishment" may seem trivial to those outside PS 100, several witnesses told this office that the message was clear and understood throughout the school. The loss of free time and the

---

[56] The organizational sheet listed all staff members and their respective assignments.
[57] Teachers reported that Board employees from across the District attended the meetings. Clearly Possner was not the only principal working for Plotnick. He was, however, one of the most successful. Plotnick was reelected to the School Board, but lost in the Democratic primary for City Council.

attached stigma had its intended effect, as virtually every single teacher attended the second meeting on April 26, and the Club voted to grant Plotnick the endorsements he sought.[58]

Educators or "Battered Women"

To truly appreciate the coercive nature of the solicitation that occurred in PS 100, Possner's management style and its effect on his staff must be understood. Several teachers described instances where Possner verbally abused students, teachers, and parents. Others reported being the victims of his graphic and aggressive sexual harassment.[59] At least one teacher described how Possner physically abused a student. Finally, this spring, the entire staff was witness to Possner's excesses. They stood by helplessly as the Principal had City Councilman Horwitz arrested and removed in handcuffs for attempting to attend kindergarten graduation, all because, as community residents reported, Horwitz chose to support Sheldon Plotnick's long time opponent Howard Lasher.

These reports led investigators to question why teachers would remain without complaining to the outside world. In response, one teacher likened the staff to "battered women" who see no way out of their destructive environment. Instead, teachers remain and do whatever they can to stay out of Possner's way and avoid being summoned to his office at all costs. Repeatedly, teachers expressed the belief that Possner was too "well connected" to be disciplined even if their allegations came to light. At the same time, those who have cooperated have expressed great trepidation about the repercussions they would suffer if their participation in the investigation became known. Both the belief in Possner's invincibility and the fear of retribution are understandable under the circumstances. In 1986, when Possner was convicted of a crime directly related to his duties as principal, the local board took no disciplinary action. Since that time, when teachers at PS 100 have complained about the Principal's abusive behavior to their union representative, Myra Abramowitz, she has refused to support their complaints.[60] At the same time, the slightest hint of disloyalty is treated harshly. Several of Possner's closest aides learned first hand during this investigation how their fortunes could change if they did not give their first allegiance to their Principal. After Micki Davis, Elyse Schneider, and Naomi Fritz testified under oath before this office, Possner immediately summoned them to find out what questions they were asked and what responses they gave. When they refused to answer his questions, they each found that on the next staff organizational chart they had new, more onerous classroom assignments.[61] We hasten to acknowledge that everyone, including teachers and other school personnel, has the right to voluntarily take part in the election of Community School Board

---

[58] Possner apparently felt that this "punishment" was a success because he used it again to punish those who defied his wishes and refused to attend a dance held after school on April 2. The following Monday a movie was shown to give teachers preparation time. Again, the teachers who had not attended the dance were assigned to supervise the movie.

[59] Several teachers who agreed to cooperate only after being assured that they would not be identified in this report testified under oath that Possner made sexually harassing comments and demands in one-on-one situations either in his office or their classrooms. Those who gave such testimony did so with a great deal of specificity. However, to repeat their descriptions in any detail here would be tantamount to disclosing their identities.

[60] Teachers told us that time and time again, she has suggested that Possner was "only joking" and otherwise discouraged them from pursuing formal action.

[61] As explained earlier in this section, Davis, Schneider and Fritz had to that point had few if any classroom assignments. This change was noted by several witnesses and cited as another example of the ways Possner could punish those who defy him. As a result, Schneider has transferred to another school in the District.

members. On the other hand, no teacher or school board employee should be forced to participate. The request by a supervisor of a subordinate to contribute time or money to a political cause is inherently coercive and thus prohibited by law. Where, as here, that "request" is actually a demand, its impact on the educational system is even more corrosive and must not be tolerated.

District 9

In District 9, a district with a history of corruption and influence peddling, employees have long complained that they are routinely pressured into making contributions of time and money. Given that atmosphere, the strong-arm tactics described in District 21 were unnecessary. District 9 employees knew from experience what was expected of them. Our investigation revealed that Carmelo Saez, a long time power both on the Board and behind the scenes, enlisted well placed employees in the district to coordinate his campaign and raise money for him and his slate of candidates.[62] And when Carmelo Saez or his representatives came calling, District 9 employees gave of their time and money in large numbers.

Saez's primary vehicle for raising money was through an organization called the "Comite Pro Representacion Hispana." Witnesses described how he used district employees to organize a fundraising event on behalf of the "Comite" and solicited contributions in support of it. The event, billed as a "Fundraiser/Dinner/Dance," was held at the restaurant "Chez Sensual" on April 23. For a donation of $25 per person, patrons enjoyed two bands and a D.J., a hot buffet and drinks. According to a number of witnesses, at any given time several hundred people were in attendance, including "principals of practically every school" in the District.[63]

Exactly how much money Saez or the "Comite" pocketed from the event remains a mystery. The "Comite" did not file a Financial Disclosure Form with the Board of Elections as required by law, thus no information about the receipts of the fundraiser is available. Instead, Saez filed a form indicating that money was raised on his behalf by an organization called "Friends of Carmelo Saez," but claimed that the group need not itemize since it raised less than $1000.[64] Those who attended Chez Sensual on April 23, expected that at least Saez, if not all the Comite candidates, would benefit from the event. Thus, unless those in attendance were deceived as to the recipient or were wildly inaccurate in their crowd estimates, the mystery with respect to the proceeds is one that is being perpetrated in violation of all disclosure rules.[65] Indeed, the lack of documentation makes it difficult to determine whether any of the

---

[62] Carmelo Saez is a former Board member in District 9 who was removed for improper use of school facilities in May 1992. He was reelected in May 1993, and the new Board selected him as its President.

[63] The event was run much like the A-Team fundraiser we described in our April 1993 report on corruption in District 12. Saez, like District 12's Kenneth Drummond, made use of his power base in the local school district to raise money. And like the A-Team fundraiser in 1991, the Comite's party raises questions about how much money was raised and where that money went.

[64] to Election Law Section 14-124(4), candidates who raise less than $1,000 must file but need not itemize. If they raise more than $1,000, School Board candidates must itemize every receipt no matter how small. See Education Law section 2590-c(6)(b). Notably, although Saez claimed money raised on his behalf was done by "Friends of Carmelo Saez," he was one of two individuals authorized to withdraw money from the "Comite" account.

[65] Based on testimony or other information provided, we can account for over fifty purchased tickets representing $1,250. At least one third of those tickets were sold to teachers in District 9.

money was spent on the campaign or if it merely lined Saez's pocket.[66] A conservative estimate of the fundraiser attendance is two hundred fifty people -- many of whom paid cash at the door. The resulting amount raised would be $6,250. Nevertheless, only $345 in cash and $2,000 in checks were deposited in the "Comite" bank account.[67]

Whatever the actual financial reward Saez reaped from the evening at Chez Sensual, there is no question that it was achieved with the aid of numerous district employees. Frank Rodriguez, the Assistant Director of Bi-Lingual Programs, Hilda Gutierrez, the Principal at PS 35, Nancy Vasquez, a teacher at CS 90 and the wife of successful candidate Benjamin Ramos, and Angel Crespo, a teacher at IS 147, were enlisted to organize the event or sell tickets to it.[68]

Saez enlisted Frank Rodriguez to find a suitable location and solicit contributions. Rodriguez chose Chez Sensual and met Saez there on a Tuesday in March. Although he arranged and attended the meeting, he denies participating in the exchange between Saez and the owner. In his words, he was there "just to be there."

Rodriguez did more than handle logistics. At Saez's behest, he solicited his associates' attendance. He admitted that Saez gave him twenty tickets to the fundraiser to sell. Of those twenty, Rodriguez distributed thirteen to members of his own unit, including the Director and other staff members.[69] Aside from the Director, those receiving tickets were all subordinate to Rodriguez and thus susceptible to improper coercion.[70]

Hilda Gutierrez, the Principal of PS 35, was another cog in the Saez machine.[71] She helped arrange for the food that was to be served at the fundraiser and bought numerous tickets in addition to attending on her own. Though much of her testimony before this office was internally inconsistent or incredible on its face, it is clear that she was substantially involved in the fundraiser.[72]

---

[66] According to the records of Chemical Bank, the "Comite" account was opened on April 27, 1993, four days after the fundraiser, by Saez and his sister-in-law Carmen Abarca, a District 9 employee. On that date, $345 in cash and $1,845 in checks were deposited. An additional $175 in checks was deposited on May 4th; the account was closed on June 11, 1993.

[67] While obviously there were some costs involved in throwing the fundraiser, the food was donated and the bar was cash only after 9:00 p.m.

[68] Like Drummond in District 12, Saez cut down on costs and maximized his profit by using his allies throughout the District to carry out virtually every task needed to hold the fundraiser.

[69] According to Rodriguez, he sold the seven other tickets to friends outside the district and bought three more himself on the night of the event.

[70] A clear illustration of the potential for coercion is described in the section immediately preceding this one. Moreover, the City Charter, which applies to Board of Education employees, recognizes the dangers of coercion by supervisors and therefore forbids any public servant to "directly or indirectly compel, induce or request any subordinate to pay any political assessment, subscription or contribution." City Charter Chap. 68, Sec. 2604 (11) (c) (emphasis added).

[71] Prior to being named principal of PS 35, Ms. Gutierrez was the Deputy Superintendent in District 9.

[72] For instance, when initially asked by investigators who sold her the ticket to the fundraiser she stated that she got it from Frank Rodriguez. Later, in sworn testimony, she said that Carmelo Saez called her at home and asked her if she was interested in "Hispanic unity." According to her, she then told Saez to send her seven tickets. When asked why she originally said Rodriguez sold her the ticket, she replied, "I don't know." In addition, under oath, she first denied having anything to do with the food at the fundraiser. Later in her testimony she confirmed that she had helped Angel Crespo coordinate that activity.

At Carmelo Saez's direction, Angel Crespo, a teacher in District 9, solicited Gutierrez' assistance with the food provisions. As she ultimately admitted, Crespo called her at school to enlist her help. Although, according to her, she preferred to talk at home, she discussed with Crespo how much and what type of food would be needed. In fact, Gutierrez offered to "set up a plate or two." Thereafter, she enlisted parents to cook some of the dishes and arranged for Crespo to pick up the food outside the school.

Gutierrez claimed that she was unaware of the true nature of the Chez Sensual event, maintaining that she had attended a "party," rather than a fundraiser. This claim is incredible. First, and most obviously, the face of the ticket she admits to purchasing read: "Fundraiser/Dinner/Dance." Even if that description went unnoticed, Gutierrez's actions belie her claim of ignorance. Though she made conflicting statements about where she got her tickets and what was said to her when she got them, she was consistent about the fact that she agreed to purchase seven tickets at $25 each. She claimed that besides herself, she bought the tickets so that her husband, her daughter, and certain parents who had been helpful at her school could attend. However, her explanation makes little sense. No monetary commitment was necessary until party-goers actually arrived at the door on the night of the event. Yet, despite the fact that of her intended beneficiaries she alone attended, Gutierrez paid $175 that night. If her sole motivation was paying to entertain her friends and family at a "party," she would have only paid for one ticket when they found other diversions.

The fundraising effort was not limited to the efforts of Rodriguez, Gutierrez and Crespo. Nancy Vasquez, a teacher at CS 90 and the wife of Saez slate-member Benjamin Ramos, actively solicited contributions from numerous fellow employees at her school.[73] CS 90 Principal Richard Wallin was aware of Vasquez's activity and had received the Chancellor's memorandum forbidding campaigning in the schools, but he took no steps to stop it. Indeed, Wallin ultimately attended the fundraiser using a ticket that Vasquez had sold to CS 90 science teacher Eugene Mendelsohn.

As Election Day neared, Saez enlisted still other employees to bring his campaign into the District schools. He personally delivered a cardboard box filled with flyers to the principal's office at PS 109. From there, Principal Angelo Sanchez turned over the task of distributing flyers to a paraprofessional in the school, Miguelina Morales. Then, come Election Day, Ms. Morales and Mrs. Fuentes, a teacher at PS 109, handed out flyers in front of the school on school time. At the same time, Principal Sanchez stood on the school steps imploring voters to vote for Saez.

Seemingly determined to use any available school employees to further his political campaign, Saez sent unsolicited packages of tickets to other principals who did not "volunteer" their time. Certain District 9 principals whose names are known to this office, but who asked for anonymity out of fear of retribution, reported receiving packages addressed: "Attention Principal" at their office. The packages contained tickets to the fundraiser at Chez Sensual. Those receiving the unsolicited tickets knew from

---

[73] Vasquez testified that she sold 20 tickets that were given to her by Saez. Approximately 12 of those were sold to Board of Education employees, and she bought one herself. Her customers paid in cash. According to her, she collected a total of $500 which she turned over to Saez. Although many others also collected cash contributions, a total of only $325 in cash was deposited in the "Comite" account.

experience that they were expected to sell their quota. Sadly, District 9 educators have learned that they must pay their political dues in order to ensure their professional success.

PETITION REVIEW PROCESS

We have demonstrated the negative repercussions that occur when undue political influence infiltrates the local school district. Brazen political insiders are afforded an edge when they use the manpower and resources of the district they control to further their campaigns. In other areas of the election process, too, we have found that the playing field is not level and that those without political connections will face an uphill fight. Petition review is one such process that insiders can manipulate to their own advantage. In order to secure a place on the ballot in one of the thirty two local contests, a candidate needed to get two hundred registered voters to sign a nominating petition.[74] He or she could obtain the signatures personally or have a supporter, registered in the district, obtain them in the candidate's name. Either way, obtaining the signatures was only the beginning of a torturous, time consuming, and often secretive process. In order to survive, each candidate had to beat back all challenges to the validity of his signatures and at the same time do his or her own checking to ensure that others played by the same rules. This process, governed by state statute and administered by the Board of Elections, was played out in an arena replete with arcane rules and secrecy that at the very least appeared to favor political insiders.

The statutory scheme for the review of candidates' petitions does not confer on the Board of Elections the power to independently investigate each candidate's petitions to verify that they are valid and sufficient.[75] Rather, it assumes that the competing interests of opposing candidates will lead to a form of self-policing. Each candidate is given the opportunity to review and challenge the validity of his opponent's filing. Only if a candidate's petition is "challenged" will the Board of Elections review it. If there is no challenge there is no review. If an objection is made to a candidate's petition, the clerks of the borough offices of the Board of Elections conduct a preliminary review and send a report on their findings to the elections commissioners. The clerks make specific factual findings and tabulate each candidate's valid signatures. Then, the Board of Elections holds hearings on the challenged petitions and makes final determinations as to who will remain on the ballot.

The manner in which those decisions were made in this year's Community School Board Election raises serious questions about the integrity of the process. In several cases, the commissioners disregarded the factual findings and tabulations made by their own borough clerks. Moreover, they often made their decisions behind closed doors, in secret "executive sessions," and announced them without comment or explanation. The appearance of impropriety was aggravated by the fact that, in one case, a commissioner passed judgment on the petitions of incumbents who were overseeing programs in which he had a financial stake, without disclosing the connection or recusing himself.

---

[74] The signers had to be registered in the district where the candidate was running or have a child attending school there.
[75] In fact, Election Law Section 6-154(1) states clearly that "any petition filed with the officer or Board charged with receiving it shall be presumptively valid if it is in the proper form and appears to bear the requisite number of signatures."

District 12: The Board of Elections' New Math

The review of candidate petitions in District 12 raised serious questions of conflict of interest. In closed door meetings, the Board of Elections commissioners, including one who was at the time doing business in District 12, overruled their own clerks and ruled eligible candidates whose petitions were clearly insufficient. To do so, in one case they had to make 174 equal 200 and in another 155 became 200.

In order to understand the Board of Elections "new math," investigators from this office tried to reconstruct just what occurred in the review of the District 12 petitions. Unfortunately, many of the Board's practices and procedures impeded that reconstruction. First, the Board did not record in any manner the hearings at which objectors and candidates were afforded the opportunity to plead their cases to the presiding commissioners. Second, many of the commissioners' decisions were made in private, unrecorded "executive sessions." Third, no formal record of the vote of commissioners was kept. Finally, when the Borough Clerk calculations were overruled or disregarded, the commissioners were not required to give an oral or written explanation. Thus, investigators were left with the memory of Board of Elections commissioners and employees as well as witnesses who had attended their hearings.[76]

What is clear is that in their initial review, the Bronx clerks found that two incumbent candidates running for reelection in District 12, Randy Glenn and Ed Cain, had less than two hundred valid signatures.[77] Yet, both ended up on the ballot on May 4. How that occurred has yet to be satisfactorily explained.

Sandra Parness, a clerk in the Bronx borough office of the Board of Elections, determined that Randy Glenn had 174 valid signatures and Ed Cain had 155. She recorded those figures on the "Clerks' Report," the official document which is forwarded to the commissioners of the Board of Elections for ratification.[78] According to Kay Amer, the Chief Clerk in the Bronx, after her clerks sent their report "downtown," they had no further involvement in the process until they received copies of the same official documents back with a succinct notation on each. In the space where the final decision of the Board is indicated, someone had put a check mark next to the word "in." This notation appeared without any further explanation in writing and without any change in the clerk's calculations. Based on scant recollections and limited documentation, we tried to figure out exactly what occurred at the Board of Elections' hearings. On March 4, 1993, the commissioners met to consider the District 12 petitions along with many others. According to witnesses, each matter was called individually. In most cases, objectors and candidates were given the opportunity to address the commissioners in a public forum. However, when Cain's and Glenn's cases were announced, Commissioner Vincent Velella immediately announced "second call" and the commissioners retired to an "executive session." When the commissioners returned, Velella announced that Cain and Glenn would be on the ballot. No evidence was accepted or discussed in public and no explanation was

---

[76] Board of Elections counsel, Steven Denkberg and John LoPresto, claim that in the wake of our investigation, the Board's procedures have changed. They claim that hearings are now recorded.
[77] Following the issuance of our April, 1992 report on corruption in District 12, then Chancellor Fernandez removed the entire Board and replaced them with his trustees. Thus, by May 4, Glenn and Cain were no longer incumbents. By May 15, they had lost their bids for reelection.
[78] See Clerks' reports at the end of this section.

given for the discrepancies between the Bronx clerk's tabulations and the commissioners' determination.[79] Indeed, when Commissioners Velella and Mejias were interviewed by this office, neither could remember anything about the proceedings involving Cain and Glenn. Even after being shown the Clerk's Reports they could provide no explanation for how the two candidates were allowed on the ballot. Even if there was a logical and legitimate explanation for the commissioners' decision, the manner in which it was made and announced cast a shadow of suspicion in the participants' minds.

Behind the Scenes: District Leader Fred Brown

The shadow of suspicion created by the secretive processes and the Commissioners' failed memories lengthened when this office obtained secretly recorded conversations suggesting that political influences were exerted and unsavory back-room deals were cut. In conversations with candidates Edward Cain and Randy Glenn, Fred Brown, a Republican District Leader in the Bronx, and his associates described exactly how Brown used his influence with Elections Commissioner Vincent Velella to ensure Cain's and Glenn's places on the ballot.

First, in a recorded conversation on the very day that the petitions were reviewed, Fred Brown's associate Earl Hayde told Ed Cain:

> ...Y'all was completely off. It was no ifs ands or buts about it. You were off because of the mistakes...because of the mistakes, Mr. B had to go and get that Senator and they went in a room... Senator wanted to know was y'all important enough. Otherwise they would walk away from it... This is how you got back on....it cost a helluva big chip... I mean, to get y'all both back on there, alright, and this is through the Senator Guy Velella and people down there.

Then, four days later, on March 8, Fred Brown told Randy Glenn:

> Cain was down to 155 signatures and you were down to 174. I had placed a call in down to 32 Broadway [Board of Elections]...saying we want a Republican priority on you and Cain... A call was placed back to Guy Velella, who's the Bronx County Republican Chairperson, he placed a call back down to his father Vince Velella, who is one of the commissioners there... You were yesterday's history... Then Vince went on to make a motion for a recess and then to make a motion to go into exec[utive] session, and really deal behind the scenes with the Commissioners.

---

[79] Two other candidates, Lydia Velez, an incumbent, and Louis Maldonado, were present and testified to the manner in which the Cain and Glenn petitions were handled. Mildred Bonilla, a community activist in District 8, and Jerome Koenig, an election law specialist working for the State Assembly's Committee on Election Law, were also present and corroborated the candidates' general descriptions of the events of March 4, including the Board's use of "executive sessions" and its summary announcements of its decisions. Alice Sachs, then a commissioner from New York County, could not recall nor explain how Cain's and Glenn's petitions were approved. However, she did indicate that, in most cases, the Board accepted the findings contained in the Clerks' Report. According to her, this is particularly true when no one appears to challenge the clerk's findings.

Consistent with Brown and Hayde's statements, Commissioner Velella was the one who announced the "second call" of Cain and Glenn's petition challenges, and the one who, without explanation, announced the Board's decision to overrule its own local clerks. We are unable to say with certainty that Velella's actions were influenced by the approaches Fred Brown made on behalf of Cain and Glenn.[80] Nor have we corroborated the fact that the approach even took place, merely that Brown and Hayde made contemporaneous statements indicating that a deal had been cut. However, under the circumstances, and without documentation justifying the reversal of the Clerks' Report or other satisfactory explanation from the Board, the integrity of the entire process is suspect.[81]

District 8: An "Open and Shut" Case is Reopened

The secrecy and creative accounting that characterized the review of District 12 petitions was repeated during the review of District 8 petitions. Two candidates in that district, Steven Eskow and Ciro Guerra, were allowed to remain on the ballot despite a Bronx clerk's determination that they had only 165 and 157 valid signatures respectively.[82] However, in the cases of Guerra and Eskow, the Board of Elections had more difficulty balancing their books.

In fact, when their cases were first called by the Board of Elections on March 4, both candidates were ruled "out." However, their ouster was short-lived. The Guerra matter was "second called" almost immediately and, without comment or explanation, the initial determination was reversed. Eskow had to wait longer for his reinstatement. He remained off the ballot until March 9. On that date, at the Board of Elections' regular Tuesday meeting, the commissioners inexplicably recalled Eskow's case, reexamined his petitions, and ruled him back on the ballot -- all without notice to his challenger, Mildred Bonilla.[83]

Not surprisingly, the process bewildered newcomers to school politics such as Bonilla. She was stymied despite the fact that she had followed all the rules, including filing her objections in a timely fashion and appearing at the proper time and place to argue her case. According to Bonilla, when the Guerra and Eskow matters were called on March 4, she was the only one to appear. The Clerks' Reports indicating that Guerra and Eskow did not have sufficient signatures were presented to the commissioners and, without argument, without a second call, and without any indication that their decision was revocable, they ruled the two candidates out.[84] Understandably, Bonilla left the hearing room assuming that the issue was closed. When she later learned that the commissioners had revisited both cases in her absence and

---

[80] In an interview before this office, Commissioner Velella denied being contacted by Brown or his representatives. Beyond that, the Commissioner stated that he could not recall any of the deliberations relating to Cain or Glenn's petitions and could offer no explanation for the reversal of the Clerk's Reports.

[81] Fred Brown refused to answer our questions about his activities in connection with the 1993 Community School Board Election.

[82] Actually, the Bronx Board of Elections came up with two different calculations and two different Clerks' Reports for candidate Steven Eskow. In one, he was found to have 165 valid signatures and in another the clerks validated only 138. Both reports were forwarded to the commissioners.

[83] Bonilla contested some of Eskow's nominating signatures because the subscribing witness who vouched for them was not a registered voter.

[84] The Clerks' Report on Mildred Bonilla's objections to Steven Eskow's petition indicated that the candidate had 138 valid signatures. Likewise, the Clerks' Report on Bonilla's challenge to Ciro Guerra's petitions indicated that the candidate had 157 signatures.

overturned their initial decision, she was shocked. No one from the Board of Elections had informed her that the cases would be, or even could be, "second called," and no one gave her an opportunity to argue her case. To make matters worse, the explanation she received from the Bronx Board of Elections was, quite simply, wrong.

Kay Amer, the Bronx Clerk, claimed to have no direct knowledge of how her office had been overruled. All she could do was refer Bonilla to the returned Clerks' Reports. Each one was returned with notations purporting to reflect the commissioners' actions. In the Guerra matter, two separate annotated reports were returned. The first merely noted a "second call." The portions of the report that normally list the parties present and the Board's decision were left blank. The second report purportedly reflected the final decision. In the place left for explanations, someone wrote: "sub witness was registered...Cand. gets back 76 signs...157+76=233," and next to the word "decision," the word "out" was crossed out and the word "in" was checked. Documentation in the Eskow matter is equally scant. The returned Clerks' Report indicates that the Board heard the matter on March 4, and decided that the candidate was "out." However, a notation appearing in the explanation section contradicts the decision. Someone wrote: "Candidate is registered and SW is reg...In...3/9/93." Translation: the candidate and the subscribing witnesses are registered voters. The candidate is in.

Bonilla knew from her own review of Board of Elections files that the subscribing witnesses to whom she objected were not in fact registered to vote at the time they collected signatures and she also knew that the Board of Elections' own computers reflected that fact. Thus, she concluded that the explanation appearing on the face of the reports could be nothing more than a false pretext.

Incredibly, when Bonilla complained publicly, the Board all but conceded that she was right, but stuck to their position anyway. Daniel DeFrancesco, the Executive Director, writing on behalf of the commissioners, explained:

1. Candidates ruled off on First Call were frequently allowed a second call to present evidence and arguments in support of their petition for ballot status;

2. In the case in question, a second call was allowed and argument presented that the subscribing witnesses were registered as parent voters;

3. Acting on information and belief, the Commissioners allowed the candidates in question to proceed forward.

4. Notwithstanding <u>the fact that the information and belief that the Commissioners acted upon appears to be incorrect</u>, there does not now appear to be any way that the Board can administratively remove the names of the candidates in question from the ballot. (Emphasis added)[85]

The Board's admission of error was small consolation for someone like Bonilla who took the time and effort to be involved in this process only to be arbitrarily shut out in the end. Moreover, it only served to reinforce many parents' views that the system is closed to all but political insiders. The appearance of

---

[85] See Letter from Daniel DeFrancesco to Mildred Bonilla, dated April 14, 1993.

impropriety is heightened by the Commissioners' total lack of recall with respect to who provided the erroneous information.[86]

Commissioner Mejias: A Man Wearing Two Hats

While Fred Brown was attempting to influence Commissioner Velella, another commissioner who deliberated behind closed doors on the District 12 and 8 petitions had, and continues to have, financial interests in both districts. Paul Mejias, the other commissioner from the Bronx, is the Executive Director of the Community Housing and Economic Development and Management Corporation (CHEDMC), a community-based organization (CBO) that provides services to school children in the Bronx. Since 1991, CHEDMC has contracted with the United Way to provide dropout prevention programs in specific schools in Districts 8 and 12. However, it is, in effect, sponsored by the individual districts and can continue to function only with the local boards' continued endorsement and support.

In the spring of 1991, Mejias began pitching his projects to District 12. Though he sought no funds from the Community School Boards directly, he no doubt recognized that without district support, it would be difficult to receive outside funding and would be impossible to use district facilities. "If they were going to use district facilities they would need its blessing," Superintendent Robert Henry explained. Moreover, in the application to the United Way, the agency administering the program, CHEDMC submitted written approvals of the "workplans and budget" from representatives of the District and the individual schools in which the programs would operate.[87]

Early in 1991, when Henry was Deputy Superintendent, he attended a meeting at which Mejias and an associate presented their proposals to representatives of several Bronx districts. Henry was not impressed. He came away from the meeting believing that the program would do little to benefit his district. He told this to then Superintendent Alfredo Mathew. However, it was clear that Mathew and the Board wanted Mejias' organization to operate in the district. In a document dated April 19, 1991, which was submitted to the United Way, Alfredo Mathew formally approved the CHEDMC workplan and budget for his district. Then, the Board, including Randy Glenn, formally passed a resolution accepting the program to be run by Mejias' organization.[88] As a result, CHEDMC received $90,000 for the 1991-92 school year for programs run in two schools in District 12.[89] Since that time, its contract with the United Way has been renewed annually at the same level of funding.

Commissioner Mejias' connection to District 8 is just as substantial. Since 1991, CHEDMC has, with United Way funding and District 8 approval, run dropout prevention programs in two schools. The superintendent, Max Messer, approved and supported the organization's original application in 1991

---

[86] In interviews with this office, Commissioners Sachs, Mejias, and Velella could not recall who provided the information that led to their decision.

[87] As former Superintendent Alfredo Mathew, now deceased, once explained to a board member in District 12, "he [Mejias] doesn't work for us, he was elected by the United Way but we had to agree to take his services."

[88] A resolution accepting the Mejias program was passed at the October 22, 1991 Public Meeting. Edward Cain was not present for the vote.

[89] See United Way-New York City Board of Education CAPS Final Report for 1991-1992, Section IV.

and again last year.⁹⁰ With the district's approval then, CHEDMC was paid $112,500 for the 1991-1992 school year.⁹¹

For the 1991-1992 school year alone, CHEDMC received $202,500 from the United Way to operate in four schools in Districts 8 and 12.⁹² During that same time, Mejias, as Executive Director, received $67,750.⁹³

This investigation has not established that Mejias' votes on the petition challenges in Districts 8 and 12 were either a quid pro quo for continued support for his programs or a payback for past support.⁹⁴ Nevertheless, the potential that his judgement would be influenced by his own pecuniary interest is obvious. Even if his judgement was pristine, the appearances were not. When secretive decision-making such as we have described here involves one who has such close ties to the participants, the specter of impropriety is inevitable.

Candidate Herbert Suss: Victim of Selective Enforcement?

Board of Elections officials have attempted to justify the outcomes in the Cain, Glenn, Eskow, and Guerra matters by expressing a concern that citizen participation be maximized. Indeed, in Daniel DeFrancesco's letter to Mildred Bonilla, he emphasized that "the overriding concern of the Board [in considering the Eskow and Guerra petitions] was to give the candidates the maximum leeway allowed by law so as to maximize citizen participation." Commissioner Mejias suggested the same thing when he privately told candidate Louis Maldonado that, challenges notwithstanding, everyone would be allowed to run. Finally, former Commissioner Alice Sachs echoed this lenient bent when she said that if a candidate was within ten or so signatures of the 200 name threshold, commissioners would often accept their petitions as valid. Yet, the experience of at least one candidate, Herbert Suss, suggests that just how much leeway a candidate received depended on who were his or her friends.

Suss, long active in parent associations in District 10 but never before a candidate, got fed up this year with the way his local Community School Board was administering its schools. So he decided to run for the school board himself. To acquaint himself with the process, Suss read all the literature available to prospective candidates, including material distributed by the Board of Elections, the Board of Education and the Public Education Association (PEA). He was determined to play by the rules.⁹⁵

Without a campaign organization to do much of his legwork, Suss went door to door collecting his own nominating signatures. In so doing, he unwittingly sowed the seeds of his own destruction. On

---

⁹⁰ In a document filed with the United Way on April 30, 1991, Messer and other representatives of the district indicated that "we have reviewed the information contained herein and support this application."
⁹¹ See United Way-New York City Board of Education CAPS Final Report, Section IV.
⁹² Ibid, Section IV.
⁹³ This figure is based on information disclosed by CHEDMC in IRS Form 990 for 1991.
⁹⁴ In testimony before this office, Commissioner Mejias stated that he had no recollection of the deliberations regarding the Cain, Glenn, Eskow or Guerra petitions. However, he denied being influenced by the business interests he had in their districts.
⁹⁵ The PEA, with input from the Board of Elections, including Commissioner Alice Sachs, prepared and distributed handbooks intended to "walk" the candidate through the process from petitioning to voting to counting to financial disclosure. When in doubt, Suss called the Board of Education and Board of Elections for clarifications.

January 5, 1993, Suss not only witnessed signatures on his own petitions, he signed a petition to nominate a friend, Isobel Rooney. In the weeks that followed, he continued to collect and witness signatures on his own petitions. Finally, after amassing 477 signatures, more than twice the 200 needed to get on the ballot, Suss filed with the Board of Elections.

Unfortunately for Suss, all the handbooks and instruction books he consulted failed to mention one rule -- once an individual signs a nominating petition for one candidate, he or she can no longer validly serve as another candidate's "subscribing witness."[96] Thus, once Suss signed to nominate his friend, Isobel Rooney, any signatures he collected and witnessed in support of his own candidacy were invalid.

Ironically, the challenge to Suss' petitions on this point was heard on March 4, 1993, the same day that the commissioners considered the Cain, Glenn, Eskow and Guerra matters. Both sides argued their case and then the Board retired to an executive session. However, unlike those of the other candidates, Suss' petitions did not survive the challenge. The law was clear and he was out.

The provision of the law that went undisclosed to candidates and ultimately eliminated Suss would seem to be just the sort of arcane rule that the Board of Elections would bend in the interests of "maximum citizen participation." However, the commissioners demurred this time, citing a lack of discretion. By secretly, and without explanation, approving the candidacies of Cain, Glenn and Guerra on the same day that it removed Suss from contention, the Board sent a clear signal to the electorate.[97] Commissioner Mejias may tell candidates that the Board will let everyone run and will ignore technical violations, and Commissioner Sachs may be willing to deviate from the 200 signature threshold, but such accommodations will be made only to those with clout and connections and all others will be held to the letter of the law.

PETITIONS

Our investigation found that candidates violate the petition rules for a variety of reasons. Some incumbents use school district employees to collect signatures for them because they know they can easily exploit the people whose job stability depends on them. Other candidates have people falsely sign as subscribing witnesses because the person who actually collected the signatures -- for some reason -- did not want to sign his or her name as the subscribing witness. Others disregard the rules merely for convenience.

In a variety of ways, candidates defeated the purpose of the petition filing requirement, which is meant to ensure that only serious candidates with a demonstrated threshold of support get on the ballot. The following section of this report describes several different petition fraud schemes that candidates executed this year.

---

[96] Any signatures obtained by a subscribing witness after he or she signs a petition for another will be invalid. Moreover, courts have even invalidated signatures obtained on the same day the subscribing witness has signed to nominate another candidate without requiring proof of which came first. See Lavelle v. Gonzalez, 74 AD2d 958, rev'd, 93 AD2d 896, aff'd, 59 NY2d 670 (1983).

[97] The Board of Elections also validated Eskow's petitions. However, that did not occur until March 9.

Sister Kelliher

Sister Elizabeth Kelliher, a Community School Board member in District 1 for thirteen years, decided to run for reelection in 1993. In order to secure the requisite two hundred nominating signatures, Kelliher repeatedly asked others to break the law and even did so herself.

Kelliher used one group of volunteers to collect nominating signatures, then asked others who were not present when the signatures were obtained to falsely swear that they had witnessed them. For example, Kelliher brought several signed petition pages to Cornelius Noonan, a neighbor, and asked him to sign as the subscribing witness. Noonan signed where Sister Kelliher asked him to, even though he did not witness the signatures and did not have "the slightest idea" who did.

In another case, Sister Kelliher brought an unsigned petition page to Brother Carl Malacalza. A few days later, she retrieved it -- now complete with ten signatures -- and added it to a stack of other petition sheets. Kelliher then had a friends of hers, William Viera, sign them all as the subscribing witness, despite the fact that he did not see Brother Malacalza, or many others, sign the pages. According to Viera, he did collect some of the signatures, but he could not remember the date he had done so. So at Sister Kelliher's direction, he filled in false dates. "She told you to just pick a date and fill it in?" Viera was asked for clarification. "Yes, for the most part," he answered.

On some pages, Kelliher herself signed as the subscribing witness, falsely swearing that she observed as each signer put pen to paper. For example, Mary Moloney, a District 1 resident, told us that when she signed to nominate Sister Kelliher, the candidate was not present. Nor was the Sister present when four others added their nominating signatures to that page. Yet, Sister Kelliher signed as the subscribing witness.

The requirement that a witness vouch for the signatures appearing on each petition page is more than a mere formality. It is meant as a deterrent against wholesale forgery.[98] Where, as here, that requirement is forsaken, fraud is inevitable. In fact, we found several forgeries in our limited survey of Sister Kelliher's filings. For example, Cornelius Noonan signed page fifteen as the subscribing witness, even though he did not actually watch anyone sign the page. Not surprisingly, our investigation revealed that several of the nominating signatures on that page are not authentic. The signature and address of Michael Palanza appear in one of the slots for nominating signatures on page fifteen. Palanza's nominating signature also appears on page three, but the two signatures do not match. Palanza told investigators that he signed page three, but that he did not sign page fifteen. Palanza's son, who lives at the same address and who is also named Michael, confirmed that the nominating signature on page fifteen is not his either.

Page fifteen also contains the nominating signature and address of Katherine Hrebluk. But Ms. Hrebluk told investigators that she did not sign the petition. Indeed, she cannot sign her name in English. Hrebluk added that she has never heard of Sister Elizabeth Kelliher, or of Cornelius Noonan, who purportedly watched as Hrebluk signed the petition page.

---

[98] Board of Elections Commissioner Mejias agreed that the subscribing witness requirement is a safeguard against fraud. In his words, "It's to verify that they took the signature, that they didn't go into a back room and create it..."

In another instance, Pedro Garcia, whose name and address appear on page nineteen of the Sister's petition, told investigators that he never signed a petition to nominate Sister Kelliher to the school board. When investigators showed Garcia page nineteen, he confirmed that although he lives at the address indicated, the signature next to the address is definitely not his. Other individuals who did sign the page said that a man witnessed their signatures. However, Sister Kelliher signed as the subscribing witness.

Through a variety of scenarios, Sister Kelliher had false witnesses subscribe to at least one third of the petition pages she filed.[99] Christine Bookin, for one, collected no more than six pages of nominating signatures, but signed as the witness on approximately eighteen pages. People who signed as false witnesses testified that they did so because Sister Kelliher, whom they trusted, asked them to. In her attempt to get her name on the ballot, Sister Kelliher paid no regard whatsoever to the integrity of her nomination. It seems that whenever she needed a "witness," she called on a friend to lie. Sister Kelliher's actions suggest that she did not care if her petitions bore phony signatures, as long as someone signed every page of her petition so she could file it with the Board of Elections. As William Viera, one of the people who swore falsely for her, said, "I guess she was just looking for anybody."

The Board of Elections was not the only entity duped by Sister Kelliher's fraudulent petition drive. To the contrary, community residents who agreed to collect signatures for Sister Kelliher were unpleasantly surprised when they discovered that their efforts to nominate Sister Kelliher ended up getting a different candidate on the ballot.

In September 1992, Kelliher's superiors agreed to let her serve the rest of her current term as a School Board member, but forbade her to run for reelection in 1993. In a letter to Sister Kelliher, the Superior General of the Franciscan Sisters of Atonement wrote, "you will not seek another term *under any circumstances*."[100] Although Sister Kelliher knew since September 1992 that she would not be permitted to run for reelection, she nevertheless embarked on a campaign to get her name on the ballot. Kelliher enlisted several supporters to circulate petitions without informing them that the Church had ordered her not to run.

In February, after learning that the Sister was defying its edict, the Order reiterated its position, reminding her orally and in writing that she was forbidden to run. Undeterred, Kelliher filed her petitions on February 16 anyway, only to turn around three days later and announce that she was dropping out of the race.[101] Why would Sister Kelliher persist in an apparently futile exercise to get her name on the ballot? The answer became clear days later, when a "vacancy committee" selected Dolores Schaefer, a longtime political ally, to replace Kelliher on the ballot.[102]

---

[99] The total number of signatures on the falsified pages exceeds two hundred, the minimum required to get on the ballot.

[100] Emphasis added.

[101] Sister Kelliher claims that until February 19, she believed that she could still appeal to the Cardinal. However, no one at the Chancery gave the Sister any indication that the Order's decision might be overturned. In fact, Bishop Henry Mansell told investigators that when Sister Kelliher arrived at his office unannounced on February 19, he heard her appeal but told her that the Cardinal supported the Order's position.

[102] Dolores Schaefer's husband Robert Schoenbohm was one of the people who falsely signed as a subscribing witness on Sister Kelliher's petition. Ironically, Schoenbohm's false signature ended up validating signatures that counted toward the nomination of his wife.

The Election Law allows for a vacancy committee, chosen by the candidate, to select a substitute should the candidate drop out of the race after she files her petitions.[103] However, those who signed to nominate Sister Kelliher as a candidate for the Community School Board were never told that the Church had forbidden Kelliher to run, and that their signatures might be used to nominate another candidate. When the volunteers who worked to nominate Sister Kelliher by signing her petitions and collecting signatures for her discovered that the Order had forbidden her to run as early as September, many of them felt that they had been duped and betrayed. Marilyn Frank, who circulated Kelliher's petition, was one such disgruntled volunteer. "I'm really mad that I was put through this," Frank said. "If they had told me that Sister was told she could not run, [that] there's a problem, I would've said, 'Well, then, I'm not taking these petitions around.'"

Christine Bookin, another community member who collected signatures for Kelliher, also felt that she -- and the people from whom she collected signatures -- had been deceived. When Bookin found out that Sister Kelliher had not been totally honest with her from the outset, she was angry that the candidate allowed her volunteers to expend so much effort on her behalf without informing them that she had been forbidden to run. "I did not collect signatures for Dolores Schaefer," Bookin said that she told Kelliher. "I collected them for you."[104]

Breaking the Rules to Consolidate Power

In District 12, two candidates enacted a petition fraud scheme so that they could more easily use school employees to collect the requisite nominating signatures. Kenneth Drummond, a former Board member who continued to exert considerable influence over School Board 12 activities even after he was kicked off the Board in 1990, and Veronica James, an incumbent Board member, flouted the rules to exploit the people whom they could most easily manipulate: District 12 employees and community residents anxious for jobs.[105]

How it Worked: Using School Employees to Collect Signatures

Drummond needed people to complete the tedious task of canvassing the District 12 neighborhood to collect signatures for his nominating petition.[106] James Gelbman, an Assistant Principal in District 12, agreed to work for Drummond's campaign because Drummond promised him a promotion.[107] But Gelbman, who lives in Westchester County, was ineligible to sign as a subscribing witness. Drummond

---

[103] See Election Law, Section 6-148.
[104] Sister Kelliher submitted to this office an unsolicited affidavit primarily focusing on her attempt to get permission to run for reelection. However, she declined our subsequent invitation to appear and answer specific questions under oath.
[105] Drummond and James were arrested on July 13, 1993 and charged with Offering a False Instrument for Filing in the First Degree and Misconduct Relating to Petitions. James, who was a sitting Board member when she committed the crimes, was also charged with requesting a subordinate to participate in a political campaign, a misdemeanor under the City Charter. They were each indicted for Offering a False Instrument for Filing and other related charges.
[106] A person who collects signatures -- known as a "subscribing witness" -- must sign the bottom of the page to swear that he or she actually witnessed people signing the petition. Subscribing witnesses must live in the District and must be registered to vote.
[107] See Power, Politics, and Patronage: Education in Community School District 12.

had Gelbman collect signatures anyway. He simply told Gelbman not to sign the bottom of the page, where the subscribing witness swears to having witnessed the signatures. After collecting signatures, Gelbman handed in his petition sheet at New Ventures Tax, Drummond's private business, where it was placed "in the bin" with other unwitnessed petition sheets.

Finding a "Witness"

Once he used school employees to collect signatures, Drummond needed someone to sign off as a subscribing witness. For this task, he turned to one of his part-time employees, Glinda Mickens. According to Mickens, she signed the petition sheets as a favor to her boss. She did not realize that she was falsely swearing that she had collected the signatures. Though she did not collect nor witness any signatures, she did sign fifteen pages as though she had. Capitalizing on his power, Drummond again made use of someone whose livelihood depends on him.[108]

When investigators told Mickens that she had been used in Drummond's fraudulent scheme, she agreed to seek an explanation from him.[109] "I just wanted you to sign off because, see, everybody does that," Drummond explained to Mickens in an attempt to justify his actions. "They just get people to sign off, OK, and you file them at the Board of Elections. If somebody wants to challenge you, that's not a crime or anything." Drummond did admit, however, that he knew that what he had asked Mickens to do was illicit. "You was supposed to carry [the petitions]," he told her.

Getting the Most from District 12 Employees

Drummond did not care whether his nominating signatures were valid, as long as he made it past the two-week period in which opponents can challenge individual signatures. Solely interested in getting the most signatures possible -- whether or not they were forgeries -- Drummond preyed on his workers' weak spots to get them to produce signatures in large quantities. To Gelbman, an aspiring principal, Drummond promised a promotion; to Robert "Ricky" White, a young Board of Education kitchen employee, and his friend Kendrick Alston, Drummond offered cash. Drummond well knew that the method he used to get signatures opened the door for fraud. But he also knew that the likelihood of getting caught was slim. In fact, by his own admission, he suspected that White and Alston forged signatures. "Maybe they got their two girlfriends and the four of them sat down there, you know, and was writing, and, if they'd a taken my butt to court and saw a whole pattern of that shit they'd throw your ass out," Drummond told a fellow candidate. Drummond elaborated on the suspected scheme, and described how White and Alston might have "collected" so many nominating signatures:

> What they might have done was take, taking the um, printouts that I gave 'em and just went to the house, you know, and just signed up, 'cause some of them sheets did look too clean to be true. I mean, that's a perfect looking, I mean every handwrite, every signature

---

[108] Mickens said that Drummond alluded to the fact that once he was elected to the School Board, he would help her get a job in District 12.

[109] Thereafter, Mickens approached Drummond, wearing a recording device.

was just fine, you know, no grease stains, no drop of water, nothing boy, I mean, you know how people write over when they make a little mistake or something. . . .[110]

Though in some cases Drummond may have "looked the other way" when he suspected that his campaigners forged signatures, when it suited him he also directly asked White to commit fraud. Drummond and James used Ricky White and his mother, a school aide in IS 200, to sign as witnesses to signatures they did not collect. Drummond summoned Ricky White to his office, where White signed as the subscribing witness on a stack of petition pages. He did not know who collected the signatures on the pages he signed, but he did confirm that he definitely did not collect the signatures on at least some of those pages. Similarly, White's mother, Rosa Mae White, carried several petition sheets for Veronica James, but at James' request she signed as the subscribing witness on 28 pages. Like Mickens, she did not read the area that explained that she was swearing to the contents of the page -- nor did James explain that to her. In fact, James herself falsely signed as a subscribing witness on at least five of her petition pages, and each of those pages contains at least one forged nominating signature.

Not an Isolated Incident

The fraud we uncovered in Districts 1 and 12 was not limited to Kelliher, Drummond, and James. Other District 12 candidates and candidates in at least one other district enacted similar schemes that went undetected by the Board of Elections.

District 12 candidate Lydia Velez explained how she, too, disregarded the rules so that she could use a school employee to carry petitions. A reluctant District 12 employee collected signatures for Velez, but the employee was too "scared" to sign off as a witness. If he worked for Velez's campaign and then she lost the election, his job stability would be at the mercy of her political opponents.[111] So Velez sent the employee out to collect the signatures, and she herself signed as the subscribing witness.

District 10

A similar false witness scheme was discovered by chance in District 10. During the petition challenge period, District 10 candidate Herbert Suss was reviewing the petition filed by his opponent Marvin Kamiel. Suss noticed that Kamiel's brother Howard had signed a page which Harriet Kamiel, the candidate's wife, had signed as the subscribing witness. Suss thought this was odd because, he explained, "Howard does not get along with Harriet and he would never sign a petition she carried."

When questioned by our office, Howard Kamiel readily admitted his dislike for his brother's wife and agreed that he would not have signed any petition she presented. However, he did recall signing a petition on behalf of Marvin. Howard remembered that he signed the petition in front of a bartender named Ed Brennan at a VFW Hall in Van Cortlandt Village. Like Kenneth Drummond and Lydia Velez

---

[110] By "printout," Drummond refers to the lists of registered voters he gave to White and Alston so they would know from whom to get signatures.

[111] In fact, early this fall, the new Community School Board 12 issued a directive that no employees are to be hired without their approval. Thus, Velez's campaign workers may well have had reason to fear retribution.

in District 12 and Sister Kelliher in District 1, Kamiel easily got someone -- his wife, a teacher in District 10 -- to falsely swear to having witnessed the signatures that someone else actually witnessed.

Other Forms of Petition Fraud

Candidates in various districts brazenly violated other petition regulations as well. However, there was no mechanism to apprehend those who violated the rules or even to discourage potential cheaters. In District 12, Drummond directed the people who gathered signatures for him to leave blank the area on the petition designated for the candidate's name. That way, whoever needed the signatures -- be it Drummond, James, or another candidate on their slate -- could write in his or her name and insert the page of ten signatures into that petition. Accordingly, people who signed the petitions thinking they were nominating Kenneth Drummond may well have been used to nominate a different candidate entirely.

Many signature collectors also left the date blank so that later, they could "backdate" the petitions. If a voter signs more than one petition, only the first signature is considered valid. Thus, candidate Lydia Velez explained, candidates or their supporters often backdate petitions so that they can be sure that even a signature obtained on the second day of petitioning is not preempted by an earlier signature on someone else's nominating petition. "Everybody already knows if you go even the day before [the filing deadline] you just alter the date to the 5th or 6th [of January]," she explained. "Everybody tries to beat each other with the date." More than a half dozen individuals from various parts of the city confirmed that campaign workers routinely fill in the dates of the signatures just prior to filing petitions with the Board of Elections. Candidates might also postdate a page to enable an individual to become a registered voter "before" he or she signed the petition, Velez explained.

In District 10, candidate Marvin Kamiel's campaign took the backdating scheme to an extreme. And as in District 12, school employees were used as agents to carry out the illicit activity. The principal of IS 118, Gerald Friedlander, asked Milt Silverstein, a retired teacher who now works as a mentor in that school, to collect nominating signatures for Kamiel. According to Silverstein, Kamiel's wife Harriet, a teacher at IS 206, brought him petitions on Sunday, January 3. Silverstein began collecting nominating signatures the next day, and he continued to do so throughout the first week in January. What Silverstein did not know was that the petitions should not have been available until January 5, and no signatures could validly be obtained before then.

Herbert Suss learned that his opponent was circulating petitions early, and he immediately notified the Board of Elections. Once the Board of Elections put on record that signatures had been collected early, the Kamiel campaign did not submit any signatures collected by Silverstein. One can only speculate about what use Kamiel would have made of the signatures collected before the official date had Suss not complained publicly.

How Kamiel's campaign team got the petitions early still remains a mystery. Milt Silverstein could say only that Harriet Kamiel gave him the petitions on January 3. Marvin Kamiel admitted that his wife got the petitions from the Bronx Board of Elections, but denied any knowledge as to when she obtained them. Bronx Board of Elections clerks Sandra Parness and Kay Amer denied releasing any petitions prior to the authorized date.

In any case, at first blush it would appear that it would do a candidate little good to obtain petitions early. Any signature that is dated before the formal start of the petition period would be considered invalid by the Board of Elections, so the forms should be of no use until the proper period begins. However, if, as Velez explained, dates are filled in later and their accuracy is rarely checked by officials, the fact that signatures were collected early could easily go undetected.

In many instances, campaign workers who circulated petitions and signed as witnesses freely admitted to investigators that they filled in dates that bore little or no relation to when the individuals actually signed the petitions. None of these individuals were exposed nor their petitions invalidated by the Board of Elections. Thus, as a practical matter, obtaining blank petitions ahead of the competition gave Kamiel a window of opportunity. His canvassers, with access to petitions prior to January 5, could gain a significant advantage by collecting signatures early, and then merely filling in "January 5" as the date of collection.

The mindset of those who abuse this system was captured by Drummond when he flippantly expressed the common belief that even if a petition is riddled with fraud, as long as it is not discovered during the two-week challenge period, the candidate is home free. "If I sat down in my living room and wrote up 500 signatures myself and nobody ever raised the issue by a certain date, they could never bring that back up," he said.

RESIDENCY

One of the most basic requirements for candidacy, that the office-seeker live in the district he or she seeks to represent,[112] was all too often ignored or circumvented in this year's election. We found that people who have minimal, if any, ties to the local school district create sham addresses, claim to live with friends or relatives, or otherwise misrepresent their true homes in order to get elected to the local school boards. As a result, those who were meant to serve on the school boards -- genuinely concerned parents and community members -- are denied that opportunity. Several candidates used these schemes to get elected this May.

Riverdale or the South Bronx?

In 1990, Kenneth Drummond was removed from Community School Board 12 because he did not live in District 12, which encompasses the Morrisania and Tremont sections of the South Bronx. After Drummond was elected to Community School Board 12 in 1989, Board of Education investigators[113] proved that Drummond actually lived in the Bronx neighborhood of Riverdale. Though Drummond never moved, he made a few cosmetic changes and ran for the school board again, winning a seat in the 1993 election.

---

[112] See Education Law Section 2590-c(4).
[113] The investigation into Drummond's residency was conducted by the Board of Education's Inspector General, before the creation of this independent office, The Special Commissioner of Investigation for the New York City School District.

Why would someone who lives in a comfortable, middle class community -- whose daughter attends school there -- want to serve on the school board in an entirely different neighborhood? Drummond's record makes it perfectly clear that it was not the three R's, but the three P's -- power, politics, and patronage -- that motivated him to run for a seat on the school board. Even after he was removed in 1990, Drummond remained an active participant in the affairs of Community School Board 12.

During the summer of 1991, Drummond orchestrated a deal with Board members and the District superintendent to give principalships and assistant principalships to candidates who had worked on his political campaigns. To get one of his preferred candidates a principalship, Drummond subverted the official principal selection process by arranging meetings at his office to sway the parents who would be reviewing resumes.[114] Drummond, by his own admission, instructed the parents as to which candidates they should recommend as their top choices.[115] In November of the same year, Drummond held a fundraiser for his re-election bid for the community school board. He used school employees to work for his campaign and to perform personal favors for him by leading them to believe that the more they contributed to his campaign, the better their chances of getting a promotion.[116]

Again this year, school employees and community members anxious for school district jobs busily worked on Drummond's school board campaign, giving him a solid chance of winning the election. But one annoying detail remained. Drummond still did not live in District 12. A few simple precautions took care of that. Drummond transferred the lease for his Riverdale apartment to his wife's name. He started to receive mail at his District 12 address. Just to be sure, Drummond installed a telephone in the apartment he rents at 810 Ritter Place, a building within the District 12 boundaries. "You know, I put a phone in around the corner," he told Board member Ed Cain in March, in a secretly recorded conversation. "I don't even know what the damn phone number is, but I had to put this phone in just in case somebody wants to challenge me later...." Apparently Drummond saw no need to move to the South Bronx to run for the local school board, as long as he could fool investigators. "I've had this phone here for about a month, maybe it's two months, six weeks at least, a good six weeks, and I don't even know the number, Eddie," Drummond confided in Cain. "Yeah, the number's only written in one place and that's on the phone bill that [my wife] pays and she's not even sure where the phone bill is, so I can call out, but nobody can call me."

When he was arrested in July for petition fraud, Drummond further revealed that he set up this dummy telephone to fool investigators. When the arresting investigator asked Drummond his address, he responded, "810 Ritter Place." But when asked his telephone number, Drummond responded, "I don't remember." His Riverdale telephone number, however, Drummond recalled without hesitation. Judging from the evidence, it would be safe to conclude that to reach Drummond at home, one should call him at his Riverdale address.

---

[114] The principal selection process is supposed to be kept entirely confidential. Each parent who serves on the resume screening committee signs a confidentiality agreement to keep the process from being tainted by outside political interests.

[115] *Power, Politics, and Patronage: Education in Community School District 12,* The Special Commissioner of Investigation for the New York City School District, April, 1993, p. 41.

[116] For a complete narrative of how Drummond masterminded the November 1991 fundraiser, see p. 93 of the April report.

Benjamin Ramos: Commuter School Board Member

Adjacent to District 12, Community School District 9 has a similar constituency to that of its Bronx neighbor. The majority of District 9 residents live below the poverty line, making the local school district a prime target for political hacks eager to enhance their power. These self-interested board members turn the community school district, with its relatively large budget for entry-level jobs, into a patronage mill for friends and political cronies. When such individuals control the community school board, budget and personnel decisions are not based on educational concerns. Instead, board members concern themselves with distributing jobs and promotions to build a political base and to consolidate their power.

Like Kenneth Drummond, Benjamin Ramos saw the tempting opportunity offered by a South Bronx community school board. Substantial evidence indicates that Ramos, who won a seat on Community School Board 9 in the 1993 election, lives in South Plainfield, New Jersey. For the purpose of running for School Board 9, Ramos claimed to live in apartment 5D at 1307 Edward L. Grant Highway, which is within the confines of District 9. However, when the Board of Elections sought to contact Ramos, their correspondence was returned with the postmark "Attempted -- [addressee] not known." The Board of Elections did not pursue the matter further, but our investigation revealed that Benjamin Ramos does not even live in New York State, let alone in District 9.

To begin with, at ROLM Inc., where Ramos worked from July 1984 until March 1993, Ramos himself listed his address as 220 Geary Drive, South Plainfield, New Jersey. His wife, who is a teacher in District 9, also filled out school records listing that address as her home. On the first day of school this year, after her husband was elected to School Board 9, she submitted a change of address card and provided a new address: 1307 Edward L. Grant Highway, Bronx, New York. However, she still wrote on her son's "Emergency Home Contact Card" that her husband could be reached at the New Jersey address.

Still other official records indicate that Ramos calls New Jersey home. He had a New Jersey driver's license until it expired in 1991, and his wife currently holds a New Jersey license. On both documents, the Ramos' list 220 Geary Drive, South Plainfield, New Jersey as their residence. If that wasn't enough, Ms. Ramos registered a car to that address, and family medical records indicate that Ramos lives with his wife and son in South Plainfield.

Upon discovering this evidence, our investigators conducted surveillance on Ramos. On two separate mornings, he and his wife left the house in South Plainfield, and his wife drove him to the train station where he caught a train to his new job in Newark. On the second day, Ramos, apparently alerted to the operation, approached our investigators and asked, "Why were you parked outside of my *summer home* this morning?" Clearly, Ramos referred to the South Plainfield house as his summer residence for the benefit of our investigators.

Indeed, Board of Elections officials were not the only ones who could not reach Ramos in the Bronx. Letters sent to Benjamin Ramos at 1307 Edward L. Grant Highway in the Bronx are returned to the sender, for the United States Postal Service has no record of a Ramos family at that Bronx address, and the mailman who delivers to that address knows of no one accepting mail on Ramos' behalf. Even the building's landlord has never heard of a Benjamin Ramos. And two of Ramos' "neighbors" -- the man living right next door in apartment 5E and the woman who lives in apartment 5B -- told an investigator

that apartment 5D is occupied by an elderly couple. Both said that they know all of their hallmates at least by sight. But when shown a photograph of Ramos, they each said definitively that they had never seen this man before. After Ramos alerted the couple who has lived in 5D for over twenty years to our investigation, they reluctantly told investigators that their daughter, who is Ramos' wife, and her son live there with them. They did not mention Benjamin Ramos.[117] That a resident of New Jersey won a seat on Community School Board 9 makes a mockery of the ideals behind decentralization. Through residency fraud, outsiders like Ramos and Drummond snatch control of New York City's local school boards from the hands of concerned community members.

Other Candidates

The phenomenon of outsiders running for seats on New York City's community school boards is not limited to the notoriously corrupt Districts 9 and 12. In District 8, Sandra Love claimed a Bronx address on documents she filed with the Board of Elections to support her successful candidacy. Only after the election did investigators learn that she lives in Westchester. When Love's son appeared as a witness in a 1987 murder trial, he testified under oath that he lives with his mother at a Mount Vernon address. Yet, the voters in the Bronx district she sought to represent had no way of knowing this when they cast their votes.

In the face of the allegations regarding her fraudulent residence, Sandra Love declined the seat to which she was elected. In still another instance, George Palermo, a School Board 9 member who was running for reelection, claimed that he lived in an apartment his parents had really moved out of months before he filed his nominating petition. However, after a local news station exposed him, Palermo was not reelected. Because candidates can so easily commit residency fraud, the local community school boards are vulnerable to manipulation by members who have minimal, if any, ties to the schoolchildren, parents, and community members of the district.

CAMPAIGN ADVERTISING

An endorsement from a reputable source can make all the difference to a candidate who hopes to be successful in an election. But what is a candidate to do when endorsements are not forthcoming? In Community School District 27 in Queens, supporters of one candidate decided to create their own.

"President Emeritus"

The weekend before the Community School Board Election, candidate Geraldine Chapey was the lucky recipient of endorsements by the Gateway Republican Club and the Parents Association of Rockaway Beach Junior High School 180, or so it seemed. Flyers printed on what appeared to be the organizations'

---

[117] Ramos' claim that he lives in apartment 5D is even more unlikely when one considers that the apartment has one bedroom. Why would Ramos squeeze four adults and one child into a one bedroom apartment when he owns a sprawling house in New Jersey?

official letterhead urged voters to "make your vote count by writing #1 for Geraldine D. Chapey."[118] This campaign literature was mailed en masse and was signed "William Sampol, President, Emeritus."[119]

The leaflets were a total fraud. In fact, both groups had explicitly decided not to endorse specific candidates for the school board.[120] Furthermore, not only is William Sampol not the "President Emeritus" of either organization, there is no such position for either group.[121] Understandably, these organizations were outraged by Sampol's brazen actions.

History Repeats Itself

William Sampol's execution of an outright fraud on the voters of District 27 is more than reminiscent of the corrupt practices that plagued the district in the past. It was part of an effort to return to power those turned out of office by scandal in 1989. In that year, the Joint Commission On Integrity In the Public Schools, commonly known as the "Gill Commission," heard testimony from Superintendent Coleman Genn about widespread illicit dealmaking.[122] In particular, Genn described how board member James (Jimmy) Sullivan pressured him to give William Sampol a job as the Administrative Assistant in charge of a "satellite" district office in the Rockaways, a plum position, yet one that Sampol was wholly unqualified to fill.[123] Genn, who was by then cooperating with the Commission, did not succumb to Sullivan's influence and Sampol did not get the promised slot. However, Sullivan did succeed in placing Eugene Pasternak, Geraldine Chapey's son-in-law, on the Board to fill a vacancy.

Following the Gill Commission report, Chancellor Fernandez ousted the entire District 27 Board, including Sullivan and Pasternak. Moreover, Sullivan was convicted of mail fraud and coercion in connection with his activities as a Board member. However, in this, the first election since the 1989 ouster, both Sullivan and Sampol reappeared as prominent supporters of Geraldine Chapey. Among other activities, they both distributed campaign material on her behalf.

This investigation has not established that Chapey knew that Sampol planned to defraud voters with phony literature. However, she did not disavow his association with, nor his efforts on behalf of, her campaign. In the meantime, Sampol resorted to any means necessary to rebuild the power base that the Sullivan forces lost in the wake of the Gill Commission investigation. The phony flyers he distributed under the letterhead of the Gateway Republicans and other groups warned that "the Fernandez Gang"

---

[118] The literature suggested that the voter choose Shalom Becker #2, Kevin L. Pruitt #3, and Richard J. Altabe #4.

[119] Another piece of literature was sent out the same weekend on the letterhead of the Conservative Party of Queens. Although unsigned, it is similar in content to the signed endorsements.

[120] Both Thomas A. Carney, President of the Gateway Republican Club and Liz Sulik, Co-president of the JHS 180 Parent Association, verified that Sampol was not the "President, Emeritus" of their respective organizations. In addition, each provided this office with meeting minutes reflecting the positions of their organizations with respect to the school board elections.

[121] Sampol was a member of the Gateway Republicans, but he held no office; he was once an officer of the Parent's Association, but he was no longer a member.

[122] Coleman Genn, the Superintendent of District 27, cooperated with the Gill Commission and recorded conversations with various school board members including James Sullivan. The James Sullivan associated with District 27 has no connection with the James Sullivan discussed in connection with Community School District 10.

[123] Genn testified that Sampol agreed to fabricate his resume so that he would appear qualified for the position at the nonexistent satellite office.

-- referring to the trustees who replaced the prior Board -- "MUST NOT BE ELECTED." With the help of such bogus endorsements, Geraldine Chapey was elected to Community School Board 27.

FINANCIAL DISCLOSURE

For a variety of reasons, we have seen candidates, their supporters, and even the officials who run the Community School Board Election violate the rules. The financial disclosure requirement is another regulation that is all too often misunderstood or even outright ignored.

The requirement that candidates state who contributed money to their campaigns, how much each contributor gave, and how the candidates spent that money was intended to give voters access to important information that may help them decide for whom they want to vote. Moreover, requiring candidates and political committees to disclose who contributed to their campaigns provides a window into the political pressure suffered by educators, making it harder for school board candidates to demand -- explicitly or implicitly -- that their employees support them financially.

But in practice, the financial disclosure rules -- much like the rules governing the petition process or the ballot count -- are rendered virtually useless. To begin with, the Board of Elections does not enforce the elaborate regulations. Candidates and political committees who raise money to support candidates are required to file three separate disclosure forms on three distinct dates. But candidates who did not file their statements or who filed them late were not penalized.[124] This year, only 185 of the 543 candidates filed all three required statements.[125] More than 25 percent of the candidates ignored the financial disclosure requirements altogether.

Even political committees were able to raise substantial funds without documenting how much money they made or how they spent it. In April, the "Comite Pro Representacion Hispana," a committee supporting a group of candidates in District 9, held a fundraiser attended by more than 250 people.[126] The tickets cost $25 each. Yet, as of November 1993, the committee did not file any of the required financial disclosure statements, and the money is totally unaccounted for.

The CSA Pic 10, another political action committee that supported fourteen District 10 candidates, including Ed McCarthy, had not filed any of the required documents even a month after Election Day. When they learned that we were looking into their finances, the committee hastily filed one of the required disclosure statements.[127] The committee's treasurer stated on the form that the committee raised $10,040,

---

[124] All figures regarding the filing of financial disclosure statements are based on documents provided by the Board of Elections. Penalties, though minor, are available but are never enforced. In fact, of the 288 winners, forty six did not file any financial disclosure forms. We examined the forms due on April 2 and April 23 that were filed by May 12. The post-election forms, which were due on May 31, we examined if filed by July 28.

[125] The names of 543 candidates appeared on the ballot, but even more were required to file financial disclosure statements.

[126] Several witnesses testified that people came and went throughout the party, and that from 200 to 250 people were present at any given time.

[127] We subpoenaed the committee's treasurer, Milton Fein. The subpoena required that he supply the CSA Pic 10's financial records to this office by June 14, 1993. Mr. Fein did not comply with the subpoena. On June 23, the CSA Pic 10 filed the disclosure statement that was due on May 31.

and that it divided the money equally among the fourteen candidates it supported, giving seven hundred dollars to each candidate. But two of those candidates stated that they received only palm cards worth much less than seven hundred dollars from the CSA Pic 10. On the other hand, one candidate disclosed that the committee donated over two thousand dollars worth of supplies to her campaign.[128]

Another problem with the financial disclosure regulations is that they are not specifically designed for the Community School Board Election. Thus, even when followed correctly, the rules do not necessarily serve their intended purpose. For example, because the rules are designed for a more costly general election, candidates only have to itemize specific contributions and expenditures if the total amount exceeds $1,000. For this year's Community School Board Election, though, almost one half of the candidates who filed at least one statement waged their campaigns without going over the $1,000 mark, or so they claimed. All those candidates had to do was sign a statement certifying that they did not raise or spend more than $1,000. Thus, voters know virtually nothing about the finances of even those candidates who do file the required statements.

RECOMMENDATIONS FOR SYSTEMIC CHANGE

The events we have chronicled in this report make clear that the present system of electing representatives to local community school boards must be changed dramatically. As it stands now, the system is too often an impediment to true community representation and participation in the educational process. The format itself is inherently confusing and thus inaccessible to all but the most sophisticated politicians. Enforcement of the rules is so lax or unevenly applied as to be an invitation to commit fraud. At the same time, politics too often invades the classroom and dictates educational decisions.

Decentralization was designed to attract and empower concerned members of a community -- parents and others -- in the education of the community's children. Its creators did not intend to establish patronage mills where, every three years, teachers and administrators are forced to become foot soldiers in their bosses' campaigns and educational priorities take a backseat to political imperatives. Unfortunately, in the current atmosphere, this is all too often the case. An arcane and inaccessible system prevents full community representation and allows a district to be held captive by self-interested politicians. Those same politicians, with their power consolidated, can exert enormous pressure on the teachers they oversee and unduly politicize the school environment. As a result, the community does not receive decentralization's intended benefit -- an effective voice in the educational process. Rather, it is saddled with an unwanted side effect: the politicizing of the schools.

---

[128] The CSA Pic 10 claimed that it received $750 from the CSA. They did not specify who donated the remaining $9,290. They simply indicated that 100 individuals each contributed $99. The CSA Pic 10 deliberately solicited contributions of no more than $99, apparently believing that if a contribution does not exceed $100, they do not have to specify where they got it. But section 2590-c(6)(b) of the Education Law, read in conjunction with the Election Law, states that any candidate or committee who raises or spends more than $1,000 for a Community School Board campaign must itemize each and every contribution.

On the eve of the twenty fifth year of the decentralization of New York City's school system, the time has come to revitalize community control by reforming its bedrock, the electoral system. In making our recommendations, we are cognizant that this report comes at the close of a year in which there has been extraordinary and intense debate over school reform in the City of New York. Thoughtful proposals have been circulated from several quarters, and most have included reforms of the electoral process. Our recommendations should and could be implemented regardless of which bureaucratic structure emerges from the current debate. They are intended to simplify the system, clarify the rules, provide uniform and enhanced enforcement, and discourage fraud.

* **RECOMMENDATION:** Proportional voting should be eliminated.

The current system of proportional voting is cumbersome, error-prone and confusing to the general public. It requires the use of paper ballots and entails a lengthy and complicated counting procedure in which ballots are transferred from pile to pile. As a result, the process by which the winners are determined takes several days, if not weeks, while police manpower and resources are drained. The process itself often gives the appearance of impropriety.

* **RECOMMENDATION:** Votes should be cast on the voting machines used in the general elections.

First and foremost, using voting machines would provide voters with a level of privacy they have a right to expect but do not currently receive. In addition, public concern about the proper handling of individual paper ballots would be alleviated. Returns and definitive results would be available almost instantaneously. And finally, Board of Elections inspectors could operate systems they are most familiar with and the need to subcontract the count procedure would be eliminated.

* **RECOMMENDATION:** The election should be moved to coincide with the general election in November, provided that upon adequate review, it is determined that this move would not further politicize or otherwise disrupt the system.

Though this year's election saw an increase in voter turnout, less than fifteen percent of those eligible actually cast ballots. If the school board election coincided with the vote on other initiatives or races for elective office, turnout could be expected to increase. However, prior to making such a move a determination must be made that sharing the ballot with other political races will not further politicize the school system. In addition, the question of whether electing a board in September or November, while school is in session, would cause undue disruption, must also be considered.

* **RECOMMENDATION:** The Board of Education should immediately begin planning a complete overhaul of the parent voter registration process. The current contradictory mandates of the Education and Election Laws with respect to parent voter certification should be reconciled.

As this report makes clear, the certification process has broken down repeatedly, simultaneously disenfranchising some while enfranchising others not eligible. This year, the effort began too late, moved too slowly, and suffered from a lack of communication. The Board of Education and Board of Elections

cannot wait until four months before the registration deadline to begin thinking about a workable plan. Nor can they hide behind the conflict in state law which on the one hand allows voters to register up to twenty five days before an election but requires parent voters to be certified at least thirty days prior to the election. While that law made it impossible to timely certify any registrants who registered less than thirty days before the election, it did not account for the errors that allowed multiple voting, the lack of compliance by principals that led to the disenfranchising of parents at 190 schools, or the failures in the distribution of the forms themselves. The Board of Education must begin immediately to reach out to parents and other concerned parties to develop a workable solution.

* RECOMMENDATION: All decisions made by the Board of Elections regarding candidates for Community School Board must be made in public and on the record.

As we documented in this report, the decisions of the Board of Elections Commissioners were often made behind closed doors and delivered without explanation. Making matters worse, such secretive decision making often appeared to contradict preliminary determinations made by the Commissioner's own clerks. Such processes corrode public confidence in the system. To rectify this, all Board of Elections hearings should be recorded either stenographically or on audiotape. A record of the actual vote must be kept; not merely an indication that a candidate is "in" or "out." And finally, when the Commissioners reach a result that differs from that of their clerks, an explanation should be provided and recorded.

* RECOMMENDATION: The financial disclosure requirements for Community School Board candidates should be tightened, clarified, and enforced. Candidates who fail to comply should not be sworn in as board members.

Financial disclosure is valuable because it affords the public an opportunity to see who is providing support to individual candidates and which candidates may be exerting pressure on school employees to participate in the political process. This year however, compliance with regulations was nothing short of abysmal. More than 25 percent of all candidates ignored the requirements entirely. Only 185 out of 543 candidates filed all the required documents. At least forty six elected board members had not filed all the required documents by the time they were seated in July. The causes are two-fold: the candidates' inability to understand the rules and their lack of incentive to follow them.

The regulations for school board candidates must be simplified and clarified so that candidates understand their obligations. It is not enough for the Board of Elections to merely adapt forms used in the general election, where different rules apply, for use by school board candidates. It must create forms that clearly explain that if candidates raise over $1000, they must itemize all receipts. If they raise less, they must understand their obligation to file an affidavit to that effect. Then, once the rules are clear, candidates must be convinced that their filings will be investigated and transgressions punished. At a minimum, those who fail to file all the required documentation should not be seated on any community school board.

*RECOMMENDATION: The Board of Education should require more detailed disclosure of residency status from Community School Board candidates.

As we have repeated in several contexts in this report, decentralization was meant to give a voice in the educational process to parents and others in their local communities. Thus, it is axiomatic that only local residents should be permitted to serve on community school boards. However, at present, too many candidates attempt to run in districts where they have minimal, if any, ties. When they are elected, they do not have the same stake in the success of the district's educational mission and historically have been tempted to pursue personal agendas. To guard against such abuse, the Board of Education should require candidates for the Community School Board to disclose the nature of their ties to the address they are claiming as their residence. This could properly include a sworn statement disclosing the length of time lived at the claimed address, the amount of time currently spent at that home, and the existence of any alternative residences.

* RECOMMENDATION: The Board of Education should extend "whistleblower" protection to the students of the New York City Public Schools and their parents.

Currently, all employees of the school system are protected from retaliation for their reporting of misconduct or wrongdoing by other employees of the system. However, parents and children in the school receive no such protection. While parents and students are often in the best position to detect and report wrongdoing, the students at least, are the most vulnerable. In fact, during the course of this investigation, certain parents expressed fears that their children would be retaliated against if they, the parents, cooperated with our inquiry. To alleviate those fears and to encourage all members of the school community to report corrupt or criminal activity, conflicts of interest, unethical conduct, or other wrongdoing in the electoral process or otherwise throughout the school system, the Board of Education's resolution of July 7, 1992 must be amended to expand protection to students and their parents.

This report clearly demonstrates that the negative impact of politics on education is not limited to any one district. Therefore, we repeat the following recommendations made in our April report on corruption in District 12:

- The Education Law should specifically state that the intentional interference in the hiring process by a board member beyond the statutorily-defined role, is misconduct that can lead to suspension or removal from office.

- The hiring power of Community School Boards should be limited to the hiring of the superintendent.

- The Chancellor should have the authority to reject, upon a written statement of reasons, candidates for superintendent submitted by the Community School Boards.

- Community School Board members should receive mandatory training in their rights and responsibilities.

DISCIPLINARY RECOMMENDATIONS

In addition to systemic changes, we recommend that the Chancellor take appropriate disciplinary action against the following individuals who violated rules and regulations, if not the law. Some are not previously named in this report.

Kenneth Drummond, Community School Board 12 member who has been indicted for submitting fraudulent nominating petitions in support of his 1993 candidacy, should be removed from his position.

Benjamin Ramos, Community School Board 9 member whose primary residence is neither in New York State nor in District 9, should be removed from his position.

Stuart Possner, principal at PS 100 in District 21, who pressured teachers and staff to participate in the 1993 Community School Board Election and otherwise acted inappropriately, should be immediately removed from his position and his employment should be terminated. It is clear from our investigation that Possner enlisted members of his staff to assist him in pressuring teachers. Those individuals may be the subject of future recommendations for disciplinary action.

James Sullivan, the director of Pupil Personnel in District 10, who orchestrated the fraudulent absentee ballot scheme, should be terminated from employment with the Board of Education.

Frank Rodriguez, assistant director of Bi-lingual Programs in District 9, participated in the fundraiser described in the Undue Political Influence section, including the sale of tickets to subordinates. **Gerald Friedlander**, principal of IS 118, requested subordinates to participate in political campaigns in District 10. His conduct is described in the Petition Fraud section of this report. They should be reminded of the conflict of interest provision in the City Charter.

Hilda Gutierrez, principal in District 9, participated in the fundraiser described in the Undue Political Influence section, but denied her involvement in testimony before this office. She should be reminded of her duty to cooperate with this office.

The following individuals should be disciplined appropriately:

Milton Fein, principal of PS 7 in District 10, who as treasurer of the political action committee CSA Pic 10 described in the Financial Disclosure section of this report, inaccurately and falsely reported the expenditures to individual candidates.

Julia Pappas, Community School Board member in District 30, sent invitations to her fundraiser to every principal in the District, in violation of the Chancellor's Special Election Circular.

Laura Liff, School Safety Officer in District 21, circulated a nominating petition for Marc Liff, her son, who was a candidate in the Community School Board Election, inside PS 100 during school hours, in violation of the Chancellor's Special Election Circular.

Pearl Ginsberg, Community School Board member in District 11, circulated her nominating petition at the district office in violation of the Chancellor's Special Election Circular.

Rosemarie Pilkington, teacher in District 31, placed campaign literature in faculty and staff school mailboxes in violation of the Chancellor's Special Election Circular.

Angelo Sanchez, principal, **Miguelina Morales**, paraprofessional, and **Mrs. Fuentes**, a teacher in District 9, violated the Chancellor's Special Election Circular by campaigning in the schools, as is described in the Undue Political Influence section of this report.

Harriet Kamiel, teacher in District 10, who in addition to the evidence reported in the Petition Fraud section, violated the Chancellor's Special Election Circular by using a "personal day" on Election Day, May 4, 1993, to campaign for her husband Marvin Kamiel.

Carmen Jiminez, Harriet Kamiel's principal at IS 206, allowed her to take time off on Election Day in violation of the Chancellor's Special Election Circular.

REFERRALS

In addition to the systemic changes and disciplinary actions we are recommending, we have referred several instances of fraud, corruption and conflicts of interest to the appropriate law enforcement agencies. To date, two individuals have been indicted and several others are under investigation.

Kenneth Drummond and **Veronica James**, who were both candidates for the school board in District 12, have been indicted by a New York County Grand Jury in connection with their filing of fraudulent nominating petitions. The prosecution is being handled by the Frauds Bureau of the New York County District Attorney's Office.

Evidence relating to the casting of fraudulent absentee ballots in District 10 has been referred to the United States Attorney's Office for the Southern District of New York. The prosecution is being handled by the Public Corruption Unit of that office.

Evidence of **Stuart Possner's** improper coercion of teachers at PS 100 in District 21 has been referred to the Kings County District Attorney's Office. The investigation is being conducted by the Corruption Investigation Division Unit of that Office.

Evidence of impropriety and conflicts of interest in the Board of Elections review of the nominating petitions of Ciro Guerra, Steven Eskow, Randy Glenn, and Edward Cain, including the improper interference with the process by Fred Brown, has been referred to the New York County District Attorney's Office, where a parallel investigation is already underway, and to the Bronx County District Attorney.

Evidence that **Sister Elizabeth Kelliher** filed a fraudulent nominating petition and swore falsely on individual pages of that petition in support of her candidacy, has been referred to the Frauds Bureau of the New York County District Attorney's Office.

Evidence relating to **Carmelo Saez's** handling of funds raised in connection with the 1993 Community School Board Campaign has been referred to the Bronx County District Attorney's Office.

Evidence that **Harriet Kamiel** fraudulently signed as a subscribing witness on a petition filed in support of her husband Marvin's candidacy has been referred to the Bronx County District Attorney's Office.

The complaint we received and substantiated regarding **William Sampol's** distribution of fraudulent campaign material was also registered with the United States Attorney's office for the Eastern District of New York and with the Queens County District Attorney's office.